PHILOSOPHY OF EDUCATION IN HISTORICAL PERSPECTIVE

Second Edition

D1466561

Adrian M. Dupuis
and
Robin L. Gordon

University Press of America, Inc.
Lanham • New York • London

Copyright © 1997 by
University Press of America,® Inc.
4720 Boston Way
Lanham, Maryland 20706

3 Henrietta Street
London, WC2E 8LU England

Library of Congress Cataloging-in-Publication Data

Dupuis, Adrian M. (Adrian Maurice)
Philosophy of education in historical perspective / Adrian M. Dupuis &
Robin L. Gordon.--2nd ed.
p.   cm.
Includes bibliographical references and index.
1. Education--Philosophy--History.   2. Education--Aims and
objectives--United States.   I. Gordon, Robin L.   II. Title.
LA21.D78 1996   370'.1--dc20   96-43224 CIP

ISBN 0-7618-0548-6 (pbk: alk. ppr.)

Dedication

To Red and Al

CONTENTS

Preface to the Second Edition

My students and I were introduced to Dr. Adrian Dupuis's text by one of his former students and my colleague, Dr. Alfred Lightfoot, Professor Emeritus, Loyola Marymount University. Philosophy of Education, is an elective course I offer in our graduate school of education. A majority of the students are classroom teachers who are completing their Master of Arts in Teaching. During the examination of the various examples of educational philosophies, they reflect on their own philosophies of education and they begin to make sense of their practices. They develop a foundation upon which they can further refine their thinking about educating children.

Dr. Dupuis has written a text that is accessible to the learner who is not a philosophy major. The inclusion of the major educational philosophies that have had an impact on Western education helps the layperson to make sense of past and current trends. Dupuis noted in the preface of the first edition that the educational pendulum was continuing to swing between opposing notions of effective education. He discussed these shifts in thinking within a historical perspective. Educational philosophies do not develop in an artificial, sterile environment. Rather, they emerge amidst social, political, and technological upheaval. Examining these philosophies in light of what was happening historically provides a more complete and logical picture of why events unfolded the way they did.

I have begun to change my thinking about these pendulum swings. Perhaps, educational practices are more reflective of a spiral model. Succeeding thinking builds upon what came before. What appears to be a return to previous practice is actually an adaptation. My students and I are presently examining this.

The reader who has used this text previously will notice a few additions to this edition. The excellent foundation chapters have been left intact with the inclusion of current references. Ideas for course discussion and writing have also been incorporated in the appendix. The most significant modification is the deletion of the chapter on the former Soviet Union and the addition of a new chapter on Postmodernism. It is intended that this revision will address current shifts in philosophy as we approach the third millennium.

People seem to have a compulsion to tinker with anything and everything. The educational community is not immune to this. Despite the various shifts between liberalism and conservatism, behaviorism and constructivism, process and product, the best way to educate children has been and continues to be the focus of all the debate. It will be interesting to see what further permutations will be recorded in the future edition of this text.

Los Angeles, California 1996
R.L.G.

Acknowledgements

This edition was made possible throught the collaborative effort of many people:

Dr. Adrian Dupuis: Co-Author
Dr Alfred Lightfoot: Consultation
Erika Swenson and the Students of EDUC 623: Research
Michael Gordon: Curriculum Examples
Manuscript: Kelly and Colin Van Gorder, Michael and Susan Gordon, Patricia Taylor ,John Crissey Jr., Lynn Austin, & Elizabeth Trietsch.

Chapter I

Philosophy
and
Education

Philosophy of education is one of the oldest yet one of the newest disciplines. It is one of the oldest since Plato- the philosopher par excellence of ancient times- devoted considerable attention to the nature, purposes, and content of education. It is one of the newest since philosophy of education began to emerge as a separate discipline only in the twentieth century. More specifically, Dewey's might be considered the first systematic treatment of philosophy of education. Since his time it has become an object of considerable study.

The current interest in educational philosophy has produced many approaches to the subject. Some widely used texts, for example, present the basic philosophical presuppositions, or assumptions, in the areas of metaphysics, epistemology, and axiology for each of the philosophical systems, such as realism, idealism and pragmatism. This statement of philosophical beliefs is followed by a discourse on the implications of such beliefs for the aims of education, its nature and content, as well as areas of educational concern.[1]

Another approach centers the discussion on major topics or problems in education, such as the pupil, aims, curriculum, evaluation, discipline, and the like. Each of these topics then is viewed from the varied philosophical perspectives.[2] Other texts propose a single point of view in philosophy of education. In these instances the author may present the philosophical

---

[1]Typifying this approach are: J.D. Butler, *Four Philosophies and Their Practice* (New York: Harper and Brothers, 1957): and TBrameld, *Philosophies of Education in Cultural Perspective* (New York: Henry Holt, 1955).
[2]See John Brubacher, *Modern Philosophies of Education* (New York: McGraw-Hill, 1962).

bases of education and then concentrate on the educational implications of only one system of educational philosophy. Alternative points of view may be presented, followed by a critical evaluation in the light of the principles espoused by the author.[3] Some authors have classified the various approaches to educational thought as traditional versus modern, or progressive versus essentialist, or democratic versus authoritarian.

Each approach to the subject has its advantages and disadvantages. For example, to broach the subject by the study of such philosophical systems as pragmatism and realism might give the beginner some insight into a coherent system of thought and many of the educational principles and practices derived from it. However, many philosophical beliefs discussed in the systems are quite irrelevant to education, and the answers to some questions in education are not found in the general philosophical beliefs.

Rather than use the systematic or another of the approaches mentioned, the issues of educational philosophy have been treated within the context of educational conservatism and liberalism. These categories are frequently used in such other fields as politics, economics, and social philosophy and are quite familiar to the reader. Nevertheless, the use of such terms involves certain semantic difficulties. For example, for some people "liberal" indicates only these beliefs and practices accepted by people of this day and age. But this definition of liberal would include such practices as environmental terrorism or polygamy along with democracy and the welfare state, since there are people today who advocate such practices. On the other hand, to define "conservative" in terms of beliefs and practices which no longer exist serves no purpose, since most conservatives advocate many practices which still flourish. Christian burial rites, corporal punishment, and the father's position as head of the family are practices of long standing; these practices, though of ancient origin, are still found today. In these examples, the conservative might be described as opposing drastic and rapid change, whereas the liberal favors such change.

We also know that the terms liberal and conservative are used both as symbols of endearment and detraction. In some circles to be labeled a liberal is the equivalent of being associated with dangerous or subversive activities. In other circumstances the liberal is regarded as the humanitarian, as the defender of the rights of others, and as having similar laudable traits.

---

[3]See John Dewey,*Democracy and Education* (New York: The Macmillan Co., 1916): F. Redden and J. Ryan,*A Catholic Philosophy of Education*(Milwaukee: Bruce Publishing Co., 1942); HarryBroudy, *Building a Philosophy of Education* (Englewood Cliffs, N.J.: Prentice-Hall, 1961).

Similarly, to be called a conservative is, for some, a sign of distinction; for others it is a symbol of selfishness, stubbornness, and reaction. The authors of this text wish to make no case for either the liberal or the conservative cause; this is for the reader to decide. Another difficulty in classifying educational theorists as either liberals or conservatives is that their educational and political beliefs do not always coincide. Thus Robert Maynard Hutchins is educationally very conservative, politically very liberal; Russell Kirk, on the other hand, is both politically and educationally very conservative. Many suburban communities which are politically conservative support educational liberalism; many politically liberal newspapers and journals are educationally quite conservative. Many European countries reflect this paradoxical situation: even though the political leaders of these countries espouse political and social liberalism, educational theory and practice remain very conservative. In England, for example, the Labor party has not strongly supported liberal educational movements. In order to clarify the meaning of the terms conservative and liberal as they apply to educational theory and practice, the characteristics of each will be noted in Chapter II. These characteristics reflect the views of the participants in the current debate on educational issues. But since many of the parties in the conflict do not treat all the problems of educational philosophy, one cannot imply that every liberal or conservative subscribes totally to each of the characteristics listed. For example, the conservative camp embraces both secularist and religious thinkers. In most cases the secularist will not espouse those notions about man and value which are primarily theological in origin, but both might agree on certain views of man's nature and value which are not rooted in theology or a specific religious creed. Then, too, they might agree on the primary purpose of the school but disagree on the ultimate purpose of all human activity.

The same might be said for some views classified as liberal. To illustrate, the seventeenth and eighteenth-century liberals emphasized individual freedom, whereas twentieth-century liberals view freedom within a social context. Yet both hold for freeing the individual from *external* authority. This initial clarification should be adequate for the present, since these differences and similarities will be noted throughout the succeeding chapters of the text.

Some designations of the meaning of "philosophy of education" might be helpful at this point. A fundamental difficulty, however, is that the definition of these terms is in itself a part of the controversy between the opponents in the debate which will be sketched in this book. In general, though, most philosophers concern themselves with questions of the nature of humanity and the universe, of the nature of knowing and truth, and with discussions of good, beauty and value. A notable exception to this general rule are the philosophers discussed in Chapters IX and X.

It is even more difficult to unearth a general definition of "education." Lest the educational issues be prejudged, it might be well to blanket all views of education under the broad operational definition: Education is what goes on, or, as some say, what should go on, by way of planned activities and the like in the schools. Although such a definition is very flexible, it should be meaningful because most readers have spent at least twelve years in school. Thus, unless specified otherwise, our major concern in this text is with formal education or schooling.

The use of the term philosophy of education assumes that there is (or might be) some relationship between the two fields of study. Just what this relationship is constitutes one of the controversies in educational theory today. Some thinkers are convinced that one can deduce a rather definite set or system of educational principles and practices from general philosophy. According to this view, a person will espouse a system of educational principles and practices reflecting certain basic philosophical beliefs. For example: Pragmatists will espouse a system of educational principles and practices which are directly derived from their general philosophy. Many of the thinkers discussed in Chapters V through VIII appear to hold this view.

Diametrically opposed to this position is the view that general philosophy bears little or no relationship to the educational enterprise. The advocates of this view admit that philosophy may be of service to education in clarifying the language used and in pointing out underlying assumptions of certain beliefs expressed in educational literature. General philosophy, however, has no direct bearing on the choice of educational principles or practices or on the acceptance or rejection of theories developed within the field of education.[4] The views expressed in Chapters IX and X reflect this position.

Somewhere between these two opposite poles lies another view of the relationship of general philosophy to education. Briefly, persons holding this view believe that general philosophy sketches the broad outlines from which educational principles might be developed, but leaves to the educational experts the task of devising policies and practices suited to the times. Thus the basic purposes of life and the nature of the educand will be

---

[4]For a thorough discussion of educational separatism, as it is called, see Ellis B. Page, "The Darkling Plain," *Educational Theory*, VIII (April, 1958), 120-26; and R.B. Wilhoyte, "Is It Meaningful to Assert that Philosophy and Education Are Logically Related?"*Educational Theory*, XV (January, 1965), 13-19.

derived from the field of general philosophy, but the tasks of deciding on the role of the school, of devising the specifics of the curriculum, of setting administrative policies, and of determining means of evaluation and methods of teaching will be left to the educational experts in the professional schools, the administrators, and the teachers on the job. As long as such policies and practices do not involve an obvious contradiction of the basic purpose of education or the nature of humanity as stated in the general philosophy, the professional educator is free in his or her choice of means. To illustrate: One's general philosophy might indicate that people have a dual nature-mind and body. If professional educators were to devise a curriculum which provided exclusively for the physical development of the student, it would obviously contradict the basic belief about this dual nature. Such a curriculum, then, must be rejected by the adherents of a dualistic philosophy whose *stated purpose of the school* is to educate the whole person. On the other hand, a curriculum which proposed to develop both physical and mental aspects of the educand would be in harmony with a dualistic concept of the nature of humanity, This view of the relation of philosophy and education is held by educational theorists of many different persuasions.

The very problem of the relation of philosophy to education is one which has interested many thinkers of the past. What we define as the conservative position in education finds its origins in Plato and his contemporaries. Plato, especially, proposed educational theory and practices which were consistent with his views of the world and of knowledge and with his ethical and political doctrines. Broudy, a respected contemporary conservative, calls his own system "classical realism," since many of his views about the nature and destiny of man are rooted in the classical philosophy of Plato and his eminent disciple, Aristotle.

It is this connection between the modern conservative and the classical thinker which will be traced in succeeding chapters, Thus after the distinguishing characteristics of conservatism and liberalism have been listed in Chapter II, the philosophical views of Plato and his con-temporaries, of the Romans, and of the early Christians will be discussed in Chapter III. Chapter IV treats that highly influential epoch in education, the Renaissance, which in its revival of classical learning brought about the full development of the humanistic educational ideal. It should be noted, however, that during this long span of educational history some thinkers did propose certain doctrines which might be classified as liberal. Even Plato, who is considered the father of conservatism, offered liberal proposals such as the right of every child, regardless of his social origin, to the benefits of fundamental education. In general, however, as Christopher Dawson and others point out, humanism remained the force uniting Western civilization until the modern era.[5]

The modern challenge to humanism is presented in Chapter V. The beginnings of liberalism, spanning the seventeenth and eighteenth centuries, are treated both as a revolt against the intellectualism of the humanistic era and as a somewhat unsystematic attempt to create a new educational philosophy. It is not implied that there were no liberal thinkers before this time, but their innovations had little effect on the mainstream of educational theory and practice. The new approach to education was subsequently given a foundation in philosophy and science by the thinkers of the nineteenth and twentieth centuries. This phase in the development of educational thought, covered in Chapter VI, reached its climax in the philosophy of Dewey and his followers in the first half of the twentieth century.

But Dewey's philosophy did not go unchallenged. Between the two great wars, and especially after World War II, a large number of critics appeared. Chapter VII discusses the most important aspects of this contemporary neo-conservative opposition to Deweyan liberalism. Many of the new conservatives mentioned in Chapter VII argue that American education under the influence of liberalism has been deficient; they maintain that European schools do a much more thorough job of educating the young. Often they argue that our school system, or at least certain features of it, should be modeled upon that of other countries which follow the conservative philosophy. Thus the educational systems of France and England, have been chosen to illustrate modern educational conservatism.

Chapter VIII offers a glimpse of a new and as yet undeveloped form of liberalism which theoretically rejects many of the beliefs of both conservatives and Deweyan liberals. Though this group of thinkers presents no unified approach to educational problems, their critical views about man and his role in an industrial, mechanized society present an interesting challenge to educational theorists.

Chapter IX represents an attempt to resolve the conflict between the liberals and the conservatives by suggesting that many of the conflicts will disappear when they are recognized as solely linguistic or logical problems, representing no real problems at all. Chapter X presents the two dominant psychologies of education which roughly represent the philosophical

---

[5]C. Dawson, *The Crisis of Western Education* (New York: Sheed and Ward, 1961), Chs. I, III; and M. Adler and M. Mayer, *The Revolution in Education* (Chicago: Univ. of Chicago Press, 1958), Ch. II.

thought of the theorists discussed in Chapters VIII and IX. Chapter XI introduces Postmodernism and its relationship to conservatism and liberalism.

BIBLIOGRAPHY

Broudy. H. S. *Building a Philosophy of Education*. Rev. ed. Englewood Cliffs, *N.J.:* Prentice-Hall, 1961. Ch. I.

Brubacher, J. S. *Eclectic Philosophy of Education*. Englewood Cliffs, N.J. Prentice-Hall, 1951, Chs. 1,11.

Brubacher, J. S. *Modern Philosophies of Education,* New York: McGraw Hill Book Co., 1962. Ch. I.

Brumbaugh, R. S., and Lawrence, H. N. *Philosophers on Education*. Boston: Houghton Miffllin, 1963. Ch. I.

Butler, J. D. *Four Philosophies and Their Practice in Education and Religion*. Rev. ed. New York: Harper and Brothers, 1957. Ch. I. *Harvard Educational Review,* XXVI (Spring, 1956), 103-12, 119-27, 139- 45, 190-99.

Kimball, S. T., and McClellan, J. *Education and the New America*. New York: Random House, 1962. Chs, II-VI.

Mason, B. E. *Educational Ideals in American Society.* Boston: Allyn & Bacon, 1960, Ch. I.

Morris, Van Cleve. *Philosophy and the American School.* Boston: Houghton Mifflin, 1961. Ch. I.

Nakosteen, Mebdi. *The History and Philosophy of Education.* New York: Ronald Press, 1965. Ch. I.

Ozmon, H. A. and Craver, S. M. *Philosophical Foundations of Education,* Columbus, Ohio: Charles E. Merril Co., 1981, ix-xiv.

Chapter II

Liberalism
Versus
Conservatism

In Chapter 1 the reader was apprised of some of the difficulties involved in the use of the terms liberal and conservative when applied to education. To remove some of the semantic problems, this chapter will give the connotation of these terms in relation to certain fundamental philosophical and educational questions which underlie much of the controversy in contemporary American education. Such questions as "What is man?" "How do we know the world about us?" "What is truth?" and "What is good?" have great significance for education, Also, educators seek answers to the following questions: "What is the purpose of the school?" "What should be taught?" "How should one teach?" "How should pupils be evaluated?" and "How are freedom and discipline to be harmonized?" Many other questions might be posed, such as "Who shall be educated?" "What constitutes academic freedom?" and "Who shall control education?" Obviously, all educational issues cannot be treated in an introductory text, but, some of these questions may be answered in terms of others of the basic questions listed, For example, the question of academic freedom might be resolved in the light of the discussions about freedom and discipline and the purpose of the school.

The following classification of philosophical beliefs and of educational principles and practices might generally characterize the conservative and liberal wings in the educational conflict, It must be remembered that in some areas, such as curriculum, these are not black-white classifications but, rather, degrees of emphasis; in other areas, however, such as the nature of man, there is at times no middle ground.

WHAT IS MAN?

The Conservative View

One of the most persistent beliefs about man's nature coming from the two dominant traditional philosophies, Platonism and Aristotelianism, posits man's dual nature. Most traditional philosophers (and educators) believe that man is composed of body and soul, or mind, The mind is the knowing aspect of man's nature; the body is the sensing and feeling aspect of his nature. The explanation of the interaction between body and mind varies somewhat among the philosophers, but all share a belief in the superiority of mind (spirit) over body (matter), both as to its nature and its governing function, The grasp of this belief is essential for understanding classical education as well as current educational conservatism. This view asserts that only "academic" subjects are worthy of the name education; any activities involving the body-such as manual skills, crafts, and vocational preparation-are not education but training. Only the activities of mind designed to develop the rational part of the composed being are truly educative.

Another belief about man refers to the spiritual nature of the soul, or mind. With few exceptions, philosophers holding this view believe that man's soul is not only spiritual hut also immortal. Plato and the Neo-Platonists, whose thinking dominated the early Christian Era, were very explicit about their belief in the eternal destiny of the soul. When later Christian thinkers adopted Aristotelianism there was no question about the acceptability of the doctrine of the spirituality and immortality of the soul. Therefore it is not difficult to perceive why the salvation of the immortal soul plays so significant a role in determining the goals and the curriculum of some forms of conservative education.

If the salvation of one's soul is the ultimate purpose of *all* activity in this life, it must be the ultimate goal of all educational activities as well. Religion is given a principal place in the curriculum; religious activities are an integral component of school life. The history of education again reveals that this close relationship between religion and education was severed only in recent years. That the content of the theological beliefs of Christians of the Protestant Reformation and post-Reformation eras differed did not change radically the close cooperation between church and school. Even at the time of this writing, Bible reading is still a vital part of some *public* school programs in the United States and many European countries.

Another belief espoused by some conservatives is the fallen condition of man. Since Hebrew-Christian theology dominated the thinking of the Western world until very recently, the view that man is a very imperfect being played a major role in the schools' attitude toward pupil behavior. Obviously, under this thinking, the student can not be allowed to do just as he pleases, since he will often choose evil rather than good. Consequently, very strict codes of behavior were established to guide the immature mind to right conduct and keep it from evil. Children are inclined to misbehave, and their native instincts and desires should constantly be held in check. If permitted to pursue their own wants they will follow the line of least resistance; if given too much freedom they will revolt against legitimate authority just as our first parents, Adam and Eve, revolted against God in the Garden of Eden. Children and youth do not know what is best for them in school or out of school. Mature adults must make choices for them until children have disciplined the unruly passions and instincts of their lower nature-until reason controls bodily desires. Seldom, until the influence of Rousseau was felt in education, was it assumed that children are naturally good and that the school should satisfy their interests and desires.

A final educationally important belief about human nature is founded on the dictum that human nature is everywhere and at all times *essentially* the same. Granted, some races are black, others are white; some people are lazy, others are ambitious; some people are warlike, others are peace-loving; but such characteristics are only accidental, not essential, to human nature, and they might be due to factors of heredity and environment, The one thing all human beings have in common is rationality, in varying degrees. Thus the main purposes of education should be the same throughout the world. And from this it follows that the formal curriculum in schools should be essentially the same, allowing some small variations due to local needs and differences, This belief accounts for the emphasis placed upon developing the rational powers of man by writers as far removed from one another in time as Aristotle and Arthur Bestor, St. Thomas and Mortimer Adler, Plato and John Keats. Reason alone differentiates man from the animal kingdom; it is the development of this reasoning power that gives education its rationale.

The Liberal View

It was noted just above that the conservative looks upon the child and adolescent as someone to be disciplined. Lurking behind this view is the belief that the educand, left on his own, will not choose what is good simply because he is inclined by nature to choose what appeals to his lower impulses. It was Rousseau who first stated the view that the child or adolescent will choose the good simply because his nature inclines him toward good.

Although many educational liberals do not hold Rousseau's extreme position which amounts virtually to saying that the child "can do no wrong," they insist, with Herbert Spencer, that the child's needs, interests, and desires are not evil in themselves but, rather, are morally neutral and can be directed toward socially acceptable and useful ends. Thus all true education is based upon the needs, interests, and natural desires of the child. Any psychologically sound curriculum will be related to the life of the student. Even when the traditional subjects of the curriculum are listed in the school program, the purpose assigned to them and the approach to teaching them is quite different from that of the intellectualist. To illustrate this liberal approach: Foreign languages are offered as electives in secondary schools to satisfy the special interests of some students; advanced sciences and mathematics are not offered as essential intellectual disciplines but as electives to serve the needs of the future engineer or research scientist.

At any rate, underlying the new approach is the belief that the young child, the adolescent, or the advanced student will not have to be forced to study if he is properly motivated. It remains the duty of education to provide for the fullest development of youth's natural tendencies. Discipline problems will disappear only when educators devise programs built upon the real needs and interests of the students at each level of their development. Discipline problems arise from what's wrong with the school program rather than from what's wrong with the student.

Another belief of the liberal school lies in the rejection of the mind-body dichotomy which dictates, in the determination of educational activities, the divorce of training of the body from education of the mind. On the contrary, the pupil is viewed as an evolving organism constituted of the same elements as nature around him. As such, man is not everywhere and at all times the same, but is in a state of continuous change and development. In this respect, man is not essentially different from other living, moving organisms, although he represents the highest stage in the evolutionary process.

The mind-body dichotomy is, the liberal argues, responsible for the onesidedness of traditional education. According to the conservative, bodily activities are considered intruders because they interfere with mental activities. Because bodily activities are viewed as having nothing to do with the mind, they constitute a distraction and an impediment to true education. Consequently, the conservative teacher tries to suppress bodily activities as being sources of mischief leading the pupil away from his true educational task, the development of the mind, For these reasons the traditional school puts a premium on silence ("Do not speak until spoken to"), rigid posture, and attentiveness.

The rejection of this credo in the progressive school's curriculum is quite apparent. Bodily activity becomes an integral part of educational activities. Physical and vocational education are not only introduced into the curriculum but are not relegated to an inferior status, Sports, social functions, club activities, crafts, homemaking, shop work, auto mechanics, and the like are considered worthy components of the curriculum.

Another way of expressing this rejection of mind-body dualism is reflected in the dictum that the whole child is the concern of the school. While the conservative teacher concentrates on developing the mind of the pupil, the liberal also shows concern for such factors as his social adjustment, emotional development, physical well-being, and vocational competence.

Related to the liberals' rejection of the primacy of mind is the explicit denial or practical disregard of the supernatural element in man. Beginning with the Greeks and Romans and continuing in the Christian Era, great stress was placed upon man's close relationship to, and dependence upon, the realm of the supernatural. This connection with the supernatural was essential, since the highest element in man was supernatural. Not until the nineteenth century was significant doubt cast upon the belief in man's supernatural origin and destiny. Even when the term spiritual values is used today, it in no way necessarily signifies connection with the realm of the supernatural. For some, spiritual values might be equated with aesthetic or ethical values. For all practical purposes, the secular school views the pupil as a child of nature, not a child of God.[1]

Still another belief of the educational liberal, which conflicts with the conservative view of man's nature, concerns the role of the will in the educational enterprise. The current emphasis is upon finding causes of misbehavior in hereditary and, especially, in environmental forces affecting the student, rather than in his ill-will. Books of child and adolescent psychology and guidance reveal the assumption that the behavior patterns of human beings are determined by hereditary and environmental factors, The roots of both acceptable and unacceptable behavior are to be sought in the

---

[1]B.J. Bell,*Crisis in Education*(New York: McGraw-Hill Book Co., 1949).

socioeconomic setting of the home and the school, in the family background, and in similar factors. If a pupil continually misbehaves, the manual of psychology will say to make a study of his home situation or even to reevaluate the school program, for it may be the cause of the misbehavior. In short, if the student is a discipline problem, correct the environment and the problem will vanish. Or, schools create discipline problems by a program failing to meet the needs of all the students.

HOW DO WE KNOW?

The Conservative View

It is true that classical philosophies are more concerned with meta-physical questions of what is real than they are with how one comes to know reality (epistemological questions). This preference, however, does not imply that the older philosophies do not develop theories of knowledge which had some effect upon school practice. In fact, the construction of theories of learning, as quite distinct from philosophical theories of knowledge, is of quite recent origin.

As one might anticipate, the classical approach to knowledge is based upon the belief in the rational nature of man, as described on p. 9. The conservative does not deny that man comes to know the world around him through experience. Animals also know something about their environment, but man's knowing activities are above those of animals since man is rational in nature. In other words, man reaches his highest potential for knowing when he uses his rational rather than his sensory abilities. Even when the teacher begins with the sense experiences of the pupils as starting points, he hopes the student will leave this realm of sense experience and arrive at a knowledge of general principles through the use of reason.

This belief that knowing is ideally centered in man's reasoning powers had two significant effects upon school practice. First, in order that students may exercise the intellectual or reasoning powers, facts are needed. For this reason the conservative school places great importance upon the students' mastery of a large assortment of factual materials. Consequently, a relatively large amount of time is spent in memorizing the materials to be employed in the reasoning process. Only when the student has mastered the basic facts is he considered ready to learn the higher principles of the subject under consideration. The second step in the knowing process is characterized by a high degree of abstraction. The student is expected to leave the world of sense experience and deal chiefly with ideas, in general found in the works of the greatest minds in the fields of literature, mathematics, history, and philosophy. Thus the conservative educator appeals to the highly verbal, the abstract, and that which is quite remote from the world of concrete reality.

The Liberal View

Whereas the conservative emphasizes the role of reason in knowing, the educational liberals place their trust in experience and science. The scientific advances of the past century have convinced many that man's surest mode of knowing is based upon his experience and the highly refined forms of experience (experimentation) found in scientific activities. The results of the empirical mode of knowing can provide all the knowledge man needs for his existence. There is no need, it is argued, to search beyond the world of things; there is no need for the rational formulation of the ultimate principles of reality (metaphysical speculation).

Thus the liberal theory of knowing (learning) rejects the unique role of abstract reasoning and relies upon experience. The implications of this view for teaching-learning method involve drastic changes in school practice. Not only the role of the teacher but also those of books and materials, of the school environment, of the curriculum, and of the student himself must be radically revised. Education must adapt to the new epistemology. The modern concern with the mode of acquiring knowledge makes epistemology the heart of the philosophical endeavor and the guide of educational practice.

One very significant difference between the conservative and the liberal approach to knowing and its relation to the educative process is based in the essentially inductive emphasis of the liberal. By solving problems which are rooted in experience, students arrive at their own conclusions. Any generalization which might apply to future experiences is based upon the solutions of specific problems. The older approach, often referred to as deductive, stresses the necessity of students mastering the general principles, which they might then apply to the solution of specific problems and from which necessary conclusions might be drawn.

WHAT IS TRUTH?

Once the nature of the knowing process has been defined, one is just a step from an understanding of the nature of truth. Both the liberal and the conservative agree that knowing the truth is of great concern to the school. But the meaning of "truth" differs for each school of thought.

The Conservative View

The conservative conception of truth is derived from the Platonic and Aristotelian conceptions of the nature of knowing. As pointed out on pp. 91. it is man's rational powers of knowing that distinguish him from lower forms of life in both Platonism and Aristotelianism. It is the truths of reason as well that are considered truly human for the educational theorists of these two schools of philosophical thought.

This conception of truth asserts that certain changeless principles constitute the core of what is worth knowing. The worthiness of these basic truths does not rest upon their usefulness but rather upon their own intrinsic value: They are, in short, worth knowing for their own sake. The conservative doe's not deny that the knowledge of such truths (the possession of wisdom) has practical value. On the contrary, he insists that the possession of such knowledge is necessary so that its possessor might become a wise statesman, lawyer, clergyman, or medical doctor. In fact, such knowledge is necessary for anyone to become truly human; such knowledge is worth having for its own sake, since it contributes to man's intellectual perfection. In opposition to this rational knowledge, the conservative places practical knowledge (vocational learning) which is not acquired for perfection of the mind or intellect but for some other purpose, such as performing a certain job or task.

For these reasons the conservative has always insisted that intellectual training is an essential prerequisite for anyone aspiring to the learned professions. One must perfect his mind or intellect first, acquire wisdom, and only then can one proceed to an *intelligent* study of the specialized materials of the professions. Herein lies the explanation for the high esteem the conservative has for the intellectual disciplines as opposed to vocational training. He believes the truths contained in these disciplines to be applicable to all geographical areas of the civilized world; such an education constitutes the only sound foundation for effective citizenship in a democracy, monarchy, or aristocracy, for it is the only type of education that leads man to true wisdom (the perfection of his mind).

One might ask whether the conservative maintains that *all* truths are absolute or changeless. A study of the history of education will show that such is not the case. Nevertheless, the traditional school concerns itself *primarily* with the transmission of those truths that are considered lasting; these constituted the very core of knowledge which produced wisdom in the student.

The Liberal View

The educational liberal is just as concerned with truth as the conservative, but his definition of truth differs basically from that of his opponent.

First, whereas the conservative emphasizes the permanent nature of the truths with which the school should concern itself, the liberal emphasizes a dynamic conception of truth. He rests his case on the belief that students should not labor under the illusion that there are certain facts, principles, laws, and theories that always were and always will be true. The student must be reminded that his daily search for knowledge will lead him to tentative conclusions; he must question even those truths held most sacred by past generations; doubt and uncertainty will be the watchwords of all the conclusions he arrives at by his experiencing and reasoning.

Second, according to its advocates, this relative view of truth is the only one in harmony with the actual state of affairs in both the physical and social universe. Who can deny that the physical universe and the social order are not undergoing constant change? The physical and social sciences have demonstrated that the truths of one era become the myths of another. Furthermore, truth is relative not only because the world is in a state of constant flux but also because of the unique viewpoint of the knower himself.

Third, this new conception of truth places upon the school (and the individual) the responsibility of developing very different attitudes toward truth. Whereas the conservative sought to achieve "certainty," the liberal espouses an attitude of uncertainty. His conclusions are only tentative solutions to problems, not absolute answers to questions. This somewhat skeptical attitude must hold sway not only in regard to truths of a scientific nature but also to the most cherished beliefs of religion, ethics, politics, and aesthetics.

The effects of the new conception of truth for academic freedom, censorship, and indoctrination are especially significant for the elementary and secondary schools. In the traditional school, children are taught and expected to master those truths considered eternal and immutable. Teachers do not question those truths, or do they veer from the accepted beliefs in what they teach. Often the beliefs of the teachers are closely scrutinized for possible deviation from the doctrines of those sponsoring the school. Such is the case not only in regard to theological knowledge but also in politics. Some freedom to teacher and student is granted in certain phases of school activity, but in the essentials, unity of mind and purpose is the motto of all concerned with the educational endeavor.

The position of the liberal school advocates teacher freedom in presenting all points of view on a specific topic, rejects censorship of materials used in schools, and encourages students to find their own answers and solutions to questions and problems in all areas of human concern.

WHAT IS GOOD?

The Conservative View

The conservative's beliefs about value are rooted in his Concept of truth and the nature of the knowing process. Just as he believes that man can and should use his reason to arrive at certain immutable truths, he argues that man must use his reason to determine a set of permanent values by which he will guide his everyday life. Like their liberal opponents, conservatives (Plato excepted) recognize that simply because someone knows what is right or wrong, beautiful or ugly, he will not necessarily always act accordingly. Nevertheless, *knowing* what is right is a necessary prerequisite to right action on the part of free man. And so the conservative's major concern as an educator is to see that the student *knows* what is right or wrong, beautiful or ugly. Other agencies such as the family, the church, and the state are expected to assist the young to translate this knowledge and to live the good life. Certainly, the conservative expects the pupils to behave while they are in school, and in reality classroom discipline is very rigorous. But knowledge of value is the prime objective in teaching values, and the school's rules and regulations are themselves means of impressing upon the student a knowledge of value.

Again, at least as far as education is concerned, it makes little difference whether the conservative school drew its beliefs from the Platonic or Aristotelian systems of thought, for both emphasize the primacy of the intellect (or reason) in the process of arriving at either a code of ethics or criteria for art. In the Platonic tradition, ethical and aesthetic values are somehow implanted in the mind of man, who has an immediate grasp of their first principles. It is the duty of man to use his rational powers to distinguish good from evil and beauty from ugliness. The very universality of such ethical principles as honesty and justice points to their absolute nature and origin. In the Aristotelian tradition reason is designated as the means whereby man discovers the natural law to do good and avoid evil and to make aesthetic judgments based on such rational principles as unity, clarity, and splendor. In the philosophies of both Plato and Aristotle reason plays the significant role in value judgments, and this element dominates the conservative view of value.

Often the conservative view of value has been interpreted to imply that there are no relative values whatsoever. Though classical philosophers generally did not make this claim, the school itself often was responsible for treating all values as absolute. Whether the value is relative or absolute it is handled by the school in such a manner that pupils cannot help getting the notion that all values are absolute and final. Regulations governing dress, classroom deportment, and grading standards in the traditional school often are treated as absolutes by teachers and pupils alike.

One final question remains about the origin of values in the conservative view. If values are found in the mind of man, as Plato said, or in the "law of nature," as Aristotle claimed, from whence did they originate? What man comes to know must exist. From whence did such knowledge come? Values find their origin in some supernatural force outside the mind of man and the universe: God or the Absolute. It is from this same supernatural source that man received his rational powers, and it is to this same source that man is responsible for his behavior.

The Liberal View

The liberal view of value is based upon a denial of any finality or absoluteness in the realm of value. In other words, no claim can be made for any sort of objective existence for values either in the mind of man or in the universe of nature. Rather, all values are rooted in man's daily activities. If man were not able to interact with his fellow man there would be no value at all; the very existence of values is dependent upon events happening within a social context. And since both the physical and social universe are characterized by change, so also the realm of value is to be characterized. Values will change as man's perceptions of the physical and social realm change. All values must be reconstructed to fit the changing times and the emerging needs of man.

This relative view of value does not imply that changes in value are rapid and sweeping. On the contrary, the modern liberal believes that most changes are gradual and at times almost imperceptible and that there is some stability from one situation to similar ones. Nevertheless, there can be no permanence in even the most cherished values.

Since, according to the liberal, one can appeal to no source outside man as the fountainhead of values, and since values are neither innate nor contained in an objective code, the everyday course of events is the context for value making. Thus most values are social in nature and origin; each value finds its origin in a Solution to a problem involving other human beings. As novel problems arise in human society, new solutions are devised which are stated as values. Old values, then, must make way for new ones; modern solutions to problems involving values will reflect the current needs and desires of those involved.

The emphasis on the social origin and nature of values is not held by all liberals. There are those who maintain that the choice of the individual and the satisfaction of individual needs are the ultimate criteria of values. Both the advocates of social and individualistic views however, agree that all value judgments must be put to the test of experience, for experience rather than authority determine their acceptability. Thus the same process is employed for arriving at values as for arriving at knowledge.

WHAT IS THE PURPOSE OF THE SCHOOL?

Our concern here is with the specific purpose of the school rather than the very broad objectives of education. Clearly, education involves agencies and institutions other than the school: the family, community, mass media of communication, religious and charitable institutions. To what extent these agencies and institutions should be involved in the work of the school is in itself one facet of the conservative-liberal controversy.

The Conservative View

As mentioned on p. 10 conservative philosophers point to man's reason as the only essential characteristic differentiating him from animals. Furthermore, the truths of reason and the merits of intellectual contemplation are extolled above the work of the hands. The intellectual virtues are assigned the highest rank in the hierarchy of virtues. Therefore they see the aim of the school as an intellectual one; other agencies could teach children to pray, sew, cook, and till the soil. They believe also that the acquisition of knowledge in a rational and systematic manner could not be supplied in most instances in the family circle or in an apprenticeship, and a special institution was needed to fulfill this mission. Thus from ancient times the school was considered the proper agency for the development of the intellectual powers of its clientele through the systematic presentation of knowledge or subject matter.

Any other aims were considered ancillary to this primary purpose. Thus when Plato recommended that all students receive adequate training in physical culture, it was not because he considered the development of physical fitness the proper aim of the school. Rather, he believed that physical fitness was prerequisite for the school to perform its primary task: One could not develop a mind in a weak or sickly body.

The aim of the conservative school, then, is simple and well defined. Teachers, administrators, and students know what they are about. Theoretically, only those possessing superior intellectual ability are admitted to the higher schools. Only those who demonstrate their ability as measured by mastery of the subject matter are permitted to remain in school. Elitism in education is necessary consequence of the aims of traditional education. Many conservatives of all eras, from the preChristian Era to the twentieth century, deny that all the children of all of the people can be educated; by far the great majority should be taught only the fundamental skills of communication and computation. Only a relatively small number can be afforded the kind of education which perfects the intellect and leads to true wisdom.

The Liberal View

Whereas the educational goal of the conservative is relatively simple because of its singleness of purpose, such is not the case with the liberal, who points to the inadequacies of the intellectualistic purpose of the school on several counts.

First, he argues, even if one grants that the intellectual goal of the traditional school was adequate at one time, it can no longer suffice for the modern school. As other institutions serving society have introduced fundamental changes into their own structures or have disappeared completely, so the school must change if it is to accord with present conditions.

Second, the school cannot and should not set up any final or ultimate goals. Therefore the goals of conservative education must give way to more flexible ends which will change as man and his physical and social environment change. The whole relationship of means and ends needs revision. Since, according to the conservative, the school's final end is the perfection of the intellect, all activities are considered means to this end. Thus a certain curricular pattern is considered a more effective means than another in achieving this end, and a rigid form of classroom discipline is considered a better means to the same end than a permissive approach to control. In the liberal view, however, the means-end relationship is one of interdependence and continuity. Ends are to be judged by the means used in attaining them, and means are to be judged in terms of their ends. In short, both means and ends in education will be dependent upon one another in the continuous flow of educational activity.

Once the conservative's purpose of the school has been rejected and a new means-ends relationship established, the liberal educational theorist is obliged to produce some statement of purpose for the vast educational enterprise of the modern world. This goal has been variously stated as the development of the whole child or the development of the person, as opposed to the development of his intellect.

Perhaps the best manner of approaching the objectives of the liberal school lies in an analysis of modern statements of these purposes. One expression of this view is the statement of the objectives of modern American education by the Educational Policies Commission of the National Education Association and the American Association of School Administrators.[2] It should be noted that the objectives listed cover the entire range of development, not only intellectual development. As such, it is representative of the whole-child approach to establishing the school's purposes.

The four general categories in the Commission's list are concerned with the objectives of self-realization, human relationships, economic efficiency, and civic responsibility. Conspicuous by their absence are such goals as development of the mind or intellect and the acquisition of knowledge for its own sake. For other lists very similar to that of the Educational Policies Commission, see *The Imperative Needs of Youth,* National Association of Secondary-School Principals, and *Organizing the Elementary School for Living and Learning,* the official statement of the Association for Supervision and Curriculum Development.

WHAT SHOULD BE TAUGHT?

Because of the similarity in course offerings in conservative and liberal schools, some observers might be led to believe that the differences between the two are insignificant. Even when there is duplication of courses offered, however, the reasons for offering them are basically quite different.

---

[2]Educational Policies Commission,*Policies for Education in American Democracy* (Washington, D.C.: Educational Policies Commission of the N.E.A. and the A.A.S.S.A., 1946).

Curriculum is one of the key areas in which the liberal's view differs radically from that of the conservative.

The Conservative View

One of the most salient features of the curriculum of the conservative school is its limited scope. Both elementary and secondary education restrict the content of the curriculum in accordance with the limited purpose of the school, namely the perfection of the intellect through specific subject matter. A perusal of educational history will show some variation in the curricular offerings of the schools of the Greeks and Romans, the early Christians, and the men of the Middle Ages, Renaissance, and the nineteenth century. But these offerings were limited *primarily* to those subjects and skills suited best to serve the purpose of intellectual development. The conservative lower schools of the present century offer training in the basic skills of reading, writing, spelling, and computation along with such subjects as history, geography, and music. The secondary school curriculum consists of the usual academic subjects taught in the classroom: languages, science, mathematics, history. Thus the term extracurricular is used to designate all school activities not directly related to the subject-matter classes. Athletics, social activities, dramatics, band, chorus, orchestra, and many similar activities are deliberately labeled extracurricular, for these activities are not proper to the school's purpose. They may take place in the school building simply because there is no other suitable edifice, not because they are part and parcel of "schooling." So central is this issue in defining a person's views one need not ask a teacher whether he is a conservative or a liberal to determine his position. Just ask him what criteria he uses to distinguish between curricular and extracurricular activities, and his position will be clear.

A second characteristic of the conservative curriculum is that it is, for the most part, prescribed and contains very few, if any, electives. Until the twentieth century the presence of electives in the curriculum of the lower schools was virtually unknown. Only at the university level did the need for choosing a profession permit the student to select a course of study. Consequently anyone who attended a conservative school took all subjects offered and in the prescribed sequence. As the student worked his way up the educational ladder the subjects became more academically abstract and difficult. If he was not able to cope with the required subjects, there were no electives to which the student might turn; he had reached the highest rung possible for him, and he usually left school for apprentice training or vocational school.

Another characteristic of the conservative curriculum has to do with control. Experts or scholars determine the curriculum content. Local school authorities, teachers, parents, and students have little or no direct influence on, or control over, the curriculum. This characteristic control from the top down is just as evident in the official curricular directives of many twentieth-century conservative educational systems as it was in those of Plato in the fourth century B.C.

These characteristics of this curriculum-its subject-matter centeredness, its academic nature, its compulsory nature, and its control by authorities-are somewhat related. If certain subjects are conceived by educational experts to be essential for developing the intellectual powers of man, all students should be expected to master them. If the primary job of the school is to develop the minds of its students, nonacademic activities have no legitimate place in the curriculum.

The Liberal View

The liberal's conception of the curriculum implies a complete rejection, not just a modification, of the entire conservative outlook. The first radical revision affects the scope of the curriculum: The liberal extends it to all activities which take place under the direction and control of the school. Some modern curriculum-makers even object to the term co-curricular as applied to nonacademic activities, since it might be interpreted as refusing to accept them as integral elements of a curriculum.

In extending the scope of the school curriculum to include all school-related activities both inside and outside the school, it is necessary to use other measures besides intellectual content to determine curricular patterns. One of the first criteria for selection of curricular offerings employed especially by early liberals, who revolted against the literary curriculum, was utility. They argued that unless a pupil could perceive the practical value of a subject he would just go through the motions of learning, and there would be no lasting effect.

A second important criterion for determining curricular content is derived from patterns of student interest. Not all students are interested in academic subjects, nor can the interest of all students in such subjects be aroused sufficiently to make the study of them worthwhile. Therefore a very wide range of subjects and activities must be offered to satisfy student interests. The aim of satisfying these twin motivational forces, need and interest, is responsible for the great variety of academic and nonacademic offerings available in the modern secondary school and the great freedom of choice permitted the student. Hosts of course offerings, ranging from calculus to machine shop, from Shakespeare to social dancing and personal grooming, are found in the new curriculum.

Curricula designed to meet the needs and satisfy the interests of students place no status rank on any course pattern. Liberal curriculum-makers are very clear on this point: One group of subjects, usually academic, should not be viewed as prestige subjects for bright students, with another group of subjects, usually nonacademic, viewed as being designed for students with low academic abilities. Rather, the student and his counselor select those subjects which the student needs to achieve his goals and in which he has genuine interest.

One final characteristic of the liberal curriculum is worthy of note. Whereas the conservative curriculum was constructed around certain subjects designed to perfect the intellect, the liberal curriculum might be said to be close to life. What happens in the school should not be removed from daily living but should be an integral part of it. The school is a community, a democratic community, where students live for at least seven hours a day. Therefore, the curriculum should be an experience in living, not solely a preparation for adult living.

HOW SHOULD ONE TEACH?

The Conservative View

Although the traditional school employs a variety of teaching-learning methods, all of these methods could be characterized as teacher-centered. One of the most honored, and perhaps most frequently used, methods is the lecture. This method needs little explanation in a book of this type, since most students have experienced it at the secondary and college level. The teacher or lecturer presents the essential facts and understandings of the subject matter to be learned, and the student puts the same materials in his notebook. The typical companion of this method is the basic textbook with questions to be answered at the end of each chapter. The teacher and the textbook possess the essential knowledge which the student should learn in order to perfect his intellectual powers. The lecture method, or some adaptation of it, is one of the best means of transmitting this knowledge to the students; and the student has no excuse for not learning the essentials since he has been given them by the *magister,* or master. The student need not wander about in an aimless search for what is worth knowing since the teacher by his intellectual maturity and teaching experience has selected what knowledge is of most worth. It remains for the student to master the subject matter presented to him. The recitation period so common in the traditional school was a means of determining the extent to which the student had understood and mastered the material presented by the teacher and the textbook.

Another characteristic of teacher-centered methods is the relatively great emphasis placed on teacher activity in the classroom. Student activity, unless it is in the form of a response to a question or order, is virtually unknown. Thus the functions of teaching and learning are considered quite distinct. The teacher is the active agent during the class periods; the student is relatively passive. He learns what he has been presented with, either in supervised study periods at school or in home study periods. There generally is no intermingling of teacher-learner roles.

The Liberal View

The methods of the liberal are pupil-centered, as opposed to the teacher-centered methods of conservatives, and therefore they place more emphasis on pupil activity. Perhaps the slogan "Learning by Doing," so much used by some educationists, characterizes most clearly this approach to learning.

One of the methods best exemplifying the shift from teacher to pupil activity in the teaching-learning process employs problem solving. Although in the traditional school students were given problems to deal with, the problem-solving method developed by educational liberals has little in common with that of the traditional school: It is based on a new approach to knowledge described on pp. 13-14, in which experience constitutes the heart of the knowing process. The project method, an adaptation of problem solving, has been used extensively for the past several decades. Various techniques of individualized and group instruction have been developed.

Because of the liberal's emphasis upon learning by actual experience, field trips, movies, recordings, and television serve as means of vicarious experience since students obviously cannot have direct contact in all phases of learning activities. The community and the school are more closely united in modern educational techniques which enables the student to have more direct contact with community life. Other examples of the application of newer techniques of pupil participation are noted in sections on the curriculum, evaluation, and classroom discipline.

HOW SHOULD PUPILS BE EVALUATED?

There is much controversy about testing, grading, and promotion in American education. However, there is one point on which the educational conservatives and the liberals are in agreement: All appraisal should be in terms of educational objectives. Therefore the reader must relate this discussion of evaluation to the section on the purpose of the school (see pp. 21-23).

The Conservative View

As seen, the primary aim of conservative education is the intellectual development of the pupils, which is usually judged in terms of their mastery of subject matter. The subject matter itself has changed over the centuries, but the modem conservative argues as did his classical predecessor: The best means of determining the student's intellectual progress is to discover how well he has learned the assigned material. This process consists in using all means to determine the extent to which the student has memorized all the pertinent facts, vocabulary, or formulae of the particular subject. It also involves testing the mastery of principles and of generalizations to be derived from the subject. Further, it may test the student's ability to apply his knowledge to other situations.

The oral examination was used almost exclusively for the evaluation of achievement in the various disciplines until the mid-nineteenth century. The teacher or the visiting examiner asked the questions and the student attempted to answer them; the questioner then passed judgment on the answers. Later, when the written essay examination was used, the evaluator looked for the same evidences of mastery of the subject as had the oral examiner. When short-answer type examinations are used, the prime objective of evaluation remains the same for the conservative: To what extent has the student mastered the subject?

The Liberal View

In the liberal school emphasis on development of the whole child calls for the evaluation of much more than the academic achievement of the student. A variety of techniques has been devised to measure personal and social development of the student and the group in which he works.

Anecdotal records, observational methods, rating scales, health inventories, sociometric techniques, projective techniques, and case studies are used to assay the very broad objectives of the new education. The extent to which the student has memorized facts and principles is not an all-important criterion. Rather, the teacher attempts to assess a pupil's growth in all phases of living. Tests of subject-matter achievement and intelligence are only a part of the evaluative process.

In general, the liberal point of view assesses the student's success according to the following: (1) The amount of change or growth in physical development, especially in those skills needed for living in an age of change. (2) The facility with which the pupil works and plays with the groups in which he finds himself, that is, social adjustment. (3) The development of problem-solving ability both in individual and group situations. (4) The possession of democratic attitudes and behavior. (5) The evidence of emotional maturity according to his age.

It is evident from the list that evaluation is relative. There are no absolute norms or standards based on the mastery of any given content. The pupil is viewed as achieving his goal when he demonstrates growth in these areas of behavior. Wherever possible, marks which reflect static and absolute norms, such as numerical grades (70-100 passing) or letter grades (A-D passing), are discontinued. Progress reports covering the whole gamut of pupil behavior are preferred to conservative report cards.

HOW ARE FREEDOM AND DISCIPLINE
TO BE HARMONIZED?

One of the problems which has always plagued teachers is classroom discipline. But discipline and freedom are correlative terms. The answer of the liberal to this very practical question varies greatly from that of the conservative.

The Conservative View

The conservative view of pupil behavior involves such concepts as discipline, authority, obedience, silence, and order. Early in this chapter the conservative view of the nature of man was discussed. That man's nature has evil tendencies or even is fundamentally evil was generally accepted by educators of the past and by many in the present. For this reason it is argued that strict discipline in school is essential to assist the child or the youth to become a disciplined person. If he is given the freedom to follow his natural inclinations, he will learn little or nothing in school and will enter adult society wholly unprepared and undisciplined. The good of the individual as well as that of society demand discipline.

In this view of school discipline, teacher authority and obedience to that authority are correlatives. The teachers and administrators acting in place of the parents have full authority over the pupils during school hours. Theoretically, the conservative admits that pupils have certain basic rights as human beings, but for all practical purposes these rights are subordinated to the discipline of the school, Therefore neither parents nor pupils may ever question the school's right to exact obedience to rules and regulations; no one denies the school's right to enact whatever rules it deems essential; no one questions the school's right to use whatever disciplinary measures seem best suited to exact obedience.

But the conservative educator wants the pupil to do more than proffer outward signs of obedience to school authorities. The school should develop in each pupil an understanding of, and a proper attitude toward, obedience to the commandments of God and man. In this respect the school is assisting the home, the church, and the state in preparing good citizens of this world and the world hereafter.

To summarize the conservative view, one might say that it draws its rationale from a hierarchical view of authority that necessitates a respect for, and obedience to, authority; a faith in rules and regulations; the necessity of punishment of some kind or other for infractions of the rules; and, finally, the value of reward for those who obey the rules.

The Liberal View

At the outset, the liberal rejects the traditional notion of authority. The teacher is not an absolute authority removed from, or ranked above, the class but is an integral element or part of the group. The teacher's relative maturity and experience give him certain prerogatives in the control of the class, but he has no authority ultimately derived from some supreme authority. In keeping with the spirit of democracy, then, the liberal rejects the authoritarian attitudes and actions of the traditional teacher in favor of freedom of movement and choice on the part of pupils. It is not silence or obedience that makes a class well disciplined but the cooperative efforts of the teacher and students engaged in learning activities.

Another aspect of discipline, according to some members of the liberal school, is derived from the social nature of man. Following the lead of social theorists who have influenced educational theory, they argue that the child is humanized by the social environment. These educational theorists point to the necessity of achieving order and discipline through the application of group standards and group pressures. For example, most youngsters want to be accepted by the group to which they belong. To foster discipline, the teacher will enlist the efforts of all the members of the class in establishing and enforcing norms of classroom and school behavior. When the student recognizes that the norms incorporate his own wishes and desires, he is more apt to abide by them than when he knows they are handed down by an external authority. Furthermore, his natural desire to be accepted by the group will restrain him from performing acts which may put him in disfavor with his classmates. Discipline, then, according to this school of thought, is a social process involving every person in the group, as contrasted with a state of affairs in which one individual exerts authority over his inferiors.

BIBLIOGRAPHY

Pratt, Daniel D. (1992). Conceptions of Teaching. *Adult Education Quarterly*, 42 (4), 203-220.

Young, Morley. (1993). The Dark Underside of Japanese Education. *Phi Delta Kappan*. (Oct.) 130-132.

Chapter III

Classical Educational Theory

By far the greatest of all educational conservatives is the eminent thinker of ancient Greece, Plato. "Back to Plato" has been the motto of many conservatives throughout the ages. His influence was felt in the Roman schools, the early Christian schools, the monastic schools, the medieval universities, and the schools of the Renaissance and humanistic eras. Twentieth-century conservatives may not be thoroughgoing philosophical Platonists, but, unwittingly (or wittingly), many of them advocate the broad outlines of Platonic educational theory.

Plato can be considered a conservative even within the political climate of his own time. Democracy had its first trial in Athens, but when Plato reached the peak of his career Athenian democracy was in the period of decline. He felt that the permissive atmosphere in Athens had led to chaos, the weakening of discipline, and the demise of morality among the citizenry. He was impressed, on the other hand, with the well-ordered situation in aristocratic Sparta, where each social class in the state recognized its function and contributed to the harmonious functioning of the state, producing a minimum of factional conflict. Thus Plato considered the Athenian experiment in democracy a failure. It was a failure, he believed, because citizens could never be equals in government, for only the few were fitted to rule. The only true government, then, was an aristocracy, the rule of the *good* men, and only the *aristoi* needed education for leadership. Thus advanced education, in the true sense of the word, was for the intellectual elite, not the average man. Because he advocated this reactionary point of view, Plato had to leave Athens in 389 B.C. Other factors place Plato in the conservative camp among both his contemporaries and modern theorists, but these will be discussed in some detail in the succeeding pages of this chapter.[1]

However, Plato did advocate some liberal notions such as equal educational opportunity for the children of all social classes. Regardless of their social origin, all should be given the chance to climb to the ranks of the rulers, provided they possessed the intellectual potential to achieve this status. Similarly, he believed that girls should be given the same educational opportunities as boys.

In this chapter we shall seek Plato's answers to the important philosophical and educational questions posed in Chapter II. The adaptations of Platonic theory by his pupil Aristotle, as well as by the Romans and the early Christians, will also be considered.

PLATO'S PHILOSOPHY

What Is Man?

To know the nature of man is to know the nature of education. Plato applied this dictum in developing his educational philosophy just as all great educational theorists have done since his time. And Plato is very clear in his description of human nature. In Platonic philosophy, the highest faculty of man, reason, is rooted in a spiritual soul. [2] The appetites and the emotions are functions of man's lower element, the body. (This view is classified as mind [soul] -body dualism.) At one time the soul of man existed in the world of pure spirit and enjoyed the highest bliss, pure contemplation. But because of some contact with evil in the world of pure spirit, the soul was condemned to become a part of a body, forming an organic unit. Being united to matter was considered the highest form of punishment that could be inflicted upon a spirit. Because the soul formed an organic unit with the body, it was then subject to weaknesses which it did not have in its heavenly existence.

When the soul was separated from the joys of the contemplation of universal patterns of truth, beauty, goodness, and justice, it retained all of these ideas, although in a somewhat hazy form. Thus at birth each person has the changeless idea of circularity, tree, house, horse, honesty, proportion, and so on (for a more complete discussion of absolute truth see

---

[1]An extensive discussion of Plato's educational theories adapted to twentieth-century education is found in R.C. Lodge, *Plato's Theory of Education* (London: Kegan, Trench, Trubner, 1947), Chs. XI, XII.

[2]Plato *Laws* x. 892.

p. 35). One might compare this mental state to that of a man who has suffered severe shock and retains only a faint recollection of his past. The everyday world of things and objects is merely a fleeting, shadowy copy of the true idea which the soul carries within itself from heaven.[3] The belief that looks upon the soul and body as two separable elements, at least before and after death, was not original with Plato. It is traceable to primitive cultures which used all kinds of rituals and incantations to get the soul to return to the body of a dead chieftain, hero, or beloved one. Also, it is seen in the means used by primitives to strengthen the soul for the hardships of this world as well as for life in the next world.

The educationally significant aspect of Plato's theory of Ideas, however, lies in the actual educational practices derived from it: Ideas constitute the important content of education; man's superior faculties are attributed to the soul (mind and reason) and inferior attributes to the body (evil, change, corruption, and the like). The things of the mind are the concern of education; other activities belong to man's lower nature and should not be dignified by the term education. Rather, they should be called training, in the sense that one speaks of training an animal. [4]

Since Plato placed the life-giving principle of man in the rational soul, this soul can never be dead: It must always be characterized by life. The very idea of soul excludes death, which is the opposite of life.[5] The soul, then, must be immortal, but only its rational element will live on to inhabit the bodies.

Closely allied to this view that man is composed of two elements-one spiritual and rational, the other material and irrational, with the spiritual element in the position of prestige,-is the Platonic notion of social classes. The highest class is composed of those who possess the highest degree of reasoning power, the lowest class, of those with the lowest degree. As noted in the introduction to this chapter, Plato's aristocratic preferences impelled him to maintain that only those with the highest intellectual abilities can be considered fit to be rulers; those with less ability should be the guardians of the state, who can use their more limited intelligence as warriors; those with the lowest mental ability are expected to use what little intelligence they have as workers or providers for the two higher classes and for themselves. The upper class, the philosopher-kings, is made up of those select few

---

[3]Plato *Republic* vii. 514. It is argued that Plato employed poetic language and most of these statements are not to be taken literally.
[4]Plato *Laws* i. 643f.
[5]Plato *Phaedo* 102ff. Plato *Phaedrus* 245.

possessing the superior intellectual powers which enable them to acquire a comprehensive knowledge of the supreme good. Only by the possession of outstanding intelligence can they acquire the knowledge required to attain that virtue and goodness necessary to rule, for without such power of reasoning they cannot grasp the immutable ideas of truth, goodness, and beauty which one possesses in the world of Ideas. The masses can be happy only when ruled by the intellectuals, since they do not have the intelligence necessary to run the affairs of state, and certainly they would make a jumble of things. To emphasize the great difference between the classes, Plato likened them to gold, silver, and bronze (or clay). Differences in levels of intelligence also apply within each class: The guardian or military class, for example, has its higher and lower ranks. Those with great intellectual ability should be placed in positions of leadership; the rest of the soldiers must be habituated to following their leaders blindly. [6]

But who is to select the vessels of gold? Those entrusted with the education of youth. Paradoxically, the future leaders are to be selected from all classes. But Plato did feel that the majority of the elite would come from the noble families, since they possess the means to bring out the intellectual qualities of their offspring.

The selection of the elite from the masses was a very serious matter for Plato and would not be completed until the youth was twenty years old. Only when the young man has been selected will education for leadership commence. Also, Plato envisaged no soft life for the philosopher-kings. They have to forego the joys of family life and renounce worldly goods and the ordinary recreational activities of the lower classes, for their entire lives are to be devoted to contemplation and working for the common good. Here, too, Plato was reacting against what he considered the selfish individualism which he viewed as part of any democratic structure. Individuals would place their own good above that of the common good, but in an aristocratic social structure those dedicated to the sole purpose of ruling would place the common good above their own personal gain.

Even though his specific plan was never put into practice, Plato's view of society as an ordered division of classes has been the ideal of educational conservatives throughout the ages. Like Plato, the medieval educator believed that only the intellectually gifted should receive advanced education, and the scholars of the Renaissance scorned the idea of mass education. The modern conservative is constantly deriding the evils of mass education, especially at the higher levels, and calls for very rigorous

---

[6]Plato Republic. 374ff.

selection of candidates for advanced study according to their intellectual capacities.

Because Plato emphasized the individual differences, the notion might be conveyed that there is no human nature common to all men. Such is not the case. He made this very clear when he insisted that all men are brothers and all possess the same fundamental powers of the soul.[7] Differences are not essential, but accidental. Furthermore, as already noted, he advocated a radical equality of opportunity when he pointed up that a "golden parent" will sometimes have a "silver son," and vice versa. All the children of all the people are in the same manpower pool from which the rulers will be selected.[8] Man is to be considered first and foremost a man because he has a spiritual soul. The social class in which he is to be situated is determined by the level of intelligence which the individual soul possesses. Thus Plato believed that, although human nature is everywhere and at all times basically the same and the inequality of men is a direct result of God's creation, these differences are the harsh realities with which the rulers (and educators) must work. Only the mentally inferior desire an equality to which they are not entitled. [9]

Another important philosophical consideration with educational implications is concerned with the freedom of the human will. Plato unequivocally asserted that man's will is free. Free choice is essential to all adult human behavior.[10] Plato even suggested that there is a causal relationship between individual differences and the free will of each soul. The choice of parentage, hereditary traits, physical characteristics, and early education were made freely by the soul during its previous existence.[11] With the recognition of the freedom of the will came the acceptance of the beliefs of man's responsibility for his actions and the attendant reward or punishment for good and bad behavior. These beliefs, too, are evident in the educational theory of conservatives.

To summarize Plato's fundamental notions about the nature of man the following points might be noted: (1) Man is composed of two basic substances, matter and spirit (a body and a soul). (2) The superior substance is spiritual and immortal. (3) Evil tendencies in man are usually

---

[7]*Ibid.* iii. 415

[8]*Ibid.*

[9]Plato *Gorgias* 483.

[10]Plato *Republic* x. 617; Plato *Timaeus* 42.

[11]Plato *Timaeus* 42.

associated with matter. (4) Although there is a universal and immutable human nature, important differences are found in men; these differences are rooted in the different levels of intelligence. (5) Social classes are determined by the levels of intelligence; the intellectual elite are charged with the function of governing the masses. (6) Man possesses a free will and is wholly responsible for his behavior. (7) Reason alone gives true knowledge, and sense knowledge is wholly unreliable.[12]

Thus on every criterion listed in Chapter II regarding the nature of man, Plato's educational theory can be classified as conservative-or better, Plato's theory might be viewed as the model for conservatives throughout the ages.

How De We Know?

At least indirectly, Plato answered the important educational question "How do we know?" when he defined man's nature. Although he granted that knowing begins with sense perception, he said that true knowledge could not be attained through the senses because they do not perceive the abstract, universal Ideas. Only the mind can perceive these Ideas, but the assistance of the senses is necessary to enable the mind to recall the Ideas which it possesses at birth. Thus a person knows in the most perfect way only through the rational powers of the mind. Intellectual knowledge consists in knowing the essences of things that constitute "true reality," not just the shadows of it. Using geometry as an example, one sees that the meaning of "circle" is known only when the Idea of "circularity" has been grasped. One has perceived with the mind's eye all of the relationships involved in the Idea.

This view of knowing is most significant for an understanding of the educational conservatives' emphasis on the priority of intellectual activities. Only those studies and educational methods which involve reasoning or intellection have a place in the school; how-to-do-it courses and activities are not truly educational. Students are being educated when they go beyond the world of sense experience and indulge their minds in contemplation.

Plato's theory of knowledge is certainly much more complex than this brief description suggests. However, it was not the intricacies of his involved theory that influenced educational theory and practice throughout the ages, but rather the view that knowing is primarily a matter of reasoning rather than experiencing.   Plato's theory of knowledge was actually

---

[12]Plato *Republic* vi. 510f.

abandoned later in favor of that of his pupil Aristotle, but the belief that reason is the only avenue to true knowledge never lost its influence in philosophical or educational circles until the advent of naturalism and the scientific movement.

What Is Truth?

No one in education- or any other field for that matter- has ever questioned the dictum that children should be taught the truth. But just what truth is seems to be the eternal question to which a great variety of answers have been given. Pilate asked the question at the trial of Christ. Although it was never recorded, one can be sure that, a Roman governor's answer was quite different from a Christian's answer. Such Philosophers as Aristotle, Augustine, Hegel, Kant, Rousseau, and Dewey have given different answers to the question. Throughout this volume we shall consider the various definitions of truth. Here our task is to describe Plato's views on the nature of truth.

As one might anticipate from the preceding sections, Plato looked with suspicion upon the knowledge acquired by the senses. In fact he equated the products of sense perception and the imagination with opinion rather than truth. He did grant, however, that the knowledge produced by sense perception is *closer* to the truth than that generated by the imagination, where he placed such things as myths, dreams, and poetry, all quite subjective. Plato did not object to the use of poetic language as a means of conveying truth, but he recognized that such language creates the possibility of misinterpretation of the true meaning of the message.

Sense knowledge is less subjective than that of the imagination, since it can be checked against the experience of others, but, it must be remembered that the objects of the physical world are not the "real thing" according to Plato. This type of knowledge, then, is not to be considered *absolutely* true- it, too, is relative and subject to the inherent weaknesses of all bodily functions. Perhaps the example previously used will clarify Plato's reason for considering sense knowledge imperfect. One may see (sense perception) many circles. They are all different- some large, some small; some well drawn, others poorly drawn- but none of them give the true meaning of circularity. The perfect circle exists only in the mind. It is an Idea, not an experienced fact; it is perceived as a whole, not as isolated experiences of individual circles.

Absolute and immutable truth is found only in Ideas and/or mathematical concepts, which are the result of the direct action of the intellect and reasoning power. This rational activity is super- sensible, or essentially above the activity of the senses, and it alone produces truth in the strict sense of the word.

The belief that truth is immutable is most important in Plato's philosophy. He insisted that change is generally dangerous- except change from the bad to the good. He argued that abandonment of traditional customs and mores account for the decay in society, and he even believed that changes in the rules governing sports reflected a degeneration among those advocating the changes. He feared that deviations from the rules might give the impression that change is desirable, and therefore he considered it the sacred duty of the state to protect its citizens against change. What is good and true never should be altered.[13] If censorship is necessary to preserve the truth unsullied, then use it.

Educational conservatism throughout the ages has elevated tradition and frowned upon change. The truth is to be guarded as sacred and inviolate. Only those innovations are permitted which are somehow contained in the original truths. The influence of this notion of truth in conservative education is very evident in the curricular offering of conservative schools. Those classics which represent the best products of the human mind constitute the core of the curriculum. Subjects involving direct experience (vocational subjects) and sense perception are not respectable ingredients in a true education. Mathematics, on the other hand, because of its rational nature, is usually an important element of a good education. Only when science became an abstract, theoretical enterprise was it admitted to the family of respectable subjects.

When the Platonic curriculum is discussed in detail on pp. 41-44, the truths worth knowing will be pointed up. Suffice it to say at this time that only the knowledge acquired by reasoning and contemplation is worthy to be designated as truth. [14]

To summarize Plato's view of real truth, it has the following characteristics: (1) It is rational rather than empirical. (2) It is immutable and absolute rather than changing and relative. (3) It consists in seeing things (with the "mind's eye") as a whole or in unity rather than in isolated experiences (as the bodily eyes see objects). (4) The criterion of truth is consistency, or coherence, among the Ideas rather than sense experience.

---

[13]Plato *Laws* vii. 797f.

[14]For Plato's distinction regarding the different kinds of knowledge and truth, see Plato *Republic* vi. 509ff., vii. 514.

What Is Good?

Like all great educational theorists, Plato devoted his most serious thought to the question "What is good?" All of Plato's speculations begin with an inquiry about the good and the beautiful, and only after this did he discuss knowledge.

Plato considered the happiness of the individual the highest good. Regardless of what man does, he seeks happiness. he undergoes hardships so he can acquire something that will bring him happiness. [15]

However, Plato, being an astute student of human nature, recognized the subjectivity of such a criterion of good- one man's meat is another man's poison. The objective criterion is the Idea of good, which Plato identified with God. Thus true happiness is to be found only when man frees himself from the passions and desires of the body and acquires that wisdom which will allow him to lead a virtuous life. Only then will man be like God; only in being like God can man attain true happiness.[16] Plato did temper this rather Spartan view by asserting that there is a place in the search for true happiness for genuine pleasures free from passion such as those derived from enjoyment of the arts. [17]

What is the essential ingredient of virtue which alone can bring true happiness to man? It consisted, for Plato, in the possession of a healthy soul- one that has internal order and harmony.[18] But how does one know that he is virtuous or that his soul is healthy? When there is complete harmony or a complete absence of discord within the person. And man achieve this only when he has acquired the four main virtues: wisdom, fortitude, temperance, and justice.[19] Of these virtues, wisdom has been granted the highest rank. Placing wisdom at the top in the hierarchy of virtues has no small significance for education, for we see the close tie

---

[15]Plato *Symposium* 204f.

[16]Plato *Theatetus* 176.

[17]Plato *Philebus* 28, 60ff., 619. In the *Republic* viii. 560, x. 597, however, Plato condemned art and artists because they have been a corrupting influence.

[18]Plato *Republic* iv. 443.

[19]*Ibid.* 441f.

between the development of intelligence and reasoning power and the acquisition of virtue. The implications for the curriculum are obvious.

The reader may well agree that wisdom, fortitude, temperance, and justice seem to be desirable goals for human behavior, but it was just affirmed that human beings are very subjective in their choice of things and of actions which might bring them happiness. Plato, again recognizing the great variety of human wishes and desires, believed that there must be an appeal to a criterion which is outside or above personal, individual human choice, for the latter is too utilitarian and subjective. Again Plato's appeal was to the objectively existing *Idea* of good which can be interpreted only by the philosopher-kings; those who already possess the four cardinal virtues. to state it more bluntly, it is the duty and responsibility of the state to educate its citizens in such a manner that true virtue will be inculcated in each and every one of them. Wise rulers will know what is right or wrong and will see to it that the people are kept from evil. Thus Plato was entirely consistent when he maintained that censorship was necessary to protect the people, young and old, from the evils of bad literature, of stage performances and of the teaching of some men. [20]

The view that education should provide youth with examples of the good and not expose them to error and evil is a characteristic of conservative education throughout the ages. Conservatives do not always agree upon what is good, but they have always insisted that such things as *good* literature, *good* music and the like should be the educational fare, with those in authority determining what is good. If the authorities are of a certain religious persuasion, theological norms are applied to decide what is good for the educand and what is to be kept from him. The Renaissance humanists used other criteria, such as literary style, but here, too, the authorities decided what was good for those being educated. In other instances the political authorities were responsible for defining the good.

Since conservative education has always stressed aesthetic values, Plato's notion of beauty is pertinent. With all of the Greek art around him, one might suspect that Plato proposed a rather highly developed theory of art. Strangely enough, he did not do so, even though he had more to say about it than the Greek philosophers.[21] Perhaps the most generally accepted interpretation of Plato's aesthetics is that he considered it a part of the theory

---

[20]*Ibid.* ii. 377; Plato *Gorgias* 501ff.

[21]See Plato *Ion* 533ff. Here Plato suggested that creativity is a gift from God. As such, the educator can do nothing to develop this gift; the person who possess it needs no tutoring.

of ethics. Thus something has to be *good* before it can be considered *beautiful*- only that which is good can be beautiful. The converse- that which is beautiful is ipso facto good- is not necessarily true. Perhaps this is the reason for Plato's belief that art should be censored. Any art which portrays evil simply cannot be tolerated, or better, any piece of work in the various art forms which portrays evil is not art. Plato maintained, however, that the beautiful is more easily grasped by the human mind than the good, since the mind easily perceives the harmony, symmetry, and order in art, these criteria being purely rational. the beautiful, then, should be used as a vehicle for reaching the good.

Plato considered the beauty found in natural things- trees, sunsets, mountains, human bodies- the lowest forms of beauty. As one moves away from the objects of sense one comes closer to absolute beauty. Poetry might be considered more beautiful than a picture of a sunset because it is more abstract than the portrayal of something observed by the senses. Mathematics moves beyond poetry for the same reason. Music, too, is a higher art form than poetry since it further removed from the world of things than poetry.

It seems evident that Plato did not apply his notion of beauty to art alone. Art is a secondhand imitation of the real. Art is not an essential activity of man such as dialectic (thinking) or governing; rather, it is merely a handmaid of more important human activities, for its only function lies in the pleasure and recreation it affords the tired mind. For this reason it must be controlled by the authorities so that it does not get out of hand. Art can never be permitted to become a vehicle for dissemination of evil. [22]

If one scrutinizes the history of education, one can detect the Platonic view of art in much of conservative education: An art piece is usually judged on the basis of its moral goodness rather than any independent and artistic criteria. The student is exposed to art works that teach a moral lesson and is not permitted to read or view immoral art, be it literature, drama, painting, sculpture, or music. The fine arts are to serve as instruments for achieving a rational grasp of moral goodness.

In summarizing Plato's views on the nature of the good and of the beautiful, several points are worth noting: (1) Each person seeks those goods which will bring him happiness. (2) The individual's choice of good is subjective and therefore relative and changing. (3) Absolute and immutable good is found only in the abstract Idea of Good- or God. (4)

---

[22]Plato *Phaedrus* 273; Plato *Republic* ii. 377.

Reason alone leads one to the knowledge of absolute good. (5) Those possessing the highest level of rational power (philosopher-kings) shall determine what is good for the rest of the people. (6) Evil must be suppressed by those in authority. (7) The beautiful is an aspect of the good; it does not stand alone but is judged in terms of good, for ethical judgments are prior to the aesthetic.

WHAT IS THE PURPOSE OF THE SCHOOL?

It has already been mentioned that Plato considered the attainment of happiness, climaxed by final unity with God, to be the ultimate purpose of all human endeavors. Consequently the ultimate purpose of education, taken in its broadest sense, consists of assisting man to achieve this lofty goal. In the *Laws*, he averred that education should lead youth to "that principle which is pronounced right by the law and confirmed as truly right by the experience of the oldest and most just."[23] But Plato realized, as did other educational theorists, that such an abstract goal gives teachers little guidance in the day-to-day operation of schools, regardless of how informal the situation may be. Even a teacher who functions as a private tutor to the son of a nobleman needs a more concrete goal for his instruction than happiness or a right principle.

Plato set several specific goals for the lower schools. The first is the determination of the intellectual level of all children to identify those with superior ability. While accomplishing this goal the school also should give all children minimum training in the basic skills, [24] a knowledge of the essentials of tradition and the character education necessary to be a good member of the state. Preparation for worthy membership in the community is a very important goal of elementary schooling. It includes all that the modern conservative means by patriotism, especially the maintenance of the status quo. As mentioned, the most important criterion used in the screening process is the ability to handle abstract materials. But the crucial point in Aristotle's ethics (as far as education is concerned) is the superiority which he assigned to the intellectual virtues of understanding, science and wisdom over moral virtues.[25]

---

[23]Plato *Laws* ii. 659.

[24]*Ibid*, vii. 809ff.

[25] Aristotle's discussions on the nature of God and evil are contained chiefly in *Nichomachean Ethics and Politics*.

As noted, Aristotle's answers to the questions of educational theory and practice are so similar to those of Plato that no substantial changes are warranted in Plato's system. His insistence upon the superiority of intellectual activities reinforces the Platonic notion that the school's major purpose is to cultivate the intellect. The "training of the hand" (vocational education) is not worthy of the name *education*. "Paid employments absorb and degrade the mind."

Aristotle's curriculum follows Platonic lines, with the early years of formal education devoted to reading, writing, arithmetic, geometry, astronomy, music, civics, and physical education. Although Aristotle admitted that these subjects had practical value for life, he insisted that knowledge acquired through them is good in itself and is necessary for intellectual perfection. Purely utilitarian knowledge is "unsuited to men that are great-souled and free."[26] Like Plato, Aristotle, in his *Politics*, advocated strict censorship of curricular materials used in the elementary schools. By being exposed solely to good literature and the like during their school years, people will be prepared to reject evil influences in later life.

The completion of the elementary school means the end of formal education for all but the gifted. Aristotle suggested no significant changes in the content of secondary and higher education. Thus the quadrivium and philosophy would constitute the curriculum of these two levels respectively.

Though Aristotle had no specific recommendations on teaching-learning methods, one might extract from his theory of logic some pertinent implications. Simply stated, Aristotle's logic is based upon formal structures in which one deduces from general truths certain particular truths. But this, too, is a *rational* or *intellectual* method just as Plato's is. Methodological techniques derived from Aristotle's logic, either in his own time or in the Middle Ages, reflected the same intellectualism inherent in Plato's dialectical method. Both stress intellectual processes; both insist that only the use of rational methods distinguishes man from animals; both teach the same lesson: Regardless of what specific techniques the teacher and student employ in the learning process, the process must be rooted in the belief that reasoning power is cultivated by rational procedures.

With respect to the problem of evaluation of pupil ability and progress, there is no evidence to indicate that Aristotle recommended any principles or practices different from those of Plato. The necessity of evaluating students' intellectual ability and achievement in the academic areas was recognized as the only means of selecting students for more advanced

---

[26]Aristotle*Politics* viii. 645

schooling. the chief criteria for such selection continued to be mastery of the content of certain intellectual disciplines and the display of a high level of abstract reasoning.

Aristotle's view of freedom and discipline appears somewhat milder than Plato's. However, he did contend that children should not be allowed to hear indecent speech, read indecent literature, look at bad pictures, or attend unapproved dramas until they are of an age to drink strong wine. By that time their knowledge of what is right and wrong should insulate them against such evils. Since Aristotle recommended that adults who use indecent language in the presence of youth or show them indecent pictures should be flogged, one might assume that he would recommend some kind of punishment for children who persist in following such bad examples.[27] At least Aristotle felt that those who were able to drink strong wine in public places should be allowed to read questionable literature and attend satirical comedies whereas Plato advocated strict censorship for even the adult population.

To summarize Aristotle's views, the following points should be made: (1) He reiterated the dualistic nature of man and attributed to reason or intellect the highest rank among human abilities. (2) Although he believed that the knowing process begins with sensation of the external world, true knowledge is found only in universal ideas. (3) Intellectual virtues are superior to moral virtues. (4) In educational theory, he recommended no major revisions in Plato's conservatism. The purpose of the school is basically intellectual; curricular content is mostly abstract or academic; methodology is intellectualistic in structure and purpose; evaluation is generally in terms of mastery of content and use of intellectual skills; pupil freedom is limited, and discipline tends to be severe.

ROMAN EDUCATIONAL THEORY

Roman education sometimes is viewed as representing a radical break with the conservative pattern of Greek education. Such a generalization is, of course, misleading. One must remember that the early period of Roman history antedates the work of Plato and Aristotle by several centuries. But, during this early period in Italy, little or nothing existed by way of formal education, as most citizens confined their activities to farming and fighting their enemies. Thus the educational needs of the early Romans were met within the family. Here they learned the skills needed to provide a livelihood

---

[27]*Ibid.* vii. 17.

and to defend their lands. In addition to these very practical pursuits, informal education introduced the young to the ancestral customs which guided the social life of the communities.

Once Rome began extending her influence and borders beyond the Italian peninsula, it soon engulfed the entire area including Greece (146 B.C.). Expansion brought about great economic and social changes. The small, independent agrarian communities gave way to a national state made up of huge estates owned by wealthy aristocrats. Commerce and industry (production of tools, machinery, furniture, and the like) flourished. This spread of Roman power and influence accounts for the introduction of non-Roman cultural ideals into Italy, for when the Romans became conquerors they were wont to bring back to Rome much of the culture and riches of the conquered. Since Rome of the preconquest period had little by way of an educational tradition, it is not surprising to find that Greek educational ideals were adopted (and adapted) by the Romans. For this reason Horace, the great Roman poet, maintained that *Greece conquered Rome*-culturally.[28]

In spite of numerous changes, Roman society retained very definite class distinctions throughout its history. The aristocracy (patricians), the descendants of the old Roman families, were at the top of the social ladder and undoubtedly had economic control as well as the greatest influence in political matters. The plebeians occupied a social position between the patricians and the slaves. Some of them even owned small plots of land but usually they were not able to compete with the owners of large estates who employed slave labor. By the fourth century AD all of the economic wealth and political power was concentrated in the hands of the nobility. The plebeians either entered the army or joined the ranks of industrial workers in the cities.

Thus the structure of Roman society lent itself well to the Greek pattern of education according to social classes. One can see the strong strains of Platonic theory in the Roman philosophy. In the succeeding paragraphs both similarities and differences between the Greek and Roman patterns will be noted.

What Is Man?

That Roman thinkers held a dualistic view of man is evident. Cicero, for example, taught that the soul is of supernatural origin and is essentially different from the material of which the body is made. The superiority of the

---

[28]Horace *Epistle* ii. 1, 156.

soul and its faculties of intellect and will was affirmed by Cicero. He used Platonic arguments to prove the immortality of the soul and the freedom of the will. Man's origin and destiny are other-worldly. Like the Greek philosophers he followed, he taught that social classes are ordained by God. Educational elitism was just as acceptable to Cicero and his fellow Romans as it was to Plato and Aristotle.

Cicero and other Roman philosophers, then, made no revisions in the Greek conception of man. For educational purposes, the primacy of reason and intellect still dominated theory and practice.

How Do We Know?

Like Plato, Cicero held that the mind contained knowledge before birth. The essential truths of mankind are antecedent to experience and not dependent upon the senses for their verification. Thus one arrives at knowledge and truth through the exercise of reason.

Truths, once reason has reached a grasp of them, should be applied in the practical order for the good of the state. Plato, too, had insisted that knowledge should not remain sterile but should find its practical application in government. Therefore, Roman thinkers like Cicero can claim no originality even on this point, in spite of the fact that the Romans actually did concentrate the major portion of their efforts on the solution of practical problems. But the training given to youth prior to their entrance into the active fields was intellectual.

What Is Truth?

Regarding the notion and definition of truth, an apparent conflict between theory and practice is noted in Roman culture. All the evidence points to the Roman acceptance of the Greek notion of truth. Cicero himself admitted that "he merely clothed the Greek doctrines in Roman dress."[29]Perhaps it is more accurate to say that most Romans did not concern themselves with such problems as the nature of truth and - concentrated on the business of building roads, aqueducts, government buildings, armies, and the Empire. This concern for the practical can be noted in the curricular patterns of Roman education to be discussed.

In theory, then, the Romans held that truth is contained in universal, innate ideas. It was fashionable (and necessary) for a Roman making any

---

[29]Cicero*Epistle to Atticus*xii. 52.

claim to being educated to have a thorough knowledge of Greek literature as well as to use the elegant style of the Greek men of letters. The notion that the well-educated person was the possessor of the wisdom contained in universal ideas of beauty and truth applied to the new aristocracy as well as to the old. But in practice, truth appeared as that eclectic collection of ideas, values, and ways of doing things which produced tangible results. Some historians aver that the Romans were the first to apply the notion that that which works or produces measurable results is true. The rapid expansion of the Empire and the tremendous success of their manifold undertakings seems to bear out this contention. In this respect, the Romans foreshadow the thinking and action of the liberal philosophy of America which resulted in this country's rapid rise to a position of a world power and great domestic prosperity.

Perhaps a feasible explanation for this apparent contradiction lies in the Roman eclectic spirit of selecting from the works of the Greeks and from their own rural traditions those elements that fit best in an emerging culture. Thus, they could hold to the Greek ideal that truth is intellectual in origin and content without sacrificing the down-to-earth notion of their hard-working ancestors that intelligence also implies getting the job done.

What Is Good?

Popular literature and the movies give one the impression that the Romans considered personal pleasure the highest possible good for man. Stories of Roman feasts, orgies, and gladiatorial duels in the Coliseum make one believe that the Romans were a wholly undisciplined lot. Of course, this picture is partially correct. But Roman ethical doctrine, especially as expounded by Cicero, rejects the view that man's highest aim in life is to have a good time. In fact, he advocated a moderate form of stoicism, which demands rather rigorous self-discipline. Accordingly, *virtue* is considered the highest good for man. But the Platonic and Aristotelian modifications, namely, that external goods properly used can assist one to achieve virtue, became an integral part of Roman ethical theory. This view might be compared to the modern American notion that one cannot be happy or morally good unless he has a full stomach, adequate clothing, and a roof over his head, plus a little extra money to enjoy the finer things-the theater, advanced education and leisure time. Note that the finer things of life for the Romans were intellectual-literature, the arts, the theater-things of the mind had more prestige than the pleasures of the body.[30] The crass sensualism which was so characteristic of decadent Rome was no more in harmony with the classical Roman view of the good life than it was for Plato.

Roman ideals of beauty, too, were patterned after those of the Greeks. Symmetry, harmony, and unity were the criteria applied in artistic judgment. Certain adaptations of the Greek notion of beauty are found in Roman sculpture, architecture and literature but the Greek influence is much in evidence. It can be conceded that the major adaptation of the Romans involved certain utilitarian purposes. But the purely practical never became the dominant focal point of Roman art. Beauty and its appreciation retained its intellectual character.

What Is the Purpose of the School?

It was noted previously that the Roman conquerors carried back to Rome the riches of the conquered. The greatest of these riches was the Greek scholars and teachers who were enslaved by the Romans and given the task of teaching the sons of the nobility. Recognizing the talents and worth of these educated slaves, the Roman nobles soon emancipated most of them. These Greek teachers continued to serve as hired tutors, but also opened schools in Rome.

As one might expect, these teachers carried with them Greek ideas concerning the purpose of the school. Furthermore, Roman parents did not need to hire the Greeks to teach them the best methods of agriculture or the practical arts since the Romans themselves excelled in these areas. Thus both the teachers and the parents of the children considered the cultivation and formation of the intellect the primary goal of the school. The future orator and civic leader had to submit to an intellectual discipline which would prepare him to take his place in the senate. In reality, the Romans were even more rigorous in their interpretation of the role of intellectual discipline than the Greeks for they felt that music, dancing, and athletics distracted the student from his primary purpose.[31] Whereas the Greeks had retained them as an integral part of the curriculum of their elementary and secondary levels, the Romans felt that education of free men would do well without such frills.

The Romans, then, were the first among the long line of conservatives up to the modern era to either delete or de-emphasize the school's role in

---

[30]Cicero *De Finibus* vi.
[31]See Marrou,*op. cit*, pp. 246-50.

assuring the physical fitness and graceful manners of its clientele. From this time on, conservatives began to assign this function to other agencies such as the home and recreational organizations. The school, thus relieved of one of its former functions, could concentrate exclusively on its intellectual purpose. Even in conservative twentieth-century American schools, participation in athletics and other nonacademic activities is dependent upon the student's achievement in the required academic disciplines.

Just as in the Greek schools, the Roman elementary school had as one of its purposes the selection of the intellectually able students for the next level. Similarly, the lower schools considered it their obligation to transmit the cultural heritage, teach the basic skills, and inculcate patriotism.

What Should Be Taught?

Since there was little or no formal schooling prior to the "invasion" of Greek culture in Rome, this section is limited to a discussion of the curriculum of the established schools. Although a few historians claim some originality for the Roman curriculum, the differences between the Roman and Greek curricula are minor. Marrou claimed that "the general principles, the syllabus and the methods used in the Roman schools were simply copied from their Hellenistic prototypes...."[32] He contended that any differences which appear arise from a comparison of the old Greek schools of the sixth and fifth centuries B.C. with those of Rome several centuries later.

The Roman schools had the three educational levels roughly corresponding. to those mentioned in the program Plato recommended. The university was also added to the educational ladder. However, students did not spend as much time at each level as Plato had suggested. This matters not since the Greek schools did not follow his recommendation in this regard either.

At the elementary level reading and writing and simple arithmetic constituted the core of the curricular requirements. Reading was from simple literary works which taught love of country and other moral lessons. For example, a translation of the *Odyssey* served the dual purpose of teaching morality and reading. The pupil was expected to memorize certain selections or passages in order to exercise his memory as well as to learn the content. Not much else was accomplished in these general elementary schools since the elementary school teachers were themselves uneducated.

The next educational level was only for those who had done excep-

---

[32]*Ibid.*, p. 265.

tionally well at the first level. Plato's notion that only the best should go on to post-elementary education fit perfectly into the Roman social class structure. But the Romans based attendance at higher schools on social classes alone, not on intellectual classes. The curriculum of the secondary school included advanced training in grammar and rhetoric, literature, and, later on, the quadrivium (arithmetic, music, geometry, and astronomy). The latter, however, were taught more for their practical applications than had been done in the Greek schools.

The literature studied at this level consisted of the great classics. Before the Romans had their own great authors and poets, the Greek classics were used. At Quintilian's time (first century AD) the works of the authors of the Golden Age of Roman culture were added. Quintillion, following the lead of Isocrates, is considered the first of the great Roman classicists insofar as he argued for a return or a going back to the classics for the major portion of curricular content. This notion of *going back* to the old became the watchword of conservatives throughout the ages. Note how the humanistic educators of the Renaissance demanded a return to the Greek and Roman classics as the best means for training the minds of youth (see Chapter IV). The vulgar Latin and the vernacular were unfit for intellectuals. Many nineteenth- and twentieth-century conservatives, too, insist that the classics be the meat of literary studies.

If a Roman youth planned on a leadership career in government or law, a curriculum designed to develop oratorical skills and perfection in rhetoric was available. Along with this training the student was required to study mathematics, science, law, and philosophy. Many Roman students traveled to the Greek centers of higher learning to take advantage of the philosophic training offered in those schools. It was this educational pattern that produced the great Latin authors remembered by so many American high school students-Cicero, Caesar, Livy, Lucretius, Catullus, Virgil, Horace, and Ovid. The influence of Greek education and culture in the works of these men is evident.

Because of the great need for specialists in the days of the Empire, Roman higher education included curricula to prepare people for medicine, law, mechanics, and architecture. This professional aspect of Roman higher education was to remain an important function of university education.

In conclusion, it seems that the curricula of the Roman schools were near duplicates of those of Greek schools with minor modifications to meet the special needs of a vast empire and an increased demand for professional services.

How Should One Teach?

Marrou claimed that "Roman teaching methods were as Greek as the Roman syllabus." The student was completely passive. The teacher assigned certain selections which the student was to commit to memory and recite before the master and students, even to the point of imitating the teacher's voice, inflections, and the like. The pupil who failed to memorize his lessons was punished in various ways for his lack of diligence. From what one can gather from the history of the period, pupils hated school because of the dull teaching methods and the severe punishments employed to force them to memorize their lessons.[33]

Even the eminent educator Quintilian, who was considered progressive in his day, laid great stress on the cultivation of memory. He considered a good memory the best evidence of high mental ability and felt it should be exercised by memorizing long passages from the classics. If the student memorizes the passages perfectly, he should be able to imitate their style. Perfect imitation of the great masters of the literary tradition indicates that the student is docile and therefore receptive to the lofty ideals of intellectual perfection.

But Quintilian did have a few insights into child nature which certainly helped free the pupil from the terrible drudgery of the schools. For example, he recognized that the child's attention span is relatively short. Consequently, teachers should keep both study and recitation periods brief. He also noted that children and adolescents resist compulsion, especially when they are tired. Teachers should use ways of getting pupils to learn their lessons because they want to do so. He believed that the teacher should motivate the pupil by offering rewards rather than by threatening punishment, since pupil learning is retarded rather than aided by fear. He reminded educators that individual differences in pupils are a reality to which the teacher must make adjustments. Thus pupils are to commence the study of different subjects when their minds were "ripe" for them.

Quintilian also felt that considerable advantage accrued from having students work and study in groups; the classroom might serve as a medium of social adjustment; pupils can often learn from one another more than they can learn from the teacher. He recommended that pupils be encouraged to write themes and debate on topics which are connected with their out-of-school life.[34]

---

[33]See *ibid.*, pp. 265-73.
[34]See Quintilian *Institutes of Oratory* This major work describes Quintilian's

In conclusion, one can say that Roman teaching methods were teacher-centered, memorization-recitation oriented, and generally very formal. Modifications appeared in the late first and the second centuries which somewhat liberalized teaching procedures. In general, however, the instructional devices of the Greek schools were merely transplanted to Rome.

How Should Pupils Be Evaluated?

Since Roman educators did little by way of revising or improving Greek curricula and teaching methods, one cannot expect to find changes in evaluation techniques. Changes in the latter are essential only when something drastic takes place in the former. Thus Roman pupils were evaluated in terms of the amount of material perfectly memorized, their docility and good behavior, and their ability to reproduce the literary style of the great classics. Excellent ratings on these factors were considered an indication of superior intelligence.

Oral examinations served well to determine to what extent the pupil had memorized the material and his ability to reproduce the style of the masters. Question-answer techniques delved deeply into the specifics considered worth memorizing. The student was expected to demonstrate on his wax tablet not only his ability to write but also his knowledge of grammar and rhetoric. The blackboard, which was not used in Greek schools, became a popular means of evaluating proficiency in basic skills and mastery of content. Debates in the presence of classmates and schoolmasters would give further evidence of the student's knowledge of the required content, his proficiency in grammar, and his eloquence. Subsequent chapters will show that conservative education, although it recognizes the necessity of evaluation, has done little by way of introducing significant innovations in the area of measurement and appraisal of student progress.

How Are Freedom and Discipline to Be Harmonized?

The Roman child and adolescent experienced no freedom in the school.

---

educational theory not only for the training of the orator, but for the entire educational sequence.

Only approved classics were read and studied. Dangerous materials were banned or expurgated. Behavior was rigidly controlled. The main stimuli for learning were force and punishment. A few educators such as Quintilian bemoaned the lack of pupil freedom and the extreme cruelty of the Roman schoolmasters. Their influence, however, does not seem to have had lasting effect: St. Augustine of Hippo who attended a fourth-century Roman school said he would prefer to die rather than have to undergo again the terrors of his school days.[35] Other writers of the period mention the beatings received in their school days. The cane was the chief instrument for keeping order and forcing students to study. To add a little variety to the mode of flogging, a recalcitrant pupil would be raised on the shoulders of a companion and then caned.

However, one should not be too harsh in one's judgment of Roman methods of discipline since the same means were employed in early American schools (and some twentieth-century ones).

EARLY CHRISTIAN EDUCATION

The appearance of Christianity coincided with the period of Roman glory and power. Although this religion had its origin in Israel it was already established in Rome by 80 AD However, its cultural and educational ideals are not purely Roman in character. Judaism constitutes the main religious foundation for the beliefs of the Christians, but Oriental religions also had some influence in such areas as the great emphasis upon immortality and the concern for the afterlife.

In addition to the Judeo-Oriental and Roman roots of Christian ideology, one can detect the strong influence of Platonic philosophy in those writings of the New Testament which reveal a philosophic bent.[36] Christianity, then, especially in its cultural manifestations contains elements of Graeco-Roman thought as well as the religious beliefs of Hebrew-Oriental cultures. To these were added the changes made by Jesus of Nazareth and his immediate disciples.

It must be remembered that the Christians conducted very few schools for the first three centuries after the founding of their religion. This apparent lack of interest may have been due to the emphasis placed on attaining salvation and to the belief that the end of the world was near at hand. Those Christians who acquired formal schooling did so in the public schools of the

---

[35]St. Augustine *Confessions* i. 9.
[36]See, especially, the works of St. John the Evangelist.

Empire or from private tutors. Since a large number of the Christians came from the lower classes, they had no schooling whatsoever. Still others felt that the corrupting influences of the pagan schools were to be avoided at all costs and therefore kept their children out of school[37] (education was not compulsory in the Roman Empire). The home and the church, then, shared the responsibility for religious and moral training. Instruction in Christian doctrine was given by the church to those interested in learning about the faith and those actually preparing for baptism. These catechumenal schools, as they were called, gave no instruction in reading and writing and the other subjects taught in the public schools of the area in which the Christian communities were located.

When the Emperor Constantine freed the Christians in the fourth century, the new religion spread very rapidly and soon became the dominant ideology in the Western world. It was through this ideology that Greek and Roman culture and Hebrew monotheism became part of the warp and woof of a pattern of educational thought which predominated until the nineteenth century.

Christian schools began to flourish soon after the Christians came out of the catacombs. But, as Marrou pointed out, they did not create a completely new type of school; they simply added the study of Christian doctrine to the classical curriculum of the existing schools with some modification.[38] Thus Christian thinkers gave some original and some old answers to the important philosophical and educational questions. We shall turn now to these questions, recognizing that not all modern Christians give identical answers or the same interpretation of the doctrines taught in the early church. Discussion of these many differences would lead one into the bitter theological controversies which have beset Christianity almost from its inception.[39]

What Is Man?

Christian thinkers accepted the notion of man as a composition of spiritual and material elements. However, even greater stress was laid upon the

---

[37]See Augusta T. Drane, *Christian Schools and Scholars* (New York: Benzinger Bros., 1924), p. 20.
[38]Marrou, *op. cit.*, pp. 317f.
[39]See Hans Lietzmann, *The Founding of the Church Universal* (rev. ed.; London: Lutterworth Press, 1950).

superiority of the spiritual element within man than either the Greeks or Romans had done. The new theology was very specific in defining the nature, origin, and destiny of the soul. It is a spiritual substance vastly superior to the body to which it is joined to form an organic unit. It is incorruptible and immortal; it possesses the faculties of intellect and free will. Man's sole purpose on earth is to know, love, and serve God so as to be happy with him after death for all eternity.

One belief about man's nature which had been contained rather hazily in pre-Christian philosophy is now specifically defined, namely, that man's lower nature inclines him to evil. This inclination toward evil is due to the sin of the progenitors of the human race, Adam and Eve.[40] Each person carries within him the seeds of evil which are expressed in the desires and passions of the flesh. Prior to his fall into sin man had not experienced any conflict between the soul and body because the body was under the complete control of the intellect and will. Since the fall, however, one of man's first obligations has been to subject his animal nature (body) to the rule of the spirit.

In order to understand Christian educational theory and practice, and thus much of conservative education of the past twenty centuries, one must realize the importance of this conception of man. Mark's Gospel stated very directly that man is tainted by evil: "For from within, out of the heart of men, come evil thoughts, adulteries, immorality, murders . . . . All evil things come from within and defile man" (Mark 7:21f). In Matthew's Gospel the same view is expounded: "Therefore, if you, evil as you are, know how to give good gifts to your children ..."(Matthew 7:11).

Paul in his letter to the Romans spoke of the flesh as evil: "For we know that the Law is spiritual but I am carnal, sold into the power of sin. . . . For I know that in me, that is in my flesh, no good dwells, because to wish is in my power, but I do not find the strength to accomplish what is good" (Romans 7:14). In the same letter he pointed out the opposition between the bodily desires and God's will: "Now they who are according to the flesh, mind the things of the flesh. . . . For the inclination of the flesh is death. . . . For the wisdom of the flesh is hostile to God. . . . And they who are carnal cannot please God" (Romans 7:5-9).

Because of the evil within man, the body must be mortified and chastised. Paul likened the fight against the flesh to an athletic contest: "And

---

[40]There is a difference of opinion among Christians regarding the extent to which original sin affected human nature. Some maintain that man's nature was corrupted (depraved), others, that it was weakened (deprived).

everyone in a contest abstains from all things   I chastise my body and bring it into subjection lest perhaps after preaching to others I myself should be rejected" (I Corinthians 9:25-27). In a letter to another Christian community he admonished them to "mortify your members [body] which are on earth: immorality, uncleanness, lust, evil desires, and covetousness. . . . But now do you also put them away" (Colossians 3:5f). If one does not control natural inclinations one will be lost. ". . . for if you live according to the flesh you will die; but if by the spirit you put to death the deeds of the flesh, you shall live" (Romans 8:13).

However, the flesh is not the sole source of evil. Man's intellect and will has also been affected by the sin of Adam and Eve. Therefore, even man's higher nature needs guidance and assistance.[41] This is made available to man by the Scriptures (the word of God) as interpreted by the church and by the official ceremonies, sacrifices, and sacraments decreed by the church. The Fathers of the Church (that is, theologian-philosophers) are the chief sources in the ancient church for the interpretation of the Scriptures, the definition of doctrine, and the delineation of liturgical practices.

Early Christian educators acknowledged the great individual differences in mental and physical abilities among human beings.[42] This view, they felt, in no way constituted a contradiction to the proposition that all members of the human race are essentially the same. But individual differences in mental ability would be the grounds for selecting those destined for leadership as clergymen in the church. And, as Plato recommended, the rulers within the church must *practice* their religion as well as *know* it. The ideal bishop and priest should possess both knowledge and virtue.

In general, the early Christian educators, most of whom were Neo-Platonists, held many views similar to those of Plato about the nature of man. Adaptations and modifications in the great Greek thinkers' philosophy of man were based on theological sources and called for certain revisions in educational theory, the most important of which was that the final goal of all human activity is conformity to God's will in this life and in the next, salvation. The effects of this new supernatural goal on educational theory will be noted next.

---

[41]I Timothy 6:3; Mark 7:22; Romans 13:1-5; Acts of the Apostles 5:29.
[42]M. Dods (ed.) "On Catechizing the Uninstructed," *Works of St. Augustine* (Edinburgh: T. & T. Clark Co., 1873).

How Do We Know?

In the history of philosophy, early Christian thinkers are classified as Neo-Platonists. For them, as for Plato, mind or intellect is the primary knowing faculty in man. Sense knowledge is unreliable since it represents only imperfect imitations of the Ideas contained in the mind. Thus perfect knowledge is acquired only by reasoning. St. Augustine's discussion *On The Teacher* makes it very clear that the pupil enters school with knowledge already in his mind. It is the teacher's responsibility to motivate the pupil to bring forth or bring to life that knowledge which he already possesses. However, sense experience does play a role in reviving the Ideas in the mind.

The early Church Fathers added one mode of knowing not found in Plato's philosophy: faith. This method of arriving at knowledge is the most reliable of all since an all-perfect God cannot deceive his children in matters which involve their eternal destiny. "God can neither deceive nor be deceived." God has communicated this knowledge to his children through the Scriptures.

The authority of God and his chosen interpreters is final and absolute in all questions concerning matters essential to man's life on earth and in the hereafter. Whereas Plato had placed faith in the political ruler as the interpreter of God's will, the Christian placed his faith in the interpretation of the ecclesiastical rulers. As time passed Christian theologians and philosophers appealed to the authority of the early Church Fathers for the interpretation of doctrines of faith and morals and even the nature of the physical universe.

In arranging the ways' of arriving at knowledge in a hierarchical order, the Christian will place faith at the top of his pyramid. Reason and experience follow in that order. Mind is superior to matter (Romans 7:22).

What Is Truth?

From the preceding section it is evident that the Christian believes that "every word which proceeds from the mouth of God" is true. The most important truths are those derived from religion or theology. These truths of faith are immutable and absolute. Many of these truths go beyond human understanding, and nearly all are beyond the realm of experience. For example, the doctrine of the Trinity (three persons in one God) cannot be grasped by the human mind; belief in a life hereafter is not subject to the test of experience; the fact that the sacraments give supernatural grace is not testable by empirical means.

Yet another aspect of the Christian notion of truth is found in the corrective function assigned to theological truth. Thus if some knowledge arrived at by reason or experience is not in harmony with a theological truth, the latter is to be held as true by Christian thinkers. For example, Aristotle, using arguments from reason, taught that the world existed from all eternity. Christian thinkers maintained that such a position was de facto untenable since the Scriptures taught that God created the world *in time* and consequently it could not have existed from all eternity. Similarly, if one argues from experience that man's existence terminates with death, this simply is not true since theology teaches that man's soul (later to be reunited with the body) will exist for all eternity.

Next to the truths of revelation, the Christian Fathers placed the truths of reason. As followers of Plato they used reason to prove their doctrines about the structure of the universe and the laws governing it. It is not important that they did not always agree with Plato. The significant point is that greater certitude was found in the truths of reason than in those of experience. The effect of this position is evident in the predominance of theological and philosophical, literary and academic studies in the curriculum of the early Christian schools. An experience-centered curriculum was out of the question.

What Is Good?

In the Christian context, God is the highest good for man. Plato and Aristotle had pointed to happiness as man's summum bonum. The Christian did not disagree with this view but argued that man can never achieve ultimate happiness until he is united with God after death for all eternity. True happiness on this earth can be achieved only by conformity to the will of God. Since man's intellect and will have been adversely affected by original sin, he cannot follow his own instincts, drives, and wishes if he is to live a good moral life.

In general, the Christian had relatively little difficulty deciding what was morally right or wrong. He had inherited the Ten Commandments from the Old Testament of the Hebrews. The New Testament, authored by the immediate apostles and disciples of Christ, contains additional moral directives by which he could regulate every phase of his personal and social life. To enumerate all of these moral directives is not the purpose of this discussion, but the Christian hierarchy of values or goods must be noted in order to grasp the meaning of Christian education.

The highest values are, of course, spiritual in origin and design. "What does it profit a man if he gain the whole world but suffer the loss of his soul?" All man's words, thoughts, and actions are to be motivated by love of God and fellowmen, who are considered other Christs. Life in an early Christian community centered on religious doctrines, ceremonies, and instructions. Christianity was considered a way of life which would guide the faithful's activities in all areas of human endeavor-work, politics, and family life.

At the opposite end of the scale the Christian placed material goods and values. In reality, the early Christian despised earthly possessions, riches and bodily pleasures as derived from Christ's words: "Leave all things and follow me." Celibacy and virginity were viewed as superior to the married state. Marriage itself was sublimated by raising it to the status of a sacrament; that is, the spiritual element took precedence over the physical. Death was considered a welcome event since it liberated the soul from the shackles of the body (Philippians 1:21). The authors of the New Testament never glorified material values-riches, comfort, pleasure, food and drink.[43]

Where did the early Christian educator stand in regard to the intellectual goods which the Greek and Roman cultures had valued so highly? Many early Christian leaders believed that these should be rejected because of their pagan origin. As discussed earlier, the Greeks and Romans had placed supreme reliance on the powers of human reason. But the Christian had a higher (and safer) source, Revelation. The great apologist Tertullian preached against the acceptance of secular knowledge and felt that youth should be kept from its corrupting influence. He is a representative of the anti-intellectualist wing among early Christians.

St. Augustine, on the other hand, defended the incorporation of intellectual values in Christian education, especially those acquired through the study of rhetoric, classical literature, and philosophy. All of this content which is in harmony with the Faith should be employed by the Christian teacher to aid in the spiritual development of his students.[44] After all, the intellect is the most noble element in man, and its power is derived from the spiritual soul. The great reliance placed upon Plato's philosophy as the rational framework for early Christian theology attests to the victory of modified intellectualism over its opponents. From St. Augustine's time on, classical literature, rhetoric, and philosophy constituted the core of secular learning in Christian schools. The only prerequisite for their use was that

---

[43]See. pp. 62f in this volume.
[44]Dods, *op. cit.*, pp. 75f.

they be put to the service of the Christian faith. For example, philosophy should be the handmaid of theology; rhetoric and literary studies should equip the clergyman for his pastoral duties, especially preaching. During the Middle Ages and the Renaissance, Christian educators exalted intellectual values to the same heights which they enjoyed in Greek and Roman schools.

What Is the Purpose of the School?

Although early Christians believed that the primary goal of all educational activities is the development of the perfect Christian person, they placed most of the responsibility for achieving this goal upon the home and the church. The school's major function consisted in giving the young knowledge. Obviously, a knowledge of Christian doctrine had top priority, especially in the first schools run by the Christians. Other types of knowledge were added as the Christians broadened their educational efforts. The significant point seems to be that the transmission of knowledge claimed the superior role in formal schooling. How could the child be expected to live the Christian Faith if he did not know it? How could young and old do good and avoid evil if they did not know right from wrong? How could a ruler be a good Christian ruler if he did not know the principles of Christian justice?

Thus even the early catechumenal schools which taught only religion concentrated their efforts on giving knowledge. The moral training given in the school was only a supplement to that given in the home and the church. One cannot conclude, however, that the Christian school did not concern itself with moral behavior. Children and youth had to act as Christians in the school. Discipline, punishments, and the like reflected Christian principles. Therefore, it seems fair to assert that the primary purpose of the Christian school was intellectual (giving knowledge) and only secondarily moral. This sharpening of the intellectual powers of the student and the transmission of the Graeco-Roman and Christian heritage was to remain the goal of Christian Humanism throughout the succeeding centuries.

What Should Be Taught?

The curriculum of the first Christian catechumenal schools was very limited, and the only subject taught was Christian doctrine. The students in these schools were at two different levels: (1) those who were seeking information about the Faith, and (2) those who were receiving instructions preparatory to Baptism or official initiation into the Church. These schools did not teach reading, writing, or any of the other subjects taught in the schools of the Empire.

A later development, the catechetical school, added reading, writing, literature, history, science, and philosophy to the curriculum. With the exception of the central role of theology, these schools were much like their Greek and Roman counterparts. Early Christians of note who received their training in such schools were Clement of Alexandria, Origen, Justin Martyr, Sts. Cyril and Basil, and other Fathers of the Church. The best known catechetical schools were located in Antioch, Alexandria, Carthage, Edessa, and Jerusalem. These schools were the Christians' answer to the paganism of the state schools and offered a Christianized version of the public school curriculum. St. Augustine, for example, defended the Christianization of secular subjects:

> Moreover, if those who are called philosophers, and especially the
> Platonists have said what is true and in harmony with our Faith, we
> are not to shrink from it but claim it for our own use. . . . In the same
> way all branches of human learning contain also liberiaistruction
> which is better adapted to the use of truth and some excellent precepts
> of morality. . . .[45]

These schools might be compared to the parochial schools of twentieth - century America which follow the general curricular patterns of the public schools of the area, adding the teaching of religion and a Christian interpretation of "secular" subjects. Higher learning, especially training for the clergy, was carried on in the catechetical schools and in the cathedral schools located in the bishop's residence. The decline of both types of Christian schools (in the sixth century) paralleled the decline of Roman education. The Dark Ages which lasted from the sixth to the tenth centuries ensued. During the Dark Ages education came to a standstill and Western culture was preserved in the libraries and cloisters of the monasteries. Both clergy and laity with few exceptions were uneducated.

In conclusion, the curriculum of the Christian schools was first and foremost Christian. When the curriculum was expanded beyond Christian doctrine, it was the classical one which was adopted. As Marrou argued, in spite of the early conflict between theology and the classical Hellenistic curriculum, the Christian school was not only everlastingly affected by it but

---

[45]Dods, "On Christian Doctrine,'*op. cit*, pp. 75f.

actually accepted it and made it its own.[46] The truly great scholars of the early Christian Era, such as Origen, Sts. Jerome, Ambrose, and Augustine, were as much classicists as they were theologians.

How Should One Teach?

Apparently some of the teachers of early Christianity had heard of Quintilian's recommendations on teaching methods. St. Jerome, in a letter to a friend, suggested some of the same procedures for motivating youngsters to learn: utilizing the play-instinct, offering rewards of sweets, and praise for achievement. Also, he felt that students would find pleasure in learning if properly motivated and that compulsion was unnecessary.[47] However, the main approach to teaching consisted in the memorization-recitation pattern used in Greek and Roman schools.

St. Augustine, in *On The Teacher*, was concerned primarily with interpreting the Platonic theory of Ideas in relation to the teaching-learning process. The general conclusion drawn in this treatise is that the pupil does not learn from the teacher at all. Rather the teacher stimulates the student to bring to life the truth which already exists in his mind. The treatise does not delve into teaching methods or techniques in the modern sense of the term. However, in another work, *On Catechizing the Uninstructed*, Augustine made some recommendations for improving the lifeless teaching methods which were in use while he was a pupil. He insisted that instruction must be adjusted to individual differences; he pointed to the futility of too much memory work; he argued for pleasant and comfortable surroundings and for using the native interests of students as starting points; as a Platonist he deplored the passive teacher-centered methods in use at the time; he felt that the whole person-intellect, emotions, and attitudes-should be involved in the learning process.[48]

As with Quintilian's recommendations, little seems to have been done with those of Augustine. The teaching methods remained teacher-centered and left to the pupil a passive role in the learning process.

How Should Pupils Be Evaluated?

---

[46]Marrou, *op. cit*, pp. 318, 321ff.
[47]See St. Jerome, *Selected letters of St. Jerome*, F. A. Wright (trans.) (Cambridge: Loeb Classical Library, 1933), p. 467.
[48]Dods, On Catecheizing the Uninstructed, *op. cit*, pp. 265-335.

There is no evidence that Christian educators introduced any innovation in the evaluation techniques used by the schools of the time. The emphasis placed upon knowing one's religion (catechism) suggests that evaluation was in terms of mastery of content of the religion courses. Also, before the catechumen could be admitted to membership in the Christian community, he had to give evidence of his moral fitness for such acceptance. The decision about the candidate's worthiness was not the responsibility of teachers alone but also that of the clergy, acquaintances, and family of the person.

As the curriculum of the Christian school was expanded to include classical learning, the function of determining the moral fitness of candidates gradually disappeared since all who attended the schools already were Christians. Thus the Christian school, once it had reached maturity, like its Greek and Roman prototypes, concerned itself primarily with an evaluation of the pupils' knowledge of religion, rhetoric, classical literature, and the other subjects taught. The oral examination or recitation in use at the time lent itself well in determining to what extent the pupil knew the content of these subjects.

How Are Freedom and Discipline to Be Harmonized?

The Christian view of man's nature as weak, fallen, or inclined to evil left the educator with no alternative but to limit the pupils' freedom and apply relatively rigorous discipline.[49] In the first centuries of the Christian Era, the faithful were to shun all pagan influences including festivals, literature, and customs. When the Christian community was given its freedom and especially when Christians outnumbered pagans, the fear of pagan influences lessened. At this stage the Christian schools added the classical curriculum. But the scholars responsible for this innovation warned that only those literary works (or parts thereof) which were in harmony with or at least did not contradict the Christian notion of faith and morals, were to be used. Anything which might endanger the religious or moral beliefs of youths was to be withheld since there was ample material in the classics which did not offend Christian beliefs.

In this respect Christian educators were in complete agreement with Plato who had maintained that all reading materials be closely scrutinized lest the young mind be corrupted by the false doctrine and evil example contained in literature. Like Plato, the Christian educator felt that he was not

---

[49]Luke 17:1f.

limiting the pupil's freedom by prohibiting certain books. After all, the young had not acquired the proper knowledge and virtue to distinguish truth from falsehood and right from wrong. It was the responsibility of those who possessed both knowledge and virtue to make choices for the uninstructed. Conservative educators, in general, have always (and probably always will) considered it both their right and their obligation to pass upon the moral acceptability of what is to be taught.

With regard to the other aspect of pupil freedom, classroom discipline, there was never any question among Christian educators that discipline was necessary to control the evil tendencies in all people but especially in the young: "Folly is bound up in the child and the rod shall drive it away" (Proverbs 22:15). The inhuman disciplinary measures in vogue in Roman schools were not in harmony with the message of love and charity of the New Testament, and some great teachers such as St. Augustine had urged pedagogues to use positive motivation to achieve order and a proper learning atmosphere. However, if the recommendations of St. Augustine were ever put into practice they were short-lived. The popularity of asceticism which followed shortly upon the granting of freedom to the Christians encouraged a very rigid discipline not only among the clergy but also in the family and the school. Even though the severe mortification of the body was often self-inflicted by adult and child alike, it became characteristic of Christian education.

Silence, humility, obedience, and the subjugation of one's own wishes to the bidding of those in authority were considered highly desirable traits in pupils. Corporal punishment was used extensively for it seemed better to receive the punishment for misdeeds on this earth rather than in the hereafter. However, no evidence indicates that the corporal punishment applied in Christian schools even approached that of the Roman schools in severity. Still, the practice of using some kind of punishment as a means of maintaining classroom discipline is in harmony with the Christian view that man possesses a sinful human nature which must be bridled by external and internal controls.

In review, it might be affirmed that early Christian educational theory consisted primarily of an adaptation of Graeco-Roman notions and practices to Christian theology. Man's inclination to evil and the reliance upon supernatural revelation as the main source of truth and value constitute the major theoretical innovations. The purpose of the school was intellectual, the content of the curriculum chiefly religious and classical. Educational methodology, evaluation, pupil freedom, and classroom discipline followed the patterns of the state schools of the times.

On the surface, it seems that Christian educators did very little to change or liberalize education. But, as Luella Cole points out, certain Christian notions were to affect education centuries later. Thus the belief in the fatherhood of God and the brotherhood of man served as a theoretical foundation for equality of educational opportunity. Christian love and charity tempered the harshness of school discipline and encouraged mutual cooperation. Values, ideals, and the worth of human beings were higher than material wealth and power.[50]

CHAPTER SUMMARY

Even though many of Plato's philosophical beliefs are not held by all conservatives, the educational theory and practices which they suggested became part of the warp and woof of Roman and early Christian education, the education of the Renaissance, and post-Renaissance eras as well as that of modern Europe and to some extent of America. The Platonic influence can be noted more or less directly in the following philosophical and educational beliefs. The major emphasis is placed on intellectual and/or spiritual goals. Priority is given to traditional or academic subjects. Segregation of students is on the basis of intellectual ability. Special curricula should be designed for the gifted who are to be the leaders of the future. Classification of the practical arts and vocational subjects as noneducational activities is generally accepted. Little concern is noted for the immediately useful outcomes of instruction. There is little concern for the emotive factors in education. Memorization of the approved content by students is demanded. The mind is disciplined by abstract subject matter. Censorship of dangerous materials is advocated. Physical fitness programs either do not exist or are designed to promote mental fitness. Instructional methods are teacher-centered. Classroom discipline is relatively strict and the extrinsic motivation of reward and punishment outweighs the intrinsic.

BIBLIOGRAPHY

Adamson, J. E. *The Theory of Education in Plato's Republic.* London: Swan Sonnensehein, 1903.

---

[50]Luella Cole, *A History of Education - Socrates to Montessori* (New York: Rinehart and Co., 1950), pp. 109f.

Annas, Julia. *An Introduction to Plato's Republic*. Oxford: Clarendon Press, 1987.

Augustine, St. *The Confessions of St. Augustine*. Translated by Edward B. Pusey. New York: Pocket Books, Inc., 1951.

Barclay, William. *Educational Ideals of the Ancient World*. London: Collins, 1959.

Bigg, Charles. *The Christian Platonists of Alexandria*. London: Macmillan & Co., 1886.

Broudy, H. S., and Palmer, John R. *Exemplars of Teaching Method*. Chicago: Rand McNally & Co., 1965. Chs. II, III.

Burnet, J. *Aristotle on Education*. Cambridge: University Press, 1903.

Cole, Luella. *A History of Education-Socrates to Montessori*. New York: Rinehart and Co., 1950.

Dods, M. (ed.). *Works of St. Augustine*. Edinburgh: T. & T. Clark Co., 1873.

Drane, A. T. *Christian Schools and Scholars*. New York: Benzinger Bros., 1924.

Drever, James. *Greek Education: Its Practice and Principles*. New York: G. P. Putnam's Sons, 1912.

Ellspermann, G. L. *The Attitude of the Early Christian Latin Writers Toward Pagan Literature and Learning*. Washington, D.C.: Catholic Univ. of America Press, 1949.

Good, H. C. *A History of Western Education*. 2nd ed. New York: The Macmillan Co., 1960. Chs. IV, V.

Grant, Michael (ed.). (1978). *Latin Literature: An Anthology*. England: Penguin Books.

Gwynn, A. *Roman Education from Cicero to Quintilian*. London: Clarendon Press, 1926.

Hartt, Frederich. *Art, vol.II*. Englewood Cliffs: Prentice Hall, 1985.

Jaeger, Werner. *Paideira: The Ideas of Greek Culture*. Trans. Gilbert Highet. New York: Oxford University Press. 1986.

Jerome, St. *Selected Letters of St. Jerome*. Translated by F. A.Wright. Cambridge: Leob Classical Library, 1923.

Lodge, R. C. *Plato's Theory of Education*. London: Kegan, Trench, Trubner, 1947.

Marique, P. J. *History of Christian Education*. New York: Fordham Univ. Press, 1924. Vol. 1.

Marrou, H. I. *A History of Education in Antiquity*. Translated by G. Lamb. New York: Sheed and Ward, 1956.

Monroe, P. *Source Book of the History of Education for the Greek and*

Roman Period. New York: The Macmillan Co., 1919.

Mulbern, James. *A History of Education*. New York: Ronald Press,1962. Chs. V, VI.

Nettleship, R.L.. *The Theory of Education in Plato's Republic*. Oxford University Press, 1969.

Power, E. J. *Main Currents in the History of Education*. New York: McGraw-Hill Book Co., 1970. Chs. II-VII

Quintilian. *Institutes of Oratory*. New York: C. P. Putnam's Sons,1921. Teloh, Henry. *Socratic Education: Plato's Early Dialogue*. Notre Dame, Ind. Univ. of Notre Dame Press, 1986.

Wijesinghe, Gita. (1987). "Indian Philosophy as a means for Understanding Modern Ashram Schools". *Comparitive Education*, 23 (2), 237-243.

Chapter IV

Renaissance Humanism: The Culmination of Educational Conservatism

The advent of the Dark Ages brought to a close the era of early Christian education. From the sixth to the tenth centuries the decline of education paralleled the decline of Graeco-Roman culture, though this culture was by no means completely dead. But the barbarian inroads caused such social, political, and economic instability that educational development came to a standstill. During the medieval period a great revival of learning took place which reached its peak in the intellectual life of the great universities of Bologna, Cambridge, Montpelier, Naples, Oxford, Padua, Paris, Salamanca, Salerno, Toulouse, and others. The foundational curriculum for entrance to the universities, however, was in most instances based upon the trivium (grammar, rhetoric, and dialectic) and quadrivium (arithmetic, geometry, music, and astronomy) of the Graeco-Roman-Christian schools of the period prior to the Dark Ages. The university curriculum was professionally oriented toward law and medicine, much as it was in the Roman universities with the important addition of theology, and its handmaid, philosophy.

One type of informal education which became well-established prior to the Renaissance was the vocational training program carried on in the craftsmen's guilds. This has been recognized by historians as a most efficient means of training the young of the poorer classes in the various manual crafts and trades. Its efficiency is attested to by the fact that European countries still use the apprentice and journeyman training programs for initiating youth into many of these same skills. Even the labor unions in the United States employ a modified form of this system in such trades as carpentry, plumbing, electrician training, and printing. But the vocational educational program of the guilds was not recognized as an integral part of the overall educational scheme of the times.

Thus, even though the medieval period stands out as one of great intellectual activity in the history of human thought, especially at the university level, no major changes were introduced into educational theory. Substantially the same answers were given to the basic philosophical and educational questions posed in preceding chapters. However, many other important developments were taking place during this period which were to affect the educational scene within a few centuries. Very important among these was the gradual breakdown of the feudal system which had emerged in the seventh and eighth centuries AD as a response to the disappearance of the centralized Roman government. Under the feudal system the government was completely decentralized and each feudal lord was a ruler unto himself. His only obligation to higher political authority was the military service he rendered for the defense of an area of land larger than that under his control. The end of the medieval period witnessed the trend toward strong national governments which brought about the complete downfall of the feudal system.

As the political structure gradually changed from the feudal to the national state system, certain economic innovations can be noted. Whereas the feudal economy was primarily agricultural with little industry except that carried on in the lord's shops and only a minimum amount of interregional commerce, the later medieval period saw increased industrial and commercial activities especially in the towns. This increased trade and the military expeditions, the Crusades, did much to increase not only the exchange of goods, but, more important for education, the exchange of ideas with other lands.

The increased emphasis on industry and commerce also had its effect on the feudal social class structure. In feudal days there were two classes: the upper class, made up of landlords (nobles) and higher clergy (usually landlords); the lower class, made up of workers (slaves, serfs, and renters). But the commercial and industrial activities which began to flourish at the end of the medieval period produced a new class made up of merchants, bankers, and manufacturers. It was this class which demanded the protection and assistance of a strong central government so that business affairs could be carried on in relative security.

In this new setting the educational epoch, the Renaissance, came into being. This period might be considered the culminating phase of educational conservatism before the inroads of liberalism shook the structure to its very foundations. It was the humanistic educational goals, curricula, and methodology of the Renaissance which the early liberals attacked. It was the humanistic education of nineteenth-century America which the progressive movement sought to dislodge from its place of dominance at all levels of the educational program. It is the humanistic conception of education which some mid-twentieth-century European educators are just beginning to question.

It is true that the beginnings of humanistic education can be traced to Plato, the father of all educational conservatism, and to Isocrates, the founder of the tradition of rhetoric. More specifically, though, one might locate them in the period immediately following the decline of medieval scholasticism. During the Renaissance which roughly spanned the fourteenth, fifteenth, and sixteenth centuries, educators clamored for a return to the classics as the best means of cultivating the intellect. In this sense it was a reactionary movement. It was a reaction against the dominance of theological concerns in the lives of men; it was a reaction against subjecting the products of the human mind (the classics) to the surveillance of theology. The classics, it was believed, should stand on their own merits; whether or not they were in harmony with the Christian faith should not be the criterion for their acceptance or rejection. Thus "humanism" denotes a specific preference for purely human values engendered by the revival of learning and the renewed contact with the works of the ancient world. It indicates the effort of man to rediscover himself as a free being rather than as a child of the church or the state. In this task he sought enlightenment from the Greek and Roman classics which were more human than divine in their outlook.

This does not mean that the schools of the Renaissance, the period immediately following it, and the humanistic scholars were anti-Christian. In reality, all of the schools and most of the famed Renaissance thinkers were Christian. For example, Desiderius Erasmus was a priest, and several noted humanists were Popes: Nicholas V, Pius II, and Leo X. But there was a shift in emphasis in the higher schools away from the study of the supernatural to the humanistic studies. During the reign of Leo X there were more professorships in Greek and Latin literature (twenty-one) at the Roman University than in any other field; the nearest competitor was civil law with twenty professorships. In general it was quite fashionable for the clergy to be great classicists rather than outstanding theologians.

It is this important period, from the fourteenth century to the dawn of liberalism in the eighteenth century, in the history of educational thought that we shall consider in this chapter. The events of the Reformation stand out in political and religious history, but in educational circles it was the time when human interests became uppermost.

WHAT IS MAN?

The humanists of the Renaissance never questioned the doctrine of man's dual nature. In reality, mind-body dualism received greater emphasis at the hands of the humanists than it had in prior educational patterns. The mind is the major concern of education; it represents the superior element in man. This will become very evident when the question "What should be taught" is discussed in a succeeding section of this chapter.

Also, the humanists insisted that it is the possession of the reasoning faculty which differentiates man from other members of the animal kingdom. Thus, there is only one human nature, everywhere and at all times essentially the same-the Aristotelian notion that man is a rational animal. This pride in man's rational powers became a characteristic of humanistic scholars to the extent that some of them ridiculed the predominant notion that faith or divine revelation are legitimate sources of knowledge. For them, reason alone seemed to be the sure way to knowledge.

Simply because man as man possesses reasoning power, the humanist, like his conservative forbears, did not believe that all human beings have the same amount of rationality at their disposal. Only those with intellectual gifts sufficient to master the style of the classics could be retained in school beyond the elementary level. As Butts pointed out, education in this era was aristocratic in nature and designed for rulers and clergymen. Attempts at democratization of education begun in this era were not too successful.[1]

Since most of the scholars of the Renaissance and the Reformation were Christians, the theological notions of immortality, freedom of the will, and the existence of evil tendencies in man were accepted. It is true that the Protestant and Catholic views on each of these issues were different, but these differences seemed to have no major effect upon educational theory and practice (see sections on purpose, methods, etc.).

The most significant modification which the educators of the Renaissance and humanistic era made in the medieval structure, was the shift in emphasis from theological content and concerns which dominated medieval thought to the idea of man as a rational being The products of the human mind, chiefly those of the classics, received most of the time devoted to serious study at the preuniversity level.

---

[1]F. Butt, *A Cultural History of Western Education* (New York: McGraw-Hill Book Co., 1955), p. 175. Also see pp. 83ff. of this volume.

HOW DO WE KNOW?

As mentioned in the preceding section, some of the scholars of this era reacted against the Christian belief that divine revelation is the surest way of arriving at knowledge. But, it must be remembered that the medieval thinkers had already pointed up the role that reason must play in elevating theology to a science or a discipline. The formal logic of Aristotle and metaphysics (a purely rational discipline) were put to the service of theology. Thus the reliance of the medieval scholars on reason laid the foundation for the Renaissance and the humanistic educators belief that human knowledge, at its best, comes through the faculty of intellect or reason. This was the truly human mode of knowing. Working with the hands, except in the production of artistic works, was subhuman; revelation was superhuman. The activity of the intellect, then, was wholly human.[2]

What happened when a conflict arose between the conclusions of reason and the deposit of supernatural revelation? Unlike the medieval scholar who used revelation as a guide, many Renaissance scholars would rely upon their own reasoning rather than upon religious faith. This attitude, typified by Erasmus, reflected the spirit of the Renaissance to free the mind from external control, both ecclesiastical and civil. There were, however, great humanists such as Juan Luis Vives (Erasmus' contemporary) whose religious faith, respect, and veneration for ecclesiastical authority and Christian piety motivated them to resolve such conflicts by an appeal to religious faith rather than human reason. Similarly, the humanists of the Reformation and Counter-Reformation would resolve conflicts between faith and reason in favor of their respective theological positions.

The reliance upon the intellect as the source of knowledge had yet another important effect for educational theory. Since it was the individual mind that knew, this period saw the rapid rise of individualism. The faith placed in the individual's intellectual power to arrive at his own conclusion later gave rise to private interpretation of the Scriptures, one of the key reasons for the Protestant Reformation. Prior to the Reformation, one organization, the church, furnished the official interpretation of the sacred writings. But as the individual placed greater trust in his own reasoning power, his own interpretation was viewed as final and decisive.

One side effect of this trend toward individualism and reliance on ones

---

[2]John Symonds, *The Revival of Learning* (New York: Charles Scribner's Sons, 1912), pp. 6ff.

own decisions was the secularization of education. It was during the Reformation that education was first removed from the direct control of the church and placed under the aegis of the state. The first completely independent public school system appeared in Wurttemberg, in the Protestant section of Germany, about the middle of the sixteenth century. But the shift to secular control did not change the notion that the intellect is the prime source of knowledge. Rather, it reinforced this belief first expounded by Plato and Aristotle, modified by early Christians to make room for revelation, and again revived in the medieval schools.

Does the humanist deny any validity to sense experience as a source of knowledge? If one speaks of the activity of the senses as an independent source of knowledge, the humanist might hesitate to accept it. But, if one refers to sense knowledge as a sort of raw material to be utilized in the process of intellection. then he looks upon it with a more favorable eye. The sections on methodology and the curriculum will show, however, that sense experience in itself plays no significant role in humanistic education. No vocational subjects are found in the curriculum and experience-centered teaching methods are not employed.

WHAT IS TRUTH?

Since the humanist considers the human intellect or reason as the primary tool of knowing, it follows that the conclusions of reason constitute the major truth-content of human learning. Thus some Christian humanists, such as Erasmus, felt that reason should be the primary tool for purging Christianity of superstitions, myths, and irrational practices.[3]

One of the best means of determining what an educational philosopher means by truth is to look at the curriculum he recommends. Notably absent from the humanistic curriculum of the Renaissance and Reformation eras were the kinds of knowledge derived from experience. In fact, the farther removed from everyday experience a subject was, the higher was its place in the curriculum. Therefore, there was little science in the modern sense of the term nor were there any vocational subjects. The curriculum was purely intellectual or, as a neohumanist puts it, concerned with the pursuits of the mind. Truth, then, is not found in sense experience or direct contact with the world around one. It is reason that differentiates man from animals; it is the possession of the truths of reason that raises man above the animal level. Truth is contained in the conclusions of reason.

---

[3]See Erasmus*In Praise of Folly, Colloquies*and*Adagia.*

The humanist who was faithful to his Christian beliefs did not reject the truths of divine revelation but rendered them more meaningful by the light of reason. But this trend, begun in the Renaissance when followed to its logical limits, developed into a form of rationalism which either rejected all Christian beliefs or at least those which were not in harmony with the conclusions of pure reason.

The highly rationalistic philosophical systems, such as those of Descartes, Kant, Hegel, and Berkeley, are the legitimate offspring of the thinking of the humanists. For all of them, reason was the chief source of truth. The truths of experience must be subjected to the corrective power of reason to be purged of inconsistencies and other fallacies.

WHAT IS GOOD?

The term humanist starts to answer the question of what is good. The study of human nature itself will suggest what is good. But human nature is both rational and animal. Thus one finds early in the Renaissance a rejection of Christian asceticism in favor of a more moderate view having less emphasis on mortification and more on pleasure. Christian asceticism fosters the view that human nature, with the evil tendencies of the flesh and the pride of the intellect, has to be mortified by penance, fasting, and prayer. Only by such means can man prepare himself well for the life hereafter. The writings of antiquity do not foster such a spirit. In reality, they glorify the human body and the power of the mind. Thus a life of austerity, prayer, and contemplation of the things of the afterlife was not in harmony with the predominantly human-centered concerns of the Renaissance. Life in the courts of princes was gay and carefree. The aristocracy, who viewed the possession of literary knowledge as a symbol of distinction, sponsored the humanistic scholar and usually paid him well for his services. As a result, teachers and scholars themselves showed much more interest in the finer things of life which money and fame brought them.

For the humanist the most sublime human values are intellectual-the things of the mind. The exercise of one's intellectual powers constitutes the highest good for man. The effects of this commitment are very much evident in the schools of the Renaissance and Reformation which devoted most of their time to literary studies. The study of religion received far less time than the study of the works of the great classical authors. At one time during this period, the perfect imitation of the Greek and Roman classics was considered the primary educational good for students; it was the ultimate criterion of educational success.

From the point of view of educational theory one cannot grasp the meaning of Renaissance scholarship unless one recognizes the high esteem in which perfect literary style was held. At mid-twentieth century one still hears the complaints of neohumanists that students "do not know their grammar and have no literary skills." They know no grammar because the study of grammar and rhetoric has been abandoned in favor of life-adjustment courses. They possess no literary skills because they have not read the great classics, the products of the best minds of Western civilization.[4]

In this respect, then, the humanist had not veered from the classical philosophers' view that the intellectual virtues are the highest good for man. The medieval scholastics, following Aristotle's lead, had also held the same view, but it was tempered by those principles of Christian doctrine which pointed to the weakness of human intelligence due to original sin. To the Renaissance scholars, such a view was degrading. For them, pride in intellectual prowess became a fetish; the intellect was the new god.

The notion that intellectual values were of the highest worth had a telling effect on the school. Only purely intellectual activities were considered truly educational; the development of vocational skills had no place in educational institutions. Even religion was taught as an intellectual discipline rather than as a way of life. The great humanist, Cardinal Newman, stated this position very clearly by insisting that the school's only concern is with intellectual values.[5] Additional evidence demonstrating the high regard which the humanist had for intellectual values might be found in the time and money spent by the higher clergy and aristocracy to build libraries containing all classical and patriotic masterpieces. Without the possession of these great works, one could not be considered a true intellectual.

Because of the dominant intellectualism of the Renaissance and the almost exclusive use of the classics for building a curriculum, humanists have been accused of disregarding the moral virtues. In some instances, this charge may be valid. Obviously, the moral code espoused by most of the Greek and Roman classical authors was not in harmony with that of Christianity. Some humanists, however, with strong religious faith, believed that the classics by their sublimity could impel the young to live a virtuous

---

[4]See the statement of Dr. M. Rafferty in *Scholastic Teacher* (September 20, 1963), pp. 5-6ff.
[5]J. H. Newman, *The Idea of a University* (college ed.; New York: America Press, 1941), p. 3.

life. Vergerio, the Italian humanist of the fourteenth century, wrote an entire treatise on character development and the classical studies.[6] In this book he contended that literature is the foundation of all learning, for it requires a knowledge of grammar, rhetoric, composition, and logic. The teacher can use literature to impress the young with the necessity of good moral habits. All the great masterpieces of literature convey moral lessons, at least in a negative sense.

Vittorino da Feltre also believed that a thorough knowledge of literature and language is essential to the formation of moral virtues. Even Erasmus, one of the most prolific humanistic writers (and a "cold" scholar in the true sense of the word) advocated sound moral and religions training, especially for young children. Vives, a friend of Erasmus, proposed a method of integrating moral training with classical literature in his treatise *On the Transmission of Learning.*

Perhaps it is more accurate to say that the humanists were not anti-moralistic but believed that character formation is one of the desirable by-products of education. If the classical literature which made up the core of the curriculum were expurgated of passages which might be an occasion of sin to the student, it could be used to teach moral truth. But the bulk of the evidence indicates that humanists held the acquisition of intellectual virtues to be the first responsibility of the school. They, like the conservatives before them, placed the primary responsibility for moral training on the family unit and agencies other than the school.

Of special interest to the student of education is the Renaissance scholar's love of artistic or aesthetic values. It is not surprising, however, that the humanist was moved in that direction. Art, in all its forms, but especially in literature, is the product of man's mind, par excellence. Whereas the art of the early Christian and medieval periods had been devotional (otherworld oriented), the art of the Renaissance followed the lead of Greek and Roman art which glorified man and human nature. Obviously, then, the art forms of the Greeks and Romans would be the likely exemplars for the humanists. They emulate the Greek and Latin style of the classics; even when they wrote in the vernacular, they used the Greek and Roman classics for their themes and, to some extent, for their style. Dante's works are typical of this approach. The painting, sculpture, and architecture of the Renaissance also reflected the Greek and Roman patterns. The beauty of the human body was portrayed realistically on

---

[6]P.P.Vergerio, "On Noble Character and Liberal Studies," in W. H. Woodward, *Vittoino da Feltre and Other Humanists*(Cambridge: The University Press, 1897).

canvas and in stone much as the Greek and Roman artists had done it. Jan van Eyck, a fifteenth-century painter, came as close to reality in his works as the Greeks. Michelangelo and Leonardo da Vinci, both Renaissance artists, produced some of the most perfect portrayals of the human species. It is not implied that the writers and artists of the Renaissance simply copied the works of the Greeks and Romans (although some did this), rather, one might say they espoused the same philosophy of art.

WHAT IS THE PURPOSE OF THE SCHOOL?

Although noted humanists, such as Erasmus, Vives, and the founders and administrators of the schools, spoke of the development of moral character as an important goal of education, actual school or instructional activities were almost exclusively oriented toward the development of intellectual (and verbal) skills. The study of grammar, rhetoric, and the perfect exemplars of grammar and rhetoric, the classics, engaged the bulk of the students' energies. Briefly stated, then, the humanistic notion of the purpose of the school is the cultivation or development of the intellectual powers of the student by studying the best products of the human intellect (the classics).[7] The thinking underlying the humanist's view probably is even more intellectualistic than that of Plato. But in practice it is the same. Both are saying to the teacher: "Give us young people who have mastered the intellectual disciplines, who can write well and speak fluently, who know the works of the intellectual giants of culture, and we can make leaders and professional men of them." One must be a cultured person before he can be a good statesman, legal expert, medical doctor, or clergyman. Although the cultivation of intellectual power is the job of the school, the possession of such power does serve political and social ends. In the political domain, leadership is to be provided by an intellectual elite. These are the youth who had survived the rigorous screening process; their minds are disciplined to wrestle with the complex problems of government after they leave school. The very same kind of intellectual discipline is an essential prerequisite to the honored professions of law, medicine, and the ministry. Those who cannot master this intellectual discipline are unfit to rule or take a place in the professions.

Humanistic education also had its effect on the social stratification of the times. The peasantry and the poor in general neither needed nor received a humanistic education. Most of them received only minimal instruction in

---

[7]See pp. 85-87 of this volume.

Christian doctrine and did not even learn to read or write. Obviously they could not enter the Latin grammar schools and could not, therefore, rise out of their social class. Much the same held true for tradesmen and craftsmen. On the other end of the social scale, the royalty and nobility had both the financial resources and the time to profit from a humanistic education. Their young were tutored at home or in schools so they might gain admission to the classical schools which in turn would prepare them for positions of political influence. Thus the lower classes bad no means of bettering themselves by education, and the upper classes secured their position by a classical education. Between these two extremes on the social scale were the gentry and the merchants. For these, some upward mobility through education was possible since they possessed the financial resources necessary to take advantage of a classical education. But, very often the time required for supervising their estates and running their businesses prevented them from devoting much time to educational and cultural pursuits. The status quo was reinforced by humanistic education.

It is important to note that this conception of the school's role in society has dominated Western educational theory. European countries still expect their secondary schools to train the mind and transmit their culture to the young; professional training is a university function. Until the first decades of the twentieth century, the majority of secondary schools in America considered the development of intellect and transmission of culture their primary function. Even when vocational courses were begrudgingly admitted to the curriculum, they were held in low esteem and regarded as a concession to the presence of low-ability students in the school.

Renaissance humanists, just as their ancient and modern colleagues, made a sharp distinction between the broad purposes of education and the specific purpose of the school. Broadly conceived, education includes the activities of the family, the church, the community, the school, and other educational agencies. When all of these agencies help educate the young, then character formation, civic responsibility, and vocational competence can be considered legitimate educational goals. Erasmus and Vives, for instance, emphasized the necessity of a sound moral training in the home before the student is admitted to school. But if the school were saddled with the task of achieving all these goals, it would fail because it was expected to do too much. Consequently, the school should concentrate on the realization of its primary purpose, the cultivation of the intellectual powers of its clientele and the transmission of culture to the young.

In the boarding schools the development of good moral character and the practices of religious life received a great amount of attention. But these activities were not considered an essential part of the *instructional* program. Rather, the school was acting in place of the parents in the important function of character education simply because the students made their home on the school premises. If a boy were a model of good behavior but was not able to digest the intellectual diet of the humanistic curriculum, he was sent home. Moral virtue did not save him.

WHAT SHOULD BE TAUGHT?

As mentioned in the sections on the nature of truth and values, the school curriculum gives one the most accurate insights into what each age considers true, good, and beautiful. Erasmus, Vives, and other humanistic scholars recommended that the school devote its time almost exclusively to the study of Latin and Greek grammar, rhetoric, and the great classics of Greece and Rome, especially Cicero. Arithmetic, history, music, astronomy, and dialectic were begrudgingly given a subordinate place in the curriculum. No vocational subjects were included.

The earliest schools of the Protestant Reformation, even though they had a moral and religious orientation, concentrated on developing verbal skills in Latin and Greek. This feat was accomplished by many years of reading the classics. Melanchthon, who was Luther's educational advisor, recommended that children begin learning Latin as soon as they could read the vernacular. Latin selections from Cato and Donatus made up the beginning readers. Using these and the Latin *Fables* the students were expected to master Latin grammar. Mastery of Latin grammar was followed by reading Cicero, Virgil, and Ovid.

In the sixteenth century, the educator Sturm organized the humanistic gymnasium (secondary school) which remained the prototype for secondary education for several centuries. The vernacular was used only for teaching religion to the very young. Greek and Latin grammar and rhetoric and the classics (in Greek and Latin) made up the bulk of the curriculum. Cicero was the model for written and spoken prose. Music, astronomy, and mathematics, which had a subordinate place in the curriculum, were studied in Latin or Greek. No vocational or practical subjects were taught. The content was completely verbal and intellectual, although moral training was somehow integrated with the classical content.

In the British Isles, the curriculum was quite similar to that on the continent. Latin and Greek grammar and composition and readings from Cicero, Livy, Xenephon, Homer and other classics, and the Bible in Greek and Latin accounted for practically all of the curricular content. Again, no time was devoted to the practical arts or "training of the hand."

Perhaps the most systematically developed humanistic curriculum was found in the schools of the Jesuits, the leaders of the Catholic Counter-Reformation. The curriculum of Jesuit schools was divided into five levels or grades. Generally, it took the student seven years to complete the work of the five levels. (This curriculum would parallel the last two or three years of elementary school and the four years of secondary school in America.) When the five levels were completed, the student was eligible for admission to the professional schools of the university. The first level was devoted to the study of elementary Latin and Creek grammar with simple readings from Cicero and other Latin classics. The second level covered intermediate grammar of the classical languages with readings from Cicero's *Letters*, Caesar, Ovid, Aesop's *Fables* (in Greek), Lucian's *Dialogues* (in Greek), and other Greek writers. Advanced grammar was taught at the third level along with more difficult Latin selections from Cicero, Ovid, and Virgil. St. John Chrysostom, Aesop, and others were read in Greek. The fourth level was devoted to assuring the complete mastery of Latin and Greek fundamentals, and introduction to rhetoric, and difficult readings from the ancient and Christian classics. The fifth level was designed to develop eloquence (perfect style) in writing and speaking Latin. Cicero's best works were the ideal which every student must imitate. Thus the literature studied was taken from Cicero's works renowned for their style and those Greek masterpieces of Plato, Aristotle, Homer, and Pindar exemplifying the loftiest style and beauty of the written word.[8]

Although the primary purpose of studying the classics was to develop the intellectual and verbal skills, some emphasis was placed on their historical and philosophical content, especially at the fourth level. Besides the content of the classical readings some time was given to history, mathematics, science, and religion. But the literary, humanistic studies constituted the core of the curriculum and took up two-thirds of the time devoted to instruction. Since the Jesuit schools were, for the most part, boarding schools, physical education and Christian devotional practices were an essential ingredient of the life at the school. Also, since the clientele of these institutions were destined for leadership roles, no vocational training was

---

[8]T.A. Hughes, *Loyola and the Educational System of the Jesuits* (New York: Charles Scribner's Sons, 1902), pp. 270-74. The curriculum of the Lutheran schools contained the same patterns of courses. See H. Bernard, "Life and Educational Services of Philipp Melanchton," *American journal of education*, IV (1859), 749-51.

offered.

Although there are minor variations in the humanistic curricula just described, all are essentially alike. Latin and Greek grammar, rhetoric, and composition constitute the tool subjects; the classics provide the material upon which these tools are to be used; acquiring perfect style in writing and speaking the classical languages represents perfection of the human intellect. Further, the humanistic curriculum is designed for the intellectually gifted student, not for those with other interests or abilities. Like Plato's ideal curriculum, it was designed for future leaders, not guardians or workers. It was believed that such a curriculum was the necessary foundation for all activities which are truly human.

In the modern era the curricula of the French *Lycee* or *Academie*, the Italian secondary school, and the German classical *Gymnasium* still bear a strong resemblance to those of the humanistic period.

HOW SHOULD ONE TEACH?

The spirit of the humanistic movement called for some rather drastic changes in teaching methods. The Renaissance emphasis on human values, the power of the mind, and the development of a cultured personality, should have some bearing on how one teaches. But these liberalizing ideals never seemed to sift down to the level of practice. "Teachers taught as they were taught"-a perennial occupational malady of the teaching profession.

Thus instead of encouraging individuality and independence of spirit, the typical teacher demanded imitation rather than originality from his students, and his own teaching methods were imitations of Greek and Roman (chiefly Quintilian's) methods. Even the liberal-minded Vives based his teaching-learning methods on the doctrine of imitation.[9] Erasmus, too, insisted that teachers use certain classical masterpieces as models to be imitated by the pupils.

The only new teaching method developed was the *prelection* used in the Jesuit schools. Although it might be considered an adaptation of classical methods, it does contain definite steps not found in any works of the Greeks or the Romans which the teacher should follow in presenting the subject matter. Each level of the curriculum calls for specific techniques to be used by the teacher.

At the fifth, or highest level, the teacher worked toward the twin goals of

---

[9] W. A. Daly, *The Educational Psychology of J.L. Vives* (Washington, D.C.: Catholic Univ. of America Press, 1924).

the development of eloquence and style. He took an author such as Cicero and explained a certain passage to make sure the students understood its meaning. Then, the artistic structure of the passage was analyzed and interpreted utilizing passages from other authors which exemplify the same principles of art, narration, and persuasion. If the literary works being analyzed contained any significant information or moral principles, the teacher corroborated these by statements from other respected sources, such as philosophy or theology. At this juncture the teacher introduced any material from history, mythology, and other disciplines which pertained to the passage under consideration. Finally, the teacher commented upon each word in the passage pointing to its beauty, rhythm, variety, and the way in which it was used (grammar and syntax). The method, at this level, proceeded from a general analysis of the passage and its content to the specific analysis of each word.

At the fourth level the teacher was to accompany his analysis of the passage under consideration with praise for the beauty of the Latin language, the origin of words (etymology), their forceful use, and the various ways in which phrases could be used. With this assistance the student should have been able to imitate the style of the classical author.[10] If the classic being studied contained any historical data, the teacher was admonished to summarize the events and spend class time only on the explanation of difficult passages. This was the case especially in treating the works of Caesar, Sallust, Q. Curtius, Justin, Tacitus, and Livy.

In the three lower levels, where the study of Latin and Greek grammar engaged most of the students' time, the prelection involved techniques quite different from those of the upper levels. The teacher began the period with a translation of a passage from the classical author being studied. Since the goal of the three lower levels was the mastery of classical Latin and Greek grammar, he pointed up the grammatical structure of each sentence in the passage. Subjects, predicates, modifiers, and the like were thoroughly analyzed and explained. The proper placement of each word in the sentence was stressed; its exact meaning in the context was noted; any metaphors used were to be thoroughly explained to the students by utilizing examples familiar to them. Then the teacher selected the most elegant phrases and dictated them to the students who had to use them in their themes. Finally, the teacher translated the sentence(s), just as he did at the beginning of the

---

[10]Later (nineteenth century) users of the prelection also analyzed the style of contemporary writers who employed the vernacular to expound the same principles of style found in the classics.

period, and if need be did so over and over again.

During the period, the student was to write down only what the teacher dictated for inclusion in the student's notebook. Any assistance given outside the class by tutors was to come after the classroom teacher has covered the material; the student was not permitted to begin new lessons with anyone except his regular teacher. A great deal of drill was included in each class period, and each student had to repeat what the teacher had given in the prelection. Students were pitted against each other and expected to discuss the material given in the prelection or in their own themes. Honors were given to those students who could repeat the content of the teacher's prelection.

Another significant purpose of the prelection method, as used at the three lower levels, was the mental discipline acquired through grammar. It was believed that the study of Latin and Greek grammar supplied the best possible materials for developing the intellectual powers of the young. The analysis of the structure of Latin grammar provided the student's mind with the characteristics of the reasoning Roman mind; analysis of Greek grammar offered him insight into the artistic, graceful, and versatile Greek mind.

Finally, it should be noted that the prelection method is almost exclusively teacher-centered. The teacher made the initial grammatical analysis of the passages; the student was forbidden to go ahead on his own. The teacher determined what the pupil was to write in his notebook so that the student would not be confused by conflicting interpretations or analyses. The teacher directed drill and discussion activities which were to be modeled after his own prelection. Certainly, there was pupil activity, but it was not his own activity.[11]

HOW SHOULD PUPILS BE EVALUATED?

Since the cultivation of the intellect and achievement of eloquence and perfect literary style are the main purposes of the humanistic school, evaluation is in terms of these objectives. Other factors, such as character formation, are not proper objects of evaluation. If an applicant for admission to the classical schools were morally deficient, he was not admitted to the school. If, after gaining admission, his behavior was thoroughly unsatisfactory, he was expelled. Consequently, the task of evaluating pupils was relatively simple in the humanistic schools, since teachers had to be

---

[11]For a detailed description of the prelection, see Hughes *op. cit*, pp. 234-47.

concerned only with academic achievement.

Another factor which simplified the job of evaluation was that only the intellectual elite were admitted to these schools.[12] Elementary education in aristocratic families was given by tutors who taught the elements of reading, writing, and computation. The children of the poor either received no elementary education or acquired it in parish schools.

As in the Greek and Roman schools of antiquity, the oral examination was the chief evaluational technique of the humanistic school. Since there was no formal graduation from elementary school, as we know it today, applicants had to pass an oral examination to determine their readiness for the classical curriculum. Essay or written examinations were used only when the student's skill in writing themes was under scrutiny. Evaluation of themes centered on spelling, punctuation, grammar, and style. But even then, the pupil was subjected to an oral examination upon the essay he had composed.

The oral examinations covered the content of each grade or level and were very exacting. In the classical curriculum of the Jesuit schools, for example, it was felt that

> severity must be practiced in examinations, since it is more injurious for boys to ascend a grade, when not fit, than, if really fit, to be kept where they are; and, in addition to that, if they are advanced when not qualified, they create no slight disturbance in the upper class.[13]

Thus the student was expected to know all the spelling, grammar, syntax, vocabulary, and literature of each level before being promoted to the next grade. At the higher levels, where eloquence and literary style were emphasized, oral examinations obviously were an excellent technique for evaluating the student's progress. Not only did he have to know his Latin and Greek grammar and vocabulary perfectly, but he had to render his speeches in perfect Ciceronian Latin. In the other subjects of the curriculum, such as religion, history, and geography, the oral examination covered the actual content of these courses. However, mastery of these subjects could never qualify the student for promotion to the next grade level; knowledge of the classical grammar and literature and mastery of style were the necessary criteria for promotion.

Humanistic teachers, then, had an absolute standard according to which

---

[12]See *ibid.*, pp. 260-62.
[13]*Monumenta Germaniae Pedagogica* v. 177.

they could evaluate the student's work. It was an objective standard or criterion-usually the work of a great author. The nearer a student came to the exact imitation of Cicero or Homer, the more correct his work was.

Further, this outside criterion was also considered the best measure of a student's native ability. If he could master the classical grammar and style, he had the intelligence necessary for university matriculation. A boy's future depended wholly upon his success in passing these oral examinations.

HOW ARE FREEDOM AND DISCIPLINE TO BE HARMONIZED?

Usually, the Renaissance is looked upon as the forerunner of a general revolt against established authorities. Some humanists, such as Erasmus, argued for the limitation of the powers of the monarch. He felt the king or prince should be subject to the laws of the land and all his official actions should be for the good of all people; he should not be above the people but of the people. Erasmus was, therefore, opposed to the possession or exercise of absolute authority by any secular ruler.[14]

But humanists did not limit their attacks on established authority to the secular realm. Three very influential works of Erasmus, *Praise of Folly*, *Adagia*, and the *Colloquies*, were critical of the educational practices of the church as well as of Catholic doctrine and devotions. It is believed that these works had much to do with the Protestant revolt against the central authority of the Roman Catholic Church.[15]

Thus the freeing of the human spirit from the external bonds of absolute authorities was hinted at during the Renaissance, even though most of the humanists gave some recognition to the legitimate roles of these authorities, both ecclesiastical and secular. Such a spirit of freedom also crept into educational theory. Vives, for example, insisted that force should not be used to get students to learn. They should choose to do so freely or be permitted to remain at home. Self-activity should predominate learning activities.[16] Erasmus branded the teacher as a poor master if he relied on fear of punishment as his principal motivational device. Such behavior on the part of the teacher drove youth from learning, for which they might have

---

[14]See Erasmus, *The Education of a Christian Prince*, ed. L. H. Barn (New York: Columbia Univ. Press, 1936).
[15]See P. McCormick and F. P. Cassidy, *History of Education* (Washington, D.C.: Catholic Education Press, 1946), pp. 353-60.
[16]Daly, *op. cit*, *passim.*

a natural inclination.[17] Luther, too, complained about the lack of pupil freedom and the severity of discipline in the schools of his time.

But all of this theorizing about more pupil freedom and less brutal discipline seemed to have little effect on actual practices. In the first place, pupils were afforded no freedom of choice among curricular offerings since only the one prescribed curriculum was available to them. Also, the students played no part in selecting topics for study within each course or subject. Students were permitted to read only expurgated editions of the classics. Second, teaching-learning methods were exclusively teacher-centered and allowed for little or no self-activity on the student's part. Innovations of this type were practically unknown until Pestalozzi and other liberals opened their experimental schools.

Finally, as H. G. Good said, discipline was characterized by brutality in all schools except those of the Jesuits where it was "firm, but mild and gentle."[18]

In conclusion, it seems that the spirit of humanistic education certainly would have demanded greater freedom for teachers and pupils alike because of the trend against placing individual faith in any type of absolute authority. This same spirit should have generated a more humane approach in the general treatment of the young both at home and in school. But, in actual practice, the humanistic spirit never pervaded the schools of the times. Only a relatively few humanists practiced what they preached.

CHAPTER SUMMARY

The philosophical beliefs of humanistic educators show that only minor revisions were made in the general assumptions of the conservative educators of antiquity and the Christian and medieval eras who viewed man as possessing a dual nature (material and spiritual) and who located man's superior functions in the spiritual element, the soul. It is the intellect or reason which differentiates man from brute animals and gives him claim to freedom and immortality. Man's nature inclines him to evil, entailing rigid discipline of the young. Though men are *essentially* the same, only a relatively small number composed the elite who are capable of profiting from advanced education. The knowing process is viewed as fundamentally

---

[17]W.H. Woodward, *Desiderius Erasmus* (New York: Cambridge Univ. Press, 1904), pp. 205ff.

[18]H. G. Good, *A History of Western Education* (New York: The Macmillan Co., 1960), p. 163.

rational and the knowledge derived therefrom constitutes the noblest truth which man can acquire. The Christian humanist also recognizes the truths of revelation. Direct experience as a source of truth is held in low esteem unless purified by reason.

Intellectual values remained in the high place they held in Plato's system-perhaps higher, at least as far as the school was concerned. One could not achieve the "good life" without the exercise of reason. Humanists prized moral values but did not give the school the major responsibility for developing moral character. Interest in aesthetic values received great impetus from the humanists.

The educational beliefs of the humanists followed quite closely the pattern of their conservative predecessors. The purpose of the school was primarily intellectualistic, and both the classical curriculum and the formal teaching methodology served this. Evaluation was chiefly in terms of how one responded orally to questions designed to test mental alertness, oral fluency, and knowledge of grammar and literature. Pupil freedom was extremely limited or nonexistent, and discipline generally was severe.

BIBLIOGRAPHY

Bernard, H. "Life and Educational Service of Philipp Melanchton," *American Journal of Education*, IV (1859), 749~51.

Broudy, H. S., and Palmer, J. R. *Exemplars of Teaching Method*. Chicago: Rand McNally & Co., 1965. Ch. V.

Eby, Frederick (ed.). *Early Protestant Educators*. New York: McGraw-Hill Book Co., 1931.

Erasmus, D. *The Education of a Christian Prince*, ed. L. K. Born. New York: Columbia Univ. Press, 1936.

Erasmus, D. *In Praise of Folly*. Translated by L. F. Dean. New York: Hendricks House-Farrar, Straus & Co., 1946.

Fitzpatrick, E. A. *St. Ignatius and the Ratio Studiorum*. New York: McGraw-Hill Book Co., 1933.

Hughes, T. A. *Loyola and the Educational System of the Jesuits*. New York: Charles Scribner's Sons, 1902.

Jacobus, L.A.. Francois Rabelais: The Value of Free Will. *Humanities: the Evolution of Values*. San Francisco: McGraw-Hill (1986, pgs. 278-79).

Leach, A. F. *English Schools at the Reformation*. Westminster,England:

Constable & Co., 1896.

Painter, F. V. N. *Luther on Education*. St. Louis: Concordia Publishing House, 1928.

Postman, Neil. The Disappearance of Childhood. *Childhood Education*. Mar/Apr 1985, pgs 286-293.

Power, E. J. *Main Currents in the History of Education*. New York: McGraw-Hill Book Co., 1970. Chs IX, X.

Robinson, E. Education for the 1980s and Beyond: An Interview With Carl Rogers. *Humanistic Education*. Mar. 1985, pgs 98-110.

Smith, P. *Erasmus*. New York: Harper and Brothers, 1923.

Smith, Vincent. *The School Examined*. Milwaukee: Bruce Publishing Co., 1960.

Steinberg, L. The Sexuality of Christ in Renaissance Art and in Modern Oblivion. *The Philosophy of the Visual Arts*. New York: Oxford University Press, 1992. pgs. 216-227.

Woodward, W. H. *Studies in Education During the Age of the Renaissance*. London: Cambridge Univ. Press, 1906.

Woodward, W. H. *Vittorino da Feltre and Other Humanistic Educators*. London: Cambridge Univ. Press, 1912.

Chapter V

The Beginning of Educational Liberalism

It has been noted throughout the preceding chapters that every age witnessed some liberalizing trends in educational theory. Roman educators pointed to the value of a more utilitarian education; Christianity affirmed the basic equality of all men; Renaissance and Reformation thinkers demanded greater freedom for the individual. In practice, however, such liberal trends had little effect on the educational firing line, the school. Education remained highly intellectualistic, basic equality of opportunity was never implemented, and the individual student was not freed. Undoubtedly, certain teachers in their own classrooms or schools tried to apply a more liberal philosophy, but their influence was quite limited.

The period we will examine in this chapter, roughly covering the seventeenth and eighteenth centuries, was one characterized by a radical departure from educational conservatism. Unlike some of the other educational epochs we have discussed, much of the theory was put into practice, at least on a limited basis. Of course, there was no more unanimity among educational theorists or practitioners at this time than one can find in any other period. Thus one philosopher might be of special importance because of his views on the nature of man. Another is remembered for his answer to the question: "What is truth?" The name of another might be recorded in the annals of educational history for his contributions to the area of teaching methods. But, when all of these bits are put together, they make up a completely new fabric of educational theory and practices.

The desire for something new in education did not arise in a social or political vacuum. Rumblings of the search for a different kind of knowledge of the world are detected even in the medieval period in the scientific studies of Friar Roger Bacon. The Renaissance embodied a reaction against asceticism and the concern for the things of the afterlife which turned scholars toward human concerns. The Reformation signaled the end of the authority of the Church and, along with the rejection of the feudal system, gave rise to national states. The sixteenth century witnessed the rapid expansion of trade with the Orient and the exhilarating dreams of developing the New World which Columbus came upon in his search for a trade route to the East.

The middle-class merchants and businessmen supported a strong national state, since only under conditions of unity and peace could trade and business flourish. Thus the monarch or king was entrusted with great power in order to maintain national unity and peace. At times, however, the monarch became "too Machiavellian," so that even his supporters began to question the wisdom of giving absolute power to anyone. Add to this the large number of Protestant and Catholic leaders who demanded freedom of conscience and one finds a new emphasis on individual freedom. Political theorists of various religious creeds began to speak of the power to rule residing in the people rather than in any elite of intellect or blood. The right to depose an unjust ruler (one who violated individual rights) was voiced in public and at times demonstrated by political revolt.

Not all the innovations brought immediate contentment to the people, especially not to the poor. In reality industrialization created a new breed of poor who worked long hours in the factories in order to maintain minimum subsistence for themselves and their families. To them the benefits of education were completely out of reach. It was for them that the educational reformers were to demand a more practical education which would enable the industrial serf to rise above his unhappy lot. Social equality had to be accompanied by equality of educational opportunity in order to better the condition of the industrial worker. All of these factors were important in moulding a new educational outlook, but one especially seems to stand out: J. H. Randall suggested that science became the keystone in building the new world to take the place of that broken by the Renaissance.[1]

With this social, political, and economic setting let us see what fundamental changes appear in the answers of the educational theorists of the times.

WHAT IS MAN?

Perhaps one of the most radical doctrines to be proposed to the educational world at this time was the doctrine of the innate goodness of man.

---

[1]J. H. Randall, *The Making of the Modern Mind* (New York: Houghton Mifflin Co., 1926), p. 203.

The Hebrew-Christian notion of man which had prevailed for eighteen centuries denied that man was innately good. Plato and Aristotle, the two most important thinkers of the pre-Christian era, had also taught that man's nature was somehow influenced by evil forces. When Rousseau wrote in 1762 that "Everything is good as it comes from the hands of the Maker of the world but degenerates once it gets into the hands of man,"[2] he caused a furor (never to be equaled) among secular rulers, ecclesiastics, and educators. The book *Emile* was immediately condemned and burned because it was considered ruinous of the accepted way of life, especially the moral code; it contradicted the Biblical notion of original sin and its effects on man's behavior. Instead man's natural inclinations were to be considered the guide to right behavior. No longer could any ruler, class, or social group be considered the authority in matters involving human behavior. Man could rely upon his own tendencies to guide his behavior.

The educational import of this view of man's nature is far-reaching. It affects educational aims, methodology, curriculum, evaluation, and discipline in such a way that radical changes must be made in each area. Just what these changes are will be noted in succeeding sections of this chapter. Suffice it to say here that if nature is to be one's guide the conservative aim of education will be too narrow, the classical curriculum unreal, teacher-centered methods an obstacle to natural development, evaluation in terms of subject-matter mastery incomplete, and harsh discipline a violation of nature.

Although the proposition that man is naturally good represents the most significant change regarding the nature of the educand, other conservative views were rejected or disregarded. The naturalists of this period, such as Rousseau, emphasized the development of the natural faculties of man and paid little attention to the supernatural forces supposedly rooted in a spiritual soul. Even though no great efforts were made to prove there was no soul, the natural activities of man were at the center of philosophical and educational discussions. Discourses on the nature of the soul and a description of its activities received little or no attention in the works of the naturalists. The immortality of the soul, the nature of eternal reward and punishment were not of much theoretical concern. One might say that this period in educational history turned its back on supernatural or spiritual concerns and concentrated its theoretical and practical efforts on the development of man as a child of nature.

---

[2] W. Boyd (trans.), J. J. Rousseau's *Emile* (New York: Bureau of Publications, Teachers College, Columbia Univ., 1962), p. 8.

Since conservative educators had rooted the activities of mind in a supernatural soul, one can predict that a rejection or disregard of the spiritual element in man by the early liberals might lead to doubts about the acceptability of mind-body dualism. Rousseau's directions for educating the child make no distinction between mental and bodily training (see pp. 101-3); all are lumped together in an experience-centered curriculum. Helvetius, a contemporary of Rousseau, equated mind with experience, thus breaking down the wall which conservatives believed to exist between mental and bodily activities. Thus the dualism espoused by the Greek, Roman, and Christian thinkers began to be questioned in educational circles.

Yet another conservative notion about man's nature came under fire during this period. The belief that men are destined for certain social or intellectual classes was attacked by the early liberals. John Locke, a seventeenth-century thinker, in his treatise on *Civil Government*, argued that all men are rulers; no individual or class can lay any claim to rule others. Rousseau, in his *Social Contract*, expressed the same belief: namely, that no man has a natural authority over his fellowman. Thus the theorists of the time made the first successful move against an elitism which had dominated educational theory since the appearance of Plato's *Republic*. John A. Comenius, a seventeenth-century educational reformer proposed that all children and youth receive education in common schools. For him, social or intellectual classes should not be the chief factors in determining educational opportunity. The views of these theorists were to have a lasting effect on the broadening of educational opportunity to include all classes. For example, these egalitarian ideas were applied by the early liberal educators in America who called for free public education beyond the elementary level for all the children of all the people.

It is evident that this period in educational history witnessed the challenging of every basic conception about man's nature held by the conservatives. Man is no longer viewed as evil, or inclined to evil; the spiritual element in man is denied or disregarded in favor of an emphasis on natural man; the validity of mind-body dualism is questioned; the superiority of one man over another is rejected and replaced by an egalitarian view of freedom and authority; the limited individualism born in the Renaissance reaches adolescence in the eighteenth century and later attains maturity in the rugged individualism of the nineteenth century. Man has been freed from the restrictions of monarchs, ecclesiastics, and supernatural authority (revelation).

HOW DO WE KNOW?

Following the lead of Plato and Aristotle, conservative educators placed their reliance on reasoning as the primary mode of arriving at knowledge. The Christian added revelation as a source of knowledge superior to human reason. Even though experience plays a role in the conservative theory of knowledge, it is, indeed, a minor one. Only universal ideas (rational abstractions) are considered true knowledge.

Humanism, too, is characterized by an antiscientific bias. The best minds of the humanistic era centered their interest and scholarly activities on the unscientific and sometimes antiscientific material found in the Greek and Roman classics. The emphasis the humanistic educators placed upon grammar, rhetoric, and the classics left little time for studies of an experimental nature. Thus their concern was for man as a reasoning being rather than for the world of natural phenomena. Petrarch, for example, insisted that the study of zoology and other sciences serves no human purpose whatsoever since they throw no light on human existence.[3] Erasmus expressed the same contempt for those engaged in the pursuit of science in his *Praise of Folly*.

The early liberals questioned this reliance on reason and faith and argued that experience is the only dependable way of arriving at knowledge. Early in the seventeenth century Francis Bacon proposed a new method (*novum organum*) which he believed would enable man to divest himself of the falsehoods and idols which reason and faith had created.[4] The new approach must begin, he argued, with simple observation and experimental study of the world around one. Thus in order to acquire knowledge man must first divest himself of all preconceived ideas about the world, whether these be from faith or reason, and use his senses and the tools of science.

Bacon was not the only thinker to insist that the experimental or scientific method provides the best source of knowledge. Sir Isaac Newton, Galileo, Copernicus, and others had abandoned philosophical and speculative descriptions of physical phenomena in favor of those based on controlled observations. This period was truly the beginning of the "age of

---

[3]James Harvey Robinson and Henry W. Wolfe, *Petrarch* (New York: G. P. Putnam's Sons, 1898), pp. 41ff.

[4]Francis Bacon, "Novum Organum," *the Works of Francis Bacon*, ed. R. L. Ellis (Boston: Brown and Taggard, 1860-71), Book I, Aphorism VIII, LXIII.

science"; the "ages of faith and pure reason" began to lose ground rapidly. It should be noted, however, that men such as Copernicus and Galileo had found the first notions about their new theories in ancient writers. Copernicus discovered the heliocentric theory mentioned in the works of Cicero and Aristarchus. Galileo learned much from the writings of Euclid and Archimedes before formulating his own theories. The reliance which these early scientists placed on mathematics as a tool of science reflects the influence of Pythagoras who was likewise rediscovered during the revival of learning. The fact that many of the ancient writers proposed conflicting theories about natural phenomena forced the pioneers of the new science to make a direct study of nature to resolve the issue. Therefore, even though the majority of scholars used the works of the ancients for purely literary and humanistic purposes, at least a few found in them the starting point for the new science.

The belief that experience and the method of science are the prime sources of knowledge has great significance for educational theory. Experiments become the earmark of the liberal movement in education. These educators look to the sciences of psychology, sociology, and anthropology for their answers to educational questions. The theologian or the metaphysician is not asked for his definition of the nature of man, instead man is defined in terms of natural traits, abilities, and drives. New learning theories are based on observations of organisms engaged in learning. The effectiveness of teaching methods is judged on the basis of psychological changes in children rather than on logical or rational structure in the methodology. In short, education has found new guides -experience and science. Recognizing the importance of this shift is essential for an understanding of the various liberal movements in education for it has remained one of the major bones of contention to the present time-the conservative arguing that education is an art, the liberal that it is a science, or at least rooted in science.

Rousseau, too, reflected the same attitude toward knowledge, although he was by no means a scientist. But his recommendations for learning through direct experience rather than by verbalization are quite in harmony with the new approach to knowing. The pupil should learn natural science by observing nature, not by reading books or being told about it. In fact, Rousseau felt that the child should not learn to read until he is twelve. Thus the tutor would not be tempted to substitute verbal learning for learning by experience.[5]

---

[5]Boyd, *op. cit*, pp. 65ff.

The activity curriculum and pupil-centered teaching methods, to be discussed later in the chapter, are the logical educational adaptations of the *novum organum*.

WHAT IS TRUTH?

Whereas the conservative educator had honored the conclusions of reason and/or revelation as truths in the citadel of learning, the new liberals designated the findings of the empirical sciences and direct experience as truth. On the one hand, this change involved a rejection of the authority of Aristotle, Plato, and the Bible in matters of concern to the empirical sciences, even though these sources were retained as guides to faith and morals. For example, some scholars of the times used scientific evidence to demonstrate the falsity of certain statements in the Bible or in Aristotle. Galileo, in his noted experiment from the Tower of Pisa, disproved the Aristotelian theory of the rate of speed of falling bodies. Early anthropological studies and historical research were employed to disprove the truth of Biblical chronology. Thus, although many of the early scientists believed they could find absolute truth in their experimental studies, one can detect the tendency to abandon the traditional notion that truth is immutable.[6] This is one of the essential differences between the conclusions of experience and science and those of reason and faith. The former are probable and mutable, the latter, absolute and immutable. It is not surprising, then, to find that the liberal movement in education is characterized by the absence of finality and certainty. Its advocates are always searching for new ways of doing things, new goals for the schools, and the like. Whereas the conservative is more apt to be satisfied with the status quo in educational theory, policy, and practice, the liberal is never content to leave things as they are. He feels that without change there can be no progress. If one does not find new truths to solve the problems of the times, education will stagnate and become the stronghold of reactionism. The liberal will readily abandon what one generation considered truth if it is no longer functional. Since the truths of experience and science are tentative, such an attitude is wholly consistent with the liberal point of view.

Obviously this new definition of truth had a direct effect on the curriculum and teaching-learning methods. One can look for continuous changes in the curriculum and great emphasis upon students' finding their own truths in classrooms, laboratories, and the world outside the school.

---

[6]Randall,*op. cit*, p. 230.

WHAT IS GOOD?

The answers given by the early liberals to ethical questions could but stir the ire of conservatives. The latter had looked to reason or revelation for decisions about the good or bad of human acts. Spiritual values or those associated with intellect (mind) were given preference to values rooted in fallen human nature. In general, yielding to natural drives and desires was equated with moral imperfection, and all natural inclinations must be kept under the firm control of reason or the moral code of the Decalogue. In its most extreme form, asceticism, this attitude toward man's lower nature entailed rigorous fasts, complete control of the senses lest evil enter through them, and even self-inflicted corporal punishment.

Certainly, such beliefs about morality would be wholly unacceptable to those who view man's nature as essentially good, or at least neutral. Of course, the suggestion that nature should be one's guide in the field of morals was not original with seventeenth- and eighteenth-century thinkers, it had its roots in the ancient philosophy of Epicurianism. But the Hebrew-Christian way of life with its detailed code of ethics was so vigorous from the fourth to the seventeenth centuries that a naturalistic moral system had no chance to flourish.

Most contemporary Americans cannot comprehend the great effect that this new approach to morals had on the people, since American life is guided to a great extent by naturalistic and secular codes.   We are accustomed to hearing that certain types of home training and environment are the causes of youthful delinquency.   But when Rousseau said that because the child Emile was naturally good and should be allowed to grow and develop according to natural instincts, drives and desires, he received the following verdict:

> [This work is] calculated to overthrow natural law and to destroy
> the foundations of the Christian religion; establishing maxims
> contrary to Gospel morality; having a tendency to disturb the peace
> of empires, to stir up subjects to revolt against their sovereign; as
> containing a great number of propositions respectively false,
> scandalous. . . . erroneous, impious, blasphemous and heretical.[7]

Since the new theory of morals was so revolutionary, one might surmise that no new moral code was substituted for the old. Such was not the case, however. In the first place, even Rousseau demanded that children should

---

[7] *Oeuvres de J. J.Roussau* (Paris:Lefevre, 1819-20), X, 158.

however. In the first place, even Rousseau demanded that children should be sheltered from the evil example of their elders. (It must be remembered that the moral behavior of the upper social strata at this time was scandalous.) If the child remains close to nature, his natural goodness will not be sullied by the struggle for riches, power, glory, and illicit loves which characterized human behavior This, at least, represents a negative code of ethics. On the positive side of the ledger, educators were advised to instruct their charges concerning moderation in food and drink; preparation for the normal hardships of life caused by weather, climate, and the like; meeting the need for vocational competence and harmonious living in the family and other social groups. [8]

It is true, however, that the ethical revolutionaries did not propose a complete set of "Thou shalt and shalt nots" as traditional moralists had done. Rather. they said, "let nature and experience be your guide."

Another feature of the new morality is its dynamic character. Whereas the conservative maintains that basic moral standards were changeless, the liberal speaks of revising or completely changing norms of behavior in accordance with the satisfaction of human wants. What was considered good under a feudalistic system may be wholly unacceptable under a different mode of living. Even though the early liberal thinkers generally did not attempt a point-by-point refutation of the Hebrew-Christian moral code, the very fact that they intimated it was outmoded indicates that they favored the introduction of new moral standards.

But the question still remains: "How is one to decide what is good and what is evil?" For Rousseau, at least, the answer was quite simple. Since individual men are inherently good, their moral decisions will be good. For moral decisions involving many people, the general will shall dictate the morality of behavior.[9] Just how one determines which decisions of the general will are acceptable poses a serious ethical question. But later liberals, especially Dewey, recognizing the inherent difficulties of Rousseau's doctrine, gave serious attention to the problem of social ethics.

Plato had asserted that the knower might acquire a better understanding of the good via the avenue of the fine arts. The beauty of an object does not make it good but enhances its goodness by making it more apparent to the knower. Christians, too, had used the art forms to enhance moral and religious values. Thus, for both Plato and the Christians, aesthetic

---

[8] See Boyd, *op cit*, pp. 70-130.
[9] See J.J. Rousseau, *Social Contract* and *Discourses* (New York: E.P. Dutton & Co., 1914), pp. 25ff., 83.

experience was directed to some higher purpose. Since the early liberals shifted their emphasis from the spiritual or supernatural realm to that of nature, there was no need to direct aesthetic experiences to some higher purpose. Consequently, all aesthetic values are rooted in nature itself and never transcend it. The "natural" is beautiful and the beautiful is natural.

Little more can be said about the theories of art proposed by the early liberals simply because men like Rousseau were not so concerned with the cultural and artistic aspects of human life as they were with the practical and utilitarian.[10] Keep in mind that their revolt was against the unreality and uselessness of the educational theory and practice of the humanistic era. It is not surprising, then, that highly developed theories of art are not found in the works of these thinkers.

It is clear that the prime movers of the liberal revolt in education rejected the major philosophical tenets of the preceding twenty centuries. The validity of dualism, supernaturalism, elitism, and their attendant doctrines was challenged. Knowing by reason and revelation was replaced by experimental modes of knowing. Truth was viewed as experimental and relative rather than revealed, rational, and immutable. Moral and aesthetic values were found in nature rather than in a realm above nature. The liberals' answers to important educational questions reveal the same sweeping condemnation of traditional educational theory.

WHAT IS THE PURPOSE OF THE SCHOOL?

The limited intellectualistic goal of the school which dominated conservative education could not be considered adequate by the liberals. In the first place it was based on an unnatural dualism which assumed that the pupil's mind could be cultivated in school whereas physical and emotional needs had to be cared for elsewhere. Such a division of the child for educational purposes, liberals argued, violated nature. Hence, the whole child theory was proposed.

In the early seventeenth century, John Locke had intimated that the school had failed to educate a person if his physical, moral, and emotional development had not been cared for. For him, the learning of language, literature, and the like were considered secondary. Rousseau's recommendations were more sweeping. In discussing the five stages of the educational program (from infancy to maturity), he included all phases of

---

[10] In *Emile* Rousseau does mention the value of certain literary works, but those he held most highly are close to nature such *Robinson Crusoe*.

development. For him training in walking, speaking, hearing, seeing, tasting, smelling, and touching are truly educational. In addition to this basic sense training, he recommended activities which would prepare the pupil for a specific job, social life, and marriage. Development of emotional stability is recommended at all stages of the process but especially during the last two, adolescence and maturity.[11]

One might correctly argue that Rousseau was not speaking of the purpose of the school but of education in general. This is the crucial notion in the liberals' view: namely, that the purpose of education-be it in the home, the community, or the school-is the same for all. Pestalozzi, the eighteenth-century Swiss schoolmaster who tried to put Rousseau's theories into practice, showed how this could be done. His experimental schools at Stantz and Yverdon embodied the activities recommended by Rousseau. Pestalozzi designed these activities to achieve the harmonious development of moral, intellectual, and physical powers.[12]

Even before Rousseau's time, Comenius' *Great Didactic* had recommended that the school abandon its concentration on intellectual development and set itself to meeting all the needs of all the children. The vernacular should be used instead of Latin and only useful subjects should be taught. Students should be given the opportunity to learn a trade, develop skills necessary for living in society and receive instruction and practice in politics and economics.[13]

At least in the common schools, then, the reformers demanded that the purpose be to prepare pupils for life and give them practice in living. The common school should not have as its primary goal the preparation for the higher levels of education. Those who wish to prepare for more advanced schooling should be offered the opportunity to do so. But the presence of university-bound students in the common school should not result in a "college-prep"-oriented school which excludes all other purposes.

It seems, therefore, that the essential change proposed by the liberal reformers was the broadening of the school's purpose to include all facets of human development. These early reformers did not affirm that the schools should not develop the intellectual powers of the pupils. They simply asserted that all the activities of human life are the concern of the school.

---

[11] Boyd, *op. cit*, Books I-V.

[12] See pp. 102-103 of this volume.

[13] John A. Comenius, *The Great Didactic*, M. W. Keatinge (trans.) (London. A. & C. Black, Ltd., 1923), pp. 23, 43, 52, 256-69.

WHAT SHOULD BE TAUGHT?

If the purpose of the school is broadened to include the development of the whole child, certainly the classical, literary curriculum of the conservative school will be wholly inadequate. As noted, Comenius recommended that sense training and vocational training be added to the humanistic curriculum. Furthermore, he insisted that all curricular offerings, even Latin, serve some *useful* purpose. If an educator cannot defend the practical nature of a school subject, it should be eliminated from the curriculum.

Rousseau's philosophy of the curriculum represents a more radical break with the traditional notion than that of Comenius. From ages five to twelve, the curriculum should contain many activities aimed at developing physical fitness. The subject matter in other fields, such as natural science, should consist in the direct observation of the environment. Also, the teacher should give serious attention to the emotional development of the child at this stage. Reading could be introduced near the end of this period if the need for it arose. In general, though, Rousseau opposed the use of books since "they only teach us to talk about what we do not know."[14] It is better to teach astronomy by taking the pupil to a hill on a clear night and letting him observe the wonders of the heavens. The same is true of most of the other knowledge found in books-the student will understand the same content better if he experiences it rather than reads about it.

From ages twelve to fifteen the pupil makes a more sophisticated study of geography and natural science by a systematic observation of the "things" in his environment. This might be supplemented by reading such books as *Robinson Crusoe* which reflect "nature as it is."[15] Also, at this time, the adolescent should begin mastering a vocation of his choice. Again, the teacher must be cognizant of the great changes taking place in the emotional development of the pupil and provide activities suited to this stage of development.

The final stage in the curriculum (after the student has reached fifteen) includes sex education and preparation for family living, a study of the various religions, and any specialized subjects which meet the interests and practical needs of the youth. Field trips and travel to places of interest rather than verbal descriptions are recommended. Boy-girl relationships are developed in a natural way; social activities in a natural setting assist the

---

[14] Boyd, *op cit.*, p.83.
[15] *Ibid.*, p. 84.

youth in acquiring the proper relationship with his fellow man.[16]

The important point in Rousseau's philosophy of the curriculum is not so much the specific activities which he recommended but rather that these activities reflect the natural living of the pupil at every step of his development. The curriculum is something the pupil does, not something that is done to him. It is living as well as a preparation for life.

John Basedow, a contemporary of Rousseau and an ardent educational reformer, built a curriculum designed to meet the natural needs of the pupils. Physical and vocational education were central activities in the curriculum; only the practical aspects of science, mathematics, and language were taught. Even grammar, which constituted the heart of the classical curriculum, was practically eliminated. Dancing, music, and art were included for their recreational value or as opportunities for some pupils to follow special interests.[17] Basedow opened an experimental school with this revolutionary curriculum. The humanistic schoolmen, of course, ridiculed the entire program. But the common people looked upon it with favor. Some historians argue that Basedow stole Rousseau's ideas and vice versa. At least Basedow tried to put his curriculum to the test of experience, and, perhaps, his laboratory school would have been successful if he had not been a poor administrator.

As mentioned above, Rousseau himself was not a teacher nor did he have any close connection with educational institutions, but shortly after Rousseau's death, Pestalozzi used his philosophy of the curriculum in the construction of an activity-centered program. His schools were liberal in many ways. For example, he accepted students of all intellectual and social levels. Great freedom was enjoyed by all those attending. But because the curriculum he designed for his schools was so radically different from the typical schools of his time, it received much favorable and unfavorable attention from educators. In *Leonard and Gertrude* he averred that the activities of the school should be closely associated with home life-the curriculum was living.[18] The teacher had to be solicitous for the same aspects of growth that concern the mother of a family. Thus the pupil's physical and moral development were just as important as that of his mind. The laws of good social living were to be lived in the schools rather than taught there. His school was to be a model community which civil rulers

---

[16] *Ibid.*, Books II-V.

[17] J. B. Basedow, *Das Elementarwerk*, ed. T.Fritzsch (Dessau: E.Weigand, 1909).

[18] J. H. Pestalozzi, *Leonard and Gertrude*, ed. E. Channing (Boston: D. C. Heath & Co., 1906), pp. 115-19.

taught there. His school was to be a model community which civil rulers might adapt to the larger community.[19] This is perhaps the first statement of the notion that the school should be the model for a new social order, a theory later advocated by some twentieth-century liberal American educators.

The *activities* of the Pestalozzian curriculum included reading, writing, numbers, group singing, dancing, nature study via field trips, hiking, games of all kinds, work in the shops and fields-in reality any activity that was associated with living in a group. Thus one could not find a cut and dried course of study in Pestalozzi's schools. He knew the general purpose of the activities, but flexibility and change were more evident than any one set pattern of subjects. Everything was designed to serve some practical, useful purpose in the pupil's life.

At approximately the same time as Pestalozzi was experimenting with the curriculum for living, Benjamin Franklin was fighting against what he considered the impractical classical curriculum of the secondary schools in the New World. He, too, felt that a curriculum should meet the needs of daily living. Even though he did not discard all the subjects of the classical curriculum, his academies taught bookkeeping, surveying, navigation, drawing, mineralogy, agriculture, civics, and other bread and butter subjects.

All of the curricula mentioned, in spite of specific differences, have certain characteristics in common: (1) All contain activities or subjects of a useful nature. (2) Physical education, vocational training, and social activities are just as respectable as the academic subjects. (3) The interests, needs, and emotional conditions of the pupils guide the selection of activities rather than any preconceived program of studies. (4) Wherever possible, the student must learn from firsthand experience rather than through the vicarious experience of books or by being told.

HOW SHOULD ONE TEACH?

With the exception of Quintilian and the Jesuits, conservative educators showed little concern for *how* to teach. The purpose of the school is sufficiently limited to intellectualism and the curriculum is so book-oriented that there is no great need for concern about teaching methods. Furthermore, the teacher-centered classroom of the conservative does not permit much opportunity for variations in teaching methodology.

---

[19] *Ibid.*, pp. 150ff.

Certainly, the liberals' whole child theory and the experience-centered curriculum demand essential changes in teacher-pupil interaction. The one characteristic that all the new methods had is their pupil centeredness. Generally speaking, this means that the pupil is to assume the major responsibility for learning activities. The teacher's role is more like that of the middleman or interlocutor in a minstrel show. The pupils are the actors, the teacher is the coordinator of the various acts. The new teaching techniques of the liberals are generally designated by the term natural method.

One of the most important changes introduced into teaching methodology by the early liberals is the use of direct observation of and experience with physical and social realities. This mode of studying the world is, of course, a direct outgrowth of the new method of arriving at knowledge (see pp. 97-99). To the student of today who has taken many field trips, worked in a laboratory or shop, and visited many places of historical interest, this change may not seem especially significant. But if one recalls that such practices were unheard of in the seventeenth and eighteenth centuries it becomes evident how radical the new approach to teaching actually was. Comenius used it very sparingly for he knew that educators and parents alike would not tolerate it. Nevertheless, his opposition to the verbal approach of both scholasticism and humanism was thoroughgoing. He insisted that the only way for pupils to learn was to observe things for themselves rather than to read or be told about them.[20]

But Rousseau, who was not a teacher and had no fear of professional educators or parents, argued that the method of direct observation and experience was the best means of teaching pupils at all levels of the educational program. It was because he believed that this was the only natural way to learn that he was so opposed to the use of books-a vicarious experience could never be as effective as a direct one. He told Emile's tutor not only how to provide for this direct experience but also how to avoid the pitfalls of the unnatural methods of the humanists.

The educational reformer and contemporary of Rousseau, John Basedow, also leveled an attack on humanistic teaching methodology for its lack of contact with the real world. He, too, demanded that the teacher utilize the pupil's natural desire for play and his spontaneous interest in his surroundings as the key to developing a new methodology. For example, in his schools little children were taught language by playing word games. Rote memorization of the words was eliminated, and the students eventually

---

[20] Comenius, *op cit.*, pp.43, 185ff.

learned words simply by playing the game. Physical coordination and motor control were learned through various types of games played right in the classroom. In fact, all work was presented in the form of delightful games. The children were allowed to talk and move around freely. They were taken on field trips (object lessons) to study nature or to visit a historical site. When pupils became bored with an activity, they moved on to others of immediate interest. All activities were pupil-oriented even though teachers participated in them. In fact, the entire approach to teaching was social. His method was the forerunner of the twentieth-century socialized class.

Perhaps the feature that most angered the old schoolmasters about Basedow's play-school was the continuous chatter of the students. These conservative educators could not understand how the pupils could learn anything if they were talking all the time. But Basedow countered that: Only by discussing the objects they were studying could pupils really grasp their meaning; otherwise, they merely were parroting the words of the book or the teacher.[21]

Pestalozzi's methodology, although based on Rousseau's philosophy rather than Basedow's, is very similar to that just described. But, Pestalozzi's version of the natural method appeared to be more influential than Basedow's since educators came from all over the world to observe his experimental schools. For example, Herbart, who was an ardent advocate of Pestalozzian theory, inspired the early leaders of the American Progressive movement.

Certainly there are other educational reformers of the period who contributed to the development of new teaching-learning methods. However, they embody the same principles and characteristics of those already discussed above. Briefly, the new philosophy of method entailed the following essential points: (1) Whatever techniques a teacher uses, they must not violate the natural growth pattern of the students. Positively stated this means that all teaching-learning activities must reflect the natural method of doing things. (2) The liberal methodology is pupil-centered rather than teacher-centered. To use the jargon, the teacher is a guide rather than a director. (3) Learning by doing, by direct observation (object lessons), or by personal involvement of the pupils are essential features of the new teaching methods. (4) Motivation for learning is based upon the intrinsic interests and natural needs of the learners. (5) Any teaching-learning technique must consider the physical and emotional aspects of

[21] H. Goring, *J. B. Basedow's Ausgewhalte Schriften* (Langensalza: H.Beyer und Sohne, 1880), pp. 97-99, 265f. *passim.*

pupil behavior as well as the mental.

HOW SHOULD PUPILS BE EVALUATED?

Since the liberal proposes broader goals for the school, an activity curriculum, and pupil-centered learning methods, the evaluational devices of the conservative school are obviously inadequate if not thoroughly miseducative. The liberal cannot settle for oral or written examinations to determine the extent to which the pupil has memorized certain subject matter or developed perfect literary style and eloquence.

Although the early liberals offered very few specific evaluational techniques, they did chart the broad outlines for a new philosophy of appraisal. The first and perhaps the most significant revision calls for a new approach to evaluation encompassing the *total growth* of the individual. In evaluating a pupil, the teacher is to determine whether the pupil has shown more physical, social, and emotional maturity than he had at the beginning of this educational experience. He will ask such questions as: Does the pupil know himself better now than before? Does he get along well with his fellows? Is he better equipped to care for his economic needs than before? Are his observations of natural and social phenomena more penetrating after his recent experiences? Does he know more about the world around him than he did a year ago?

Rousseau provided an excellent example of this total approach to pupil appraisal: Emile's tutor guides him through each of the experiences which touch upon all facets of human development. The infant moves to a new educational level, so to speak, when he has learned to walk, talk, and has broken some of the ties which kept him bound to his mother. The boy is promoted to the next level when he has acquired enough physical stamina to withstand the hardships of nature, when he has trained the senses of sight, hearing, taste, speech, smell, and touch to adjust to his environment and to learn by direct contact with it. At the next level (preadolescence), he is expected to begin his mastery of a trade, be more sophisticated and accurate in his scientific studies, and be able to decide which activities will best serve his physical needs. The adolescent period is considered successfully passed when the pupil has understood the meaning of the emotional reactions of this period, when he has developed adequate social relations with his fellows and, especially, with the opposite sex, and when he has built for himself a personally satisfying set of aesthetic and religious values. The appraisal of Emile's final educational experience is based on his preparedness for marriage and family life, community living, the use of his reasoning powers and on his emotional maturity.[22]

It is worth noting that Rousseau did not employ the formal examination-either oral or written-as a means of determining the pupil's readiness for the next educational level. The wise and experienced teacher, one who has lived a full life himself, will recognize when the student should be promoted. In other words, the teacher takes a measure of the pupil's growth in all phases of human development.

Pestalozzi's experimental schools, likewise, made little or no use of formal subject-matter examinations, nor was it necessary for him to do so since subject-matter mastery was only one phase of the school program. But, when the local educational authorities sent examiners to his school, Pestalozzi graciously allowed them to test his pupils. To the surprise of many people, his poor, underprivileged orphans surpassed the achievement of their peers in the established schools not only in the required subjects of letters, spelling, and reading but also in writing, arithmetic, drawing, history, natural history, geography, and measuring.[23]

Both Comenius and Basedow had removed the fear and tension caused by the grueling oral examinations of the classical schools. Since both had insisted that school activities must be pleasant for the children, they had devised other means of determining what their charges had learned. These means usually took the form of games and other play and creative activities which gave the pupils the opportunity to demonstrate their competence in language, spelling, numbers, nature study, history, and geography. Even their mastery of Latin was measured by games.

From the work of Rousseau and Pestalozzi other principles in their philosophy of evaluation can be drawn. A very significant change from the conservative view is the relativity of all appraisal. For these educators, pupil's success was always stated in terms of relative growth. Thus when Pestalozzi accepted poor, uninstructed orphans into his schools, there was no fixed standard by which they were evaluated. Each pupil did his best in relation to his abilities, interests, socioeconomic background, and personal needs. Examinations were not used to determine which students were better than others. Nor did a student have to master any given amount of subject matter to be considered successful. The essential criterion was that he know more after his educational experiences than he knew before, i.e., some growth had taken place.

---

[22] Boyd *op. cit*, Books I-V
[23] See R. De Guimps, *Pestalozzi: His Life and Work* (New York: Appleton & Co. 1892), pp. 177f.

Though Rousseau established five educational levels and suggested certain activities for each level, he did not set forth any absolute standard which might be regarded as the criterion for success. It was the relative judgment of the tutor that determined the pupil's fitness for the next level. In fact, Rousseau's theory appears to favor continuous promotion from level to level on the sole basis of natural developmental stages rather than on the meeting of any specific standards or requirements.

One final characteristic of evaluation among the early liberals is related to the role the individual plays in the process. In the conservative schools, teachers or outside authorities devise and administer the examinations-the learner plays no part whatever in the process; in the new school of the early liberals the pupil is actively participating in his own evaluation. Basedow's teachers used several ingenious games whereby the student could determine his own level of achievement in the basic skills, crafts, and other school subjects. Both Rousseau and Pestalozzi placed much of the burden of evaluation on the pupil himself, or, better, it was a cooperative enterprise between pupil and teacher.

In summary, then, one can point to the following features of the liberal conception of evaluation: (1) It is concerned with all aspects of human development-mental, physical, emotional, and vocational. (2) No absolute or permanent standards are applied; evaluation is always in terms of relative change. (3) Evaluation is a cooperative enterprise engaging both pupil and teacher. (4) Pupil self-evaluation is more important than that of the teacher or outside authorities.

HOW ARE FREEDOM AND DISCIPLINE TO BE HARMONIZED?

Next to the shift to the natural method of teaching, the most radical change in classroom practices introduced by the early liberals involved the freeing of the child to develop in harmony with nature. This move paralleled the seventeenth- and eighteenth-century revolt against both political and ecclesiastical authority. Locke, in *Treatises of Government*, argued that *every* man was born with the perfect freedom to enjoy the rights to property, liberty, life, and choice of religious belief. A century later Rousseau's Social Contract advocated the same principles of individual freedom in opposition to the claims of privileged classes or rulers. (The book was promptly condemned by both civil and ecclesiastical authorities.) In reality, Rousseau's whole life consisted of a revolt against the social structures and mores of his time.

In *Emile* he demanded the same freedom for the child as he demanded for all citizens in the *Social Contract*. Emile's tutor never forces any activities on him. The child launches out into the world of nature and finds his own answers to questions: he is not given the truth. Even in infancy and boyhood the tutor demands for the pupil the right to make mistakes and learn from his errors. The teacher does not force the customs and moral standards of adult society upon the child but permits him to live in harmony with his own natural drives and interests.[24]

During preadolescence the youth freely chooses a vocation and follows other studies of interest to him. Only during adolescence is the pupil encouraged to choose a religion for himself. This, of course, is most significant since the choice of religion was usually made for the pupil by his parents or teachers. At later stages of his development, Emile chooses his companions and finally his life's partner.[25] Granted that the theory of educational freedom presented in *Emile* is quite idealistic, the essential message conveyed is that teachers and other educational authorities should stop dictating what the pupil is to do, when and how he is to do it; the pupil must be free to develop his own talents using his natural interests as guides.

Such fundamental changes in the conception of freedom obviously call for a complete rejection of the conservative notion of discipline. Rousseau does not view the teacher as a disciplinarian. Nature herself will discipline the child; that is, the natural consequences of an act will be their own reward or punishment. The child will learn, early in life, that he will suffer if he throws himself in a bed of thorns or attacks older children.

Perhaps even more fundamental to the new view of discipline is the belief that man is essentially good. Thus the teacher or other authorities deny the fundamental freedom of the child when they restrain him from acting in harmony with nature or punish him for doing so.

Pestalozzi's experimental schools demonstrated to the educational world that Rousseau's liberal notion of freedom could function in the actual operation of a school. His advice to his teachers was very clear on this point. He asked them to cherish individual liberty as the supreme value, to give the child the chance to learn things for himself, to make his own mistakes, and to take an active part in his own discipline. If the child appears to be intent on doing something the teacher feels is not good, warn him of the consequences, but let him make his own choice. Do not shield

---

[24] Boyd, *op. cit.*, Book II
[25] *Ibid., Books* IV-V.

him from the unpleasant results of his own freedom; only in cases of extreme danger should a command be given.[26] This was no idle advice for he himself was faithful to these precepts in his own teaching and his co-workers did their best to follow his example.

However, Rousseau and Pestalozzi were not the first to object to the restrictions placed upon the freedom of the pupils and to the severe discipline in the humanistic schools. A century before Rousseau, Comenius criticized conservative schools on these two points: He called them the terror of boys and slaughterhouse of minds. He complained that subject matter was forced upon the child or beaten into him. If a teacher has to resort to punishment to get pupils to learn or behave he will have himself to blame for not utilizing the natural interest of pupils and the inherent pleasantness of the things to be learned.[27] He gave pupils freedom of choice by offering them a tempting variety of practical subjects. He forbade his teachers to use force or roughness. The classroom and school environs should be made so pleasant that pupils would prefer to attend school than stay at home. School should be as pleasant as a fair.[28]

Basedow, also, remembering the lack of freedom and the flogging of his own school days, said that children must be allowed freedom to move about the classroom and the school grounds and should never be punished for failing to learn their lessons. Generally he attributed bad behavior and failure to learn to an unrealistic curriculum and poor teaching methods rather than to pupil laziness. If a pupil never adjusted to school life, Basedow recommended that he not be forced to attend. Punishment will never change the pupil.[29]

This period of educational history witnessed a radical change in both theory and practice regarding freedom and discipline. Even though the persons mentioned presented different recommendations for achieving harmony between freedom and discipline, several essential points are held in common by them. (1) Since children are not innately bad, one can trust that the natural choices they make will be good. Therefore, they should be given all possible freedom. (2) The harsh discipline found in conservative schools will not be necessary if an interesting curriculum and natural teaching methods are employed. (3) Under no conditions should corporal punishment be used as a means to force pupils to learn their lessons or

---

[26] R. De Guimps, *op. cit*, pp. 46ff.

[27] Comenius *op. cit*, pp. 22f., 250ff.

[28] *Ibid.*, pp. 130ff.

[29] See Goring, *op. cit., passim.*

acquire certain behavior patterns. Its use is a violation of nature.

CHAPTER SUMMARY

The seventeenth and eighteenth centuries represent a period in which the most radical changes took place in educational theory and practice. The new liberalism proposed many philosophical doctrines and educational practices which were to culminate in twentieth-century American progressivism. The following are the most important:

Man is naturally good or at least neutral. The natural element in man receives greater attention than the supernatural. Political equality (egalitarianism) is proposed in opposition to the elitism of the conservatives. Experience and science are the prime sources of knowledge and truth rather than pure reason or revelation. Truth is relative and man-made rather than absolute and divine. Man's happiness or highest good lies in living in harmony with nature. True beauty is found in nature itself.

The purpose of the school is broadened to include the development of the "whole person." Curricular content and activities are determined by utility, individual pupil interests, and needs. Teaching techniques are pupil-centered and are based on the same natural method by which children learn in out-of-school situations. All educational activities should be pleasant, and no child should be forced to learn until he is ready for and interested in such learning. Evaluation is in terms of the individual's total growth; no set standards can be determined or applied. The pupil is to be allowed maximum freedom in and out of the classroom in the choice of activities and the like. Force must never be used. Discipline should be preventative rather than remedial. Punishments will consist in the natural consequences of the pupils' acts. Corporal punishment, by teachers or authorities, should never be employed to produce desirable behavior.

BIBLIOGRAPHY

Bacon, Francis. *The Works of Francis Bacon*, ed. R. L. Ellis. Boston: Brown and Taggard, 1860-71.

Barnard, H. C. *Pestalozzi and His Educational System*. Syracuse, N.Y.: C. W. Bardeen Co., 1906.

Basedow, J. B. *Das Elementarwerk*, ed. T. Fritzsch. Dessau: E. Weigand Co., 1909.

Beck, R. H. *A Social History of Education*. Englewood Cliffs, N.J.: Prentice-Hall, 1965.

Bowen, H. C. *Froebel and Education by Self-Activity*. New York: Charles Scribner's Sons, 1901.

Comenius, John A. *The Great Didactic*. Translated by M. W. Keatinge. London: A. and C. Black, 1923.

Cole, Luella. *A History of Education*. New York: Rinehart and Co., 1950. Chs. XVI-XVII.

De Guimps, R. *Pestalozzi: His Life and Work*. New York: Appleton & Co., 1892.

Franklin, Benjamin. *The Works of Benjamin Franklin*. New York: John Bigelow Co., 1904.

Goring, H. *J. B. Basedow's Ausgewahlte Schriften*. Langensalza: H. Beyer und Sohne, 1880.

Pestalozzi, J. H. *Leonard and Gertrude*, ed. E. Channing. Boston: D. C. Heath & Co., 1906.

Rousseau, J. J. *Social Contract and Discourses*. New York: E. P. Dutton & Co., 1914.

Rousseau, J. J. *Confessions*. Baltimore: Penguin Books, 1953.

Rousseau, J. J. *Emile*. Translated by W. Boyd. New York: Bureau of Publications, Teachers College, Columbia Univ., 1962.

Steegmuller, Francis. *Sir Francis Bacon, The First Modern Mind*. Garden City, N.Y.: Doubleday, Doran & Co., 1930.

Thorpe, F. N. *Franklin's Influence in American Education*. Washington, D.C.: United States Bureau of Education, 1903.

Chapter VI

The Flowering
of Liberalism

A perusal of the history of education during the period discussed in the previous chapter will show that the revolt of the early liberals against conservative education did not have immediate, widespread effects on the schools. Some of Comenius' reforms were adopted only in isolated schools of Europe. Basedow's experimental schools were short-lived. Rousseau's work was inspirational, but he himself did nothing to put his own theories into practice. Even the highly publicized experimental schools of Pestalozzi enjoyed only temporary success.

Undoubtedly, the opposition of conservative schoolmen had much to do with the failure of the new ideas to penetrate into very many schoolrooms. Nevertheless, the new theories were being studied by many European and American educators who were dissatisfied with the aims, curriculum, and methods of humanistic education. The great surge toward more political freedom was accompanied by demands for educational freedom for both teachers and pupils. The seed which had been planted in the seventeenth and eighteenth centuries grew somewhat slowly in the nineteenth century and finally flowered in twentieth-century America.

During this period many of the somewhat ambivalent answers given by the early reformers to the fundamental questions of educational theory and practice were clarified. The new scientific outlook which became established in the preceding period now had a direct effect on education, so that both educational philosophers and practitioners were able to call on empirical studies to bolster their views. Educational psychology, rooted in the new evolutionary biology, and measurement formed the heart of a science of education which was to replace the speculation of preceding centuries on such topics as learning, "transfer and mental discipline," and the effectiveness of teaching methods. Laboratory schools to test new theories were established in many teacher training institutions.

But science and technology had wrought rapid significant changes in the whole social order. Certain social and economic conditions called for a more critical look at the notions of freedom and control as these applied to the body politic, labor management relations, community life, and the like. During this period (about mid-nineteenth century) the Industrial Revolution had reached such a state. of development that industry dominated agriculture and commerce. Emigration from the rural areas began to depopulate the countryside and overcrowd the cities. As the labor force grew larger, labor unions became stronger and recorded victories over the wealthy factory owners.

At the level of economic theory, thinkers such as John Stuart Mill questioned the validity of laissez faire capitalism and proposed government regulation of industries and the elimination of unbridled competition. These theorists could not envisage an ordered society without some restraints on individual freedom-people were too interdependent in a complex industrial structure to permit rugged individualism.

Thus, at this juncture, one notes the rise of a "new liberalism" which shifts the emphasis from individual to group or collective freedom. Educational theorists, especially Dewey and his followers, were quick to recognize the educational implications of this modification in the liberal outlook. These revisions of classical liberalism will be noted in the ensuing discussion of the basic philosophical and educational questions.

The period under consideration, then, is one which, in many respects, was built upon the belief of the early liberals discussed in the preceding chapter. Important modifications were, however, introduced by the nineteenth- and twentieth-century liberals which not only consolidated the gains of the early liberals, but also reflected the changed social and economic conditions. Finally, much of the new educational theory actually received widespread application in American public and independent schools.

WHAT IS MAN?

Perhaps the most novel theory about man's nature to be proposed since the founding of Christianity was based upon the evolution of species (including man). The Biblical story traced man's origin to the direct creative act of God. Even though early liberals such as Rousseau focused their attention upon man as a *child of nature*, they offered no new theory about his origin. Thus Rousseau could say that man "is good as he comes from the hands of his Maker" and still be in accord with one aspect of the Christian view, namely, man as a distinct species was created by God. But in the nineteenth century, Herbert Spencer, Charles Darwin, and others argued that man was not a ready-made species, but that he had evolved from lower animal forms.

There is no need here to delve into the various theories of evolution. It should be noted, however, that evolutionism has several significant implications for educational theory. The first, intimated already, is that human beings do not constitute a static species. Rather, they are not only a product of lower animal forms but are also capable of much higher levels of development than they possess now. Consequently, man is not everywhere and at all times essentially the same, as most traditional philosophers believe him to be. Second, since environment plays so significant a role in evolutionary theories, the importance of education, especially in modern complex societies, is greatly enhanced. Education becomes an essential tool for ensuring progress in human affairs through the planned improvement of the environment. Also, continuous progress in education is necessary to prevent regression in human development.

The mind-body dualism of conservative thinkers received no support from most evolutionists, Mind and body are not separate entities but different aspects of the same evolving organism. Spencer explained the composition of all beings, inanimate and animate (including man and society), by means of the principles of evolution. Thus evolutionary changes account for differences in species, individuals within a species, and in social groups. Man can make no claim to, or is there any need for, a supernatural origin or destiny for his soul or mind. These are simply manifestations of a higher level of natural development.[1]

Dewey addressed himself to the problem of dualism throughout his important work *Democracy and Education*. He argued that the mind-body (spirit-matter) dualism of classical philosophy is responsible for the unnatural cleavages in society and education such as labor-leisure, practical-intellectual, man-nature, culture-vocation, subject matter-method, ends-means, and others.[2] Dewey rejected the notion that the human mind is endowed from birth with reasoning power or that its origin is in the spiritual soul. Mind is not different from the body but one with it. All of

---

[1] Herbert Spencer, *First Principles of a New System of Philosophy* (New York: Appleton & Co., 1896). See also J. Herbst, "Herbert Spencer and the Genteel Tradition in American Education," *Educational Theory*, XI (April, 1961), 99-111.

[2] J. Dewey, *Democracy and Education* (New York: The Macmillan Co., 1916), pp. 72, 76-77, 80, 388-95, 340 *passim*. See also, J. Dewey, *Creative Intelligence* (New York: Henry Holt & Co., 1917), pp. 30, 35f.

man's functions are natural-none are supernatural. Dewey's denial of the validity of all kinds of dualism is the touchstone of his educational philosophy. For him, the removal of these unnatural dualism would give unity to education and life.

The implications of Dewey's evolutionary commitment for the curriculum, teaching methods, the purpose of the school, and the like are far-reaching. Some of the earlier American liberals, such as Franklin, had tried to mingle the classical view of education with a more pragmatic approach. But Dewey and his followers saw very clearly that a marriage of the old and the new did not get to the heart of the basic educational problems; a completely new system was needed. The structure of this new system will be described in following sections.

Another important consideration is the relationship of the individual to society. In the preceding chapter it was pointed out that the early liberals focused their efforts on freeing the individual from autocratic restrictions. Since this endeavor involved a revolt against existing social structures, it is not surprising that social theory received inadequate treatment. But the advent of the highly complex industrial and interdependent societies called for a reconsideration of the role of the individual in society. The individual could not be studied as an isolated unit. In reality, his very being was a result of the kind of society into which he was born.

Spencer and others recognized the necessity of studying this relationship by giving to sociology the form and status of a significant scientific endeavor, But it was Dewey who set about to define the "social man" in a manner that radically affected educational theory and practice. Early in his long career he published *My Pedagogic Creed*, pointing to the fundamentally social nature of education. In this document he argued that the demands of *social situations* stimulated the child to act as a member of a unity, rather than as an isolated individual.[3] This social stimulation presses him to act for the welfare of the group to which he belongs. Even the child's natural instincts and tendencies must be directed into socially useful channels. It is, therefore, impossible to determine the potentialities of an individual unless he is acting with others for the good of the group.[4]

Because conservative education was either teacher-centered or subject

---

[3]J. Dewey, *My Pedagogic Creed*   (Washington, D.C..: Progressive Education Association, 1929), p. 3. This creed appeared originally in J. Dewey, "My Pedagogic Creed," *The School Journal*, LIV, 3 (January 16, 1897), 77-80.
[4]*Ibid.*, pp. 3-6.

matter-centered, it was miseducative-it was not based on the social life of the children. Neither literature, geography, history, nor even science, he said, is the true center of correlation in the curriculum; the social activities of children must be the center of correlation.[5]

In a later work, Dewey expanded upon the view that man's nature is socially built. In rejecting the conservative notion that man is born with a ready-made mind which absorbs stimuli and knowledge from an environment, he insisted that different people react to situations in different ways because of the social milieu. Thus savages are stupid because they have backward or less highly developed social institutions. In other words, an individual derives his mental powers and other traits from society.[6] Negatively stated, if there were no social groups or societies, there could be no individual minds possessing qualities which we as associate with civilization. If a new-born child were isolated completely from society, it would never become human.

The educational significance of this view of man's nature as primarily social in origin and composition is evident. Educational activities are of prime importance. in making man what he is. In fact, some of the liberal educational theorists of the twentieth century place upon educational institutions the responsibility not only for making the social nature of the pupils but also for the reconstruction of society itself.[7]

Another important effect of the new theory that what the child is or will become depends upon society and education is seen in the redefinition of the notion of free choice. Since the liberal does not accept the conservative belief that each person possesses an antecedently existing soul with powers of intellect and will, a social explanation of the fact that men do make choices is necessary.

Spencer implied that a well-rounded education, given by teachers who understand child growth and development, will somehow predetermine the person to make choices which are in harmony with nature. Consequently, if the child has been trained to care for his physical needs, to be vocational competent, to be prepared for family living and good citizenship, and to enjoy leisure time he will, under normal conditions, make choices based on this training. A child who is educated in another manner will follow other

---

[5]*Ibid.*, pp. 9-11.
[6]Dewey, *Democracy and Education, op. cit.*, pp. 40-46.
[7]See Theodore Brameld, *Toward a Reconstructed Philosophy of Education* (New York: Dryden Press, 1956), Ch. VI.

lines of action.[8] Thus the strong environmentalist orientation of early liberalism (e.g., that of Rousseau) seems to be carried forth in Spencer's educational scheme. It is, then, riot so much the free will of the individual but rather the physical and social environment and his early training that determine the course of action he will follow.

Dewey's opposition to the traditional dualism which separated thinking and willing made him attack this age-old problem more directly than Spencer. For Dewey, habit is equated with will. Habit is essentially an "acquired predisposition to ways or modes of response." The possession of certain habits gives the person a "special sensitiveness to certain likes and dislikes." Thus will or habit involves more than the simple repetition of single acts. He clarified this notion further by stating that the will (habit) can react to external stimuli of all kinds and add new qualities as well as rearrange the stimuli.[9]

What Dewey seemed to be saying is that man's choices are almost entirely determined by environment and training. However, man possesses the freedom necessary to rearrange or redirect the stimuli which he receives. Therefore, no person can claim to be the direct cause of a certain event. Yet a person can claim that he played some part in its making since he interacted in such a way that might have changed the course of events. But one will never know to what extent one's own reactions to a situation affected the 'outcome. In the last analysis, freedom consists in the ability to interact with others in the various social groups which make up human society.

This view of social freedom has important implications for education. It underlies the activities of the democratic classroom and the community school which will be discussed in succeeding sections of this chapter. Suffice it to say at this point that Dewey's conception of human freedom tends to offset the extreme emphasis on individual freedom found in the child-centered school of the early liberals; it attempts to harmonize individual freedom with social responsibility; it recognizes that, to a great extent, man acts in response to his environment but also possesses the power to improve that environment for himself and others.

The nineteenth- and twentieth-century liberals also modified Rousseau's romantic notion about man's innate goodliness. They steered a middle

---

[8]See Herbert Spencer, *Education: Intellectual, Moral and Physical* (New York: Appleton & Co., 1866), pp. 14-29, 138.

[9]J. Dewey, *Human Nature and Conduct* (Modern Library ed.; New York: Henry Holt & Co., 1922), pp. 41f, 32f.

course between the conservative who spoke of the evil tendencies dominating man and Rousseau who said the child could do no evil if left to follow his natural tendencies. Both Spencer and Dewey argued that man's nature was neither innately good nor evil, but neutral, Hence, it is important to provide the proper environment in the school and the home so that the child's behavior will be directed along socially acceptable lines.[10]

Basedow, Rousseau, Pestalozzi, and other early liberals had initiated the struggle against the conservative notion of education according to social classes. But they never adopted a thoroughgoing democratic philosophy of education. Dewey and his followers made democratic egalitarianism the central focus in most of their discourses. Dewey's *Democracy and Education* is the first treatise in the history of education which sets out to dethrone the *Republic* and *Laws* of Plato from their position of supremacy in educational thought. Whereas Plato had taught that all men by nature fall into three distinct classes and only one of these classes is fit to rule, Dewey argued that all men have the potential to direct their own activities in association with other equals. He repudiated the view that there is any authority external to that of the people themselves. Each individual, then, in association and communication with others, is equal to all others in respect to rights, privileges, and responsibilities. Obviously, he concluded, a democratic society must see to it that equal educational opportunities are available to all so that proper direction may be given to all the affairs of individual and group living.[11]

In summary, the answers given by nineteenth- and twentieth-century liberals to the question "What is man?" contain a much more complete rejection of the conservative view than those of the early liberals. They deny the story of the creation of man as a changeless species and its attendant doctrine of soul-body dualism. Mind and body are different aspects of the same natural stuff. Man's destiny, also, is this-worldly. Man's will, too, is a function of the organism interacting with the environment, Man is not inclined to evil, but neither is he unadulterated goodness. The major departure of thinkers like Dewey from the early liberals appears in their analysis of the relationship of the individual to society, especially in a democratic context.

---

[10]Spencer, *op. cit.*, pp. 170-74, 220f. Dewey said in *My Pedagogic Creed* that the individual child's desires cannot be the sole guide for action; he must be guided in formulating proper social values. See pp. 152-54 of this volume.

[11]Dewey, *Democracy and Education, op. cit.*, pp. 94-108.

HOW DO WE KNOW?

The liberal theorists of the past two centuries agree with their seventeenth- and eighteenth-century predecessors that faith and pure reason are wholly unacceptable as sources of knowledge. Experience and the empirical sciences become the valid mode of knowing. With few exceptions, however, the early liberals did little to transfer their reliance on science into the solution of educational problems nor could one expect them to since the tools for a science of education had not yet been developed.

The pioneering work in developing a science of education was done by Herbart in the early nineteenth century. He believed that knowledge about educational aims and methodology should be firmly rooted in scientific studies, mainly psychology. Use the tools of scientific psychology, he said, to determine the nature of man, then apply sound scientific principles to determine educational aims and methodology. To demonstrate that this was more than a noble ideal, he wrote what might be considered the first scientific texts in education. Some of the titles are quite significant: *The Application of Psychology to the Science of Education, The Science of Education*, and *A Textbook in Psychology*. Because he tried to apply scientific principles to education, Herbart is considered the "father of the science of education." Also, he did much to secure for psychology a status which was independent of philosophy. Certain educational doctrines of Herbart will be considered in subsequent sections of this chapter. The important point to be made here is that Herbart viewed science as the main source of knowledge about man, the world, and educational theory and practice.

Spencer, also, was in agreement with the position that the scientific mode of knowing is the only reliable one, In his rejection of revelation and reason, he reflected much the same attitude as Auguste Comte who lived in the same century. Comte taught that the human race passed through three stages of development. In its primitive stage reliance is placed on the knowledge acquired through theology; knowledge is derived from faith in a supernatural source. In the second stage, the metaphysical, man relies on his reason rather than on faith or revelation to give him knowledge about the world. In the highest phase of his development he relies upon the experimental sciences to give him all the knowledge he needs about himself, the physical universe, and the Society in which he lives.[12]

---

[12]Comte's major work which contains this theory is: A. Comte, *Positive*

Although Dewey generally agreed with the notion that experience and science are the only ways that yield valid knowledge, he felt that certain adaptations were needed for constructing a unitary educational theory. In the preface to the first edition of *How We Think* he wrote that some might feel that the scientific attitude is irrelevant in teaching children and youth. But he insisted that "the native and unspoiled attitude of childhood, marked by ardent curiosity, fertile imagination, and love of experimental inquiry, is near, very near to the attitude of the scientific mind."[13] Perhaps, then, the feature which distinguishes Dewey's method of arriving at knowledge from that employed by the pure empirical sciences is its applicability to all problems at all different levels of development. Thus it is used by the child seeking a solution to a very simple problem, by a larger group intent on solving an ethical difficulty, or by scientists trying to solve a complex question of nuclear physics.[14] Dewey's method, then, simply is a step-by-step description of the processes which he believed men actually use in their search for the knowledge necessary to solve problems which continually arise in all phases of living.

The teacher-education student will recognize the following steps of problem solving from his instruction in methods courses: (1) felt difficulty, (2) location and definition of the problem, (3) suggestion of possible or alternative solutions of the problem, (4) determining of the bearing or probable consequences of each suggestion, and (5) further observation and test of experience leading to the acceptance or rejection of the solution.[15] In the revised edition of the same work, Dewey refined his analysis of the problem-solving mode of knowing. He spoke of two limits for every complete unit of thinking or knowing: (1) the beginning, which is characterized by a state of perplexity and confusion, (2) the close, which represents a "cleared-up, unified and resolved situation." Between the beginning and close five relatively distinct phases can be noted, In the first phase, the mind leaps forward to a possible solution based on certain suggestions. The second phase consists in the intellectual analysis of the hazy or confused situation so that it can be stated or recognized as a specific problem to be solved. In the third phase, the knower takes one after the

---

Philosophy, H. Martineau (trans.) (New York: C. Blanchard Co., 1855).

[13]J Dewey, *How We Think* (Boston: D.C, Heath & Co., 1910).

[14]In *Democracy and Education, op. cit.*, p.256, Dewey gave several examples in which he equated problem solving or reflective thinking with the method of natural sciences.

[15]Dewey, *How We Think, op. cit.*, p. 72.

other of the possible solutions or hypotheses and collects data and makes observations about each. The fourth step consists in determining the extent of the effects of each hypothesis or idea. This step Dewey called "reasoning in a limited sense." The final phase is, of course, the test of the hypothesis in action (overt or imaginative) .[16]

An important characteristic of the problem-solving mode of knowing is its adaptability to changing situations, In fact, the method presupposes that everything is in a state of flux.[17] Thus as each new difficulty arises, it can be resolved in the light of the latest factual information as well as the changing social conditions, In other words, all solutions are tentative and subject to change whenever new difficulties crop up; the method yields solutions to a current problem, not answers that will hold for all time.

Whether Dewey's description of the knowing process is basically different from the methods of the empirical sciences is a disputed point. For several reasons, however, it has been widely adopted in educational circles. Children can learn by this means just as well as the graduate research specialist. One can solve questions of the physical universe and, perhaps, more important, one can arrive at values which will guide action. Thus a physicist can use the method to resolve a difficulty in nuclear physics and also to decide, in conjunction with his fellowmen, what should be done with nuclear power.

Because some opponents of problem solving have equated it with the trial-and-error method of arriving at knowledge, the liberals who defend the method argue that trial-and-error is not a method at all. It is simply a hit-and-miss means of arriving at a solution which might apply at a very primitive level of knowing or when rational methods fail. In desperation, then, one might be forced to employ pure trial-and-error. But in problem solving, the knower sets out to resolve a very specific difficulty by utilizing all the facts and information he can acquire from his own experience or that of others to formulate hypotheses (ideas or inferences). Such hypotheses are not to be wild guesses, but each is to be evaluated in terms of its possible consequences. Thus even before a hypothesis is put to the test of experience its possible consequences have been anticipated. It is not a shot in the dark but a solution which has a reasonable chance of success.

In recent years greater attention has been given to the solving of problems affecting groups. Recognizing the great interdependence among

---

[16]*Dewey, How We Think, op. cit.* (1933 ed.), pp. 106-18.
[17]See John Childs, *American Pragmatism and Education* (New York: Henry Holt & Co., 1956), pp. 52ff.

men and utilizing the findings of social psychology and group dynamics, some educational theorists argue that all significant knowledge, especially in the realm of values, must be arrived at by group problem solving. Whenever a difficulty arises which affects many people, and educational problems are of this type, some solution which is acceptable to those involved in the situation must be sought. Thus the goal of group problem solving is a social consensus of the participants, or a common persuasion. An adequate solution will include all the different points of view which were fed into the deliberations. If a true social consensus is to be achieved, the participants will have to reconstruct their own views so that at least minimal harmony can be realized.

Following Dewey's lead, the advocates of group problem solving point to several definite phases or steps which should be followed in order to arrive at an adequate solution. The first is the "clarification of common purpose-the projection of a desired state of affairs." In other words, the group must decide what it wants. Unless there is a clear and comprehensive grasp of the end to be achieved, there is no point in talking about how to attain that end.

The second phase consists in the "survey and assessment of the existing state of affairs." A great deal of fact finding is called for during this phase. Any information or theories which have a bearing upon the problem should be studied in relation to the goal decided upon in the first phase. For example, if a community agreed to the goal of building fifty new parks and recreation areas to combat juvenile delinquency and a survey of the community showed that neither funds nor land was available for so many projects, this certainly would have important bearing upon the matter.

The third phase consists in "suiting the *ideas* employed to the claims of the situation as a whole." Ideas are instruments to be employed in the solution of the problem, that is, hypotheses which might serve as possible solutions. Each of these ideas is to be viewed in the light of the total situation, not in isolation. Referring to the example just used, each suggested solution to the problem of juvenile delinquency must be considered in connection with the whole situation, including such things as finances, human resources, desirable behavior patterns, community value systems, and the like. The importance of this phase lies in the recognition of the unitary nature of the psychology of group thinking. The group "organism" solves its problems as a unit rather than as a collection of separate individuals.

The final phase consists in the forging of a "program of action." At this step, the group makes a blueprint which is to be followed in the attempt to remove the difficulty. This blueprint will be put to the test of experience. To return to the example, the plan of action for combating juvenile delinquency might include a program of adult education for parents, a revision of the school curriculum comprising programs to meet the vocational needs and recreational demands of adolescents, and a provision for an adequate number of out-of-school activities for youth.[18]

It should be evident that the problem-solving mode of knowing is much more complex and refined than the conservative's notion of simple experience. In reality, it goes beyond the early empiricist's notion which never rose above the level of the particular, the contingent, and the probable. Consequently, the term reasoning is sometimes used to describe the method of problem solving and practical intelligence. But it must be noted that "reasoning" used in this new context is not to be associated with the traditional definition which presumed the possession by man of a separate spiritual faculty of reason.[19]

To summarize the answers to the question "How do we know?" it seems that the nineteenth- and twentieth-century liberals built upon and expanded the earlier notions of experience and science as the only valid modes of knowing. In educational circles, Dewey's problem-solving method became the most widely accepted explanation for the knowing-learning process. The reconstructionist, drawing heavily upon the findings of social psychology and Dewey's philosophy, developed the methodology of group problem solving. The application of both of these approaches to classroom practice will be treated on succeeding pages.

WHAT IS TRUTH?

The conservative philosopher can always point to a reservoir of truths which he holds with certainty. Since he believes that God can "neither deceive nor be deceived," the truths of revelation are most reliable. For those conservatives who have not had the benefits of divine revelation or rejected revelation, there is the supply of truths derived from pure reason.

---

[18]For a description and analysis of group problem solving, see R.B. Raup, B. Othanel Smith, G. Axtelle and K. Benne, *The Improvement of Practical Intelligence* (New York: Harper and Brothers, 1950), Ch. VII; and T. Brameld, *op. cit.*, Ch. IV.

[19]J. Dewey, *Reconstruction in Philosophy* (enlarged ed.; Boston: Beacon Press, 1948), Ch. IV. (Original ed. Henry Holt, 1920).

Early liberals either abandoned the truths of the theists and rationalists (or sought to de-emphasize their influence) and placed their trust in experience and science. But, in general, they failed to develop satisfactory theories to account for all the aspects of experience and science. This was the task of the nineteenth- and twentieth-century liberals.

Herbart attacked the problem by noting that philosophers, who claim to be keepers and purveyors of the truth, had segregated themselves from the activities of the empirical sciences. He argued that the opposite should be the case, namely, "all the sciences each separately and yet all united, ought to produce philosophy as their indispensable complement. . . ." To demonstrate that he practiced what he preached, Herbart's initial attack on any educational problem began with a very accurate record of experiences he had in the classroom. His second step consisted in relating the findings of physiology and empirical psychology to the construction of theories of teaching and learning. Thirdly, he gave unity and coherence to psychological theory building by applying mathematics.

It is not important for our purposes here whether or not Herbart's findings are considered true by the psychologists of the mid-twentieth century or that he had occasional lapses into the "metaphysical thinking" against which he was arguing. The significant aspects of his pioneering work lay in his search for truths derived from direct experience and the empirical disciplines of physiology and psychology. Add to this his use of mathematics in building psychological theories and the earmarks of the most up-to-date hypothetico-deductive systems appear.[20] For Herbart, then, truth is equated primarily with the contents of experience and the findings of the empirical sciences. From these basic truths one can construct a valid and workable set of educational aims, formulate adequate teaching methodology, and devise objective evaluational techniques.

Spencer, Comte, and other empirically-oriented thinkers would have had no quarrel with Herbart's notion of truth. They did, however, add sociology to the family of sciences from which significant truths could be drawn for the benefit of educational theory.

Dewey, too, would have agreed that truth must be grounded in experience and the empirical sciences. But his problem-solving method possesses sufficient novelty to call for a reconstruction of the notion of truth itself. The thinking (knowing) process is set in motion by some difficulty or perplexity and the various phases or steps are designed to remove the difficulty and return the individual or the group to a "cleared-up, unified,

---

[20]See Chapter XI of this volume.

and resolved situation"; truth is achieved only when the latter condition is met. Thus if one proposes and tests a hypothesis, the test of its truth lies in whether or not it resolves the difficulty. In Dewey's words:

> If ideas, meanings, conceptions. notions, theories, systems are instrumental to . . . a removal of some specific trouble and perplexity, then the test of their validity   and value lies in accomplishing this work. If they succeed in their office, they are   reliable, sound, valid, good, true. If they fail. . . then they are false. Confirmation,   corroboration, verification lie in works, consequences. . . . The hypothesis that   works is the true one. [21]

This conception of truth is a novel one even though C. S. Pierce had introduced the notion that the consequences determined the meaning of an idea, hypothesis, or theory, but not their truth. Dewey, too, believed that the concept of meaning is prior to, and more significant than, the concept of truth, since it is futile to speak of truth unless the meaning of a term, a hypothesis, or theory is clear. Perhaps the most striking feature of Dewey's conception of truth is its active, dynamic nature. Truth is action; truth is a solution to a problem; truth can never be known unless there are consequences or works to be judged; truth must change as situations change or as new problems arise.

Dewey recognized that equating truth with what works would be misinterpreted. Therefore, he explained what this new conception did and did not imply. Truth is not to be equated with personal, emotional satisfaction, achieving some personal gain, or satisfying a personal need. Rather, the "total situation" is to be satisfied, including public and objective conditions. For example, an outraged husband may be personally satisfied with the solution to his mother-in-law problems by poisoning her, but does this solution contribute to the public good? One must consider the consequences of this action if it were used as an "out" by all husbands with mother-in-law problems.

When truth is defined as that which is useful, it must not be interpreted as personal gain. Rather "utility refers to the extent to which an idea or hypothesis achieves what it claims to do." For example, a businessman might devise a plan that would prove exceedingly useful in eliminating his competitors. Certainly, the plan is very helpful for him but it does not render a service to the whole business world.

However, the crucial point, which Dewey believed to be the cause of the

---

[21]Dewey, *Reconstruction in Philosophy, op. cit.*, p. 156.

misunderstanding of his notion of truth, arises from the conservative belief that truth is ready-made, static, and somehow tied to the existence of a Supreme, changeless reality. The conservative believes that truth is independent of human action, that it is otherworldly, waiting to be discovered, to be found, and to be accepted. Evidently, Dewey said, this notion of truth can never be reconciled with the pragmatic conception of it. Because he recognized that his conception of truth was different from that held prior to his time, Dewey preferred to speak of warrantability rather than truth. A warranted assertion is made only after a hypothesis has been put to the test of experience and has been judged acceptable in the light of the consequences. What Dewey was removing from the traditional conception of truth by substituting warranted assertions is its independent existence and its immutability.[22]

Satisfaction of the *total situation* seems to be even more important when one views problem solving as a group process. Recall from the previous section that the goal of group thinking is a common persuasion, a social consensus. Thus it can be affirmed that some hypothesis affecting group life is true not only by the needed satisfactions which have been produced "but also by the extent to which their import is agreed upon and then acted upon by the largest possible number of the group concerned. Without this agreement, followed by actions which test the agreement, the experience simply is not 'true.'"[23]

Even though a social consensus may not be the only criterion of truth, it is as close as one can get to truth since it should incorporate the knowledge and values of all participants. Further, the plan of action should be agreed upon by all involved in the situation, and all should agree whether or not the plan solves the problem. Some argue that even the empirical sciences rely upon a consensus for the truth of their conclusions. Both the methods used and the results obtained in the experiments are "agreed upon" by scientists. In other words, if there is no consensus or agreement there is no point in speaking of truth. Even the choice of the scientific evidence or facts used in working toward a solution of the problem is dependent upon the consensus of the group using them.[24]

A summary of the main points in regard to the new conception of truth includes: (1) Truth is derived from experience and that refined form of

---

[22]See *The Philosophy of John Dewey*, ed. P. A. Schlipp (2nd ed.; New York: Tudor Publishing Co., 1951), pp. 202, 205, 566ff.

[23]Brameld, *op. cit.*, pp. 35, 217f.

[24]See Raup *et al.*, *op. cit.*, pp. 35, 217f.

experience called science. (2) For Dewey, truth consisted in the solution of a problem which satisfies the total situation and is judged in terms of the consequences. Truth is that which works. (3) When truth seeking is viewed as group problem solving, at least *one* of the essential criteria of truth is the extent to which it is agreed upon by the group. (4) All truths are dynamic and changing-"there are no absolutes." (5) Truths are "made" rather than "discovered," i.e., there are no pre-existent truths.

WHAT IS GOOD?

Rousseau and other early liberals gave a rather simple answer to the question of what is good. A good life is one lived close to, and in harmony with, nature. Those acts are good which satisfy the natural inclinations and needs of man. If man is not innately evil, then deeds performed according to natural drives are good. Man can perform evil acts only when vitiated by forces outside himself. Thus good is equated with personal satisfaction. However, Rousseau had some very specific suggestions for teachers to follow to prevent the young from choosing evil. Indirectly, then, he admitted that man can do wrong.

Some nineteenth- and twentieth-century liberals, such as Spencer and Dewey, agreed that man is not innately evil. They, too, rejected the notion of original sin. But they felt that the natural impulses of the child could not be the sole guide of behavior. For these thinkers, education assumes the important role of developing a moral sense in youth. Both appealed to the sciences of biology, psychology, and sociology for justification of moral laws; both recognized the evolutionary character of moral laws; both denied that purely personal satisfaction is an adequate criterion for good.[25]

Since Rousseau's and Spencer's views of the good were assimilated, refined, and up-dated in Dewey's philosophy, an analysis of his theory should suffice. His answers to the questions "What is good?" are part of his answers to the questions about knowledge and truth already discussed. Recall that Dewey believed that the method of critical intelligence (problem solving) is just as applicable to the resolution of difficulties involving matters of good and evil as it is to the problems of the empirical sciences. The hypothesis which "Clears up, unifies, and results in a resolved situation" is "reliable, sound, valid, good, true."[26] Note that this method of

---

[25]See Dewey, *Reconstruction in Philosophy, op. cit.*, Ch. VII; Spencer, *op. cit.*, pp. 136ff.
[26]See pp. 128ff. of this volume.

inquiry produces the good as well as the true.

Dewey made it very clear that the Divine Will, the secular ruler, the ecclesiastic, the natural law, the categorical imperative can never be the determinants of good or evil. In other words, an act can not be considered good or evil simply because some external authority or some innate moral sense so dictates. The best that can be said for such traditional standards of morality is that at some time or other in the past they represented a solution to the moral questions of the times.[27]

If there is no appeal to a universal moral law, each situation is unique and must be treated as such. Thus one cannot say an act is bad because it violates the Ten Commandments or some ecclesiastical or civil law, but because it violates' the total situation. The total situation is violated when the consequences do not resolve the difficulty. Perhaps a few simple examples will illustrate the difference. The act of stealing is not wrong because God, the Bible, or some other authority says it is wrong. It is wrong because the consequences of stealing upset the equilibrium of society. In the first place, there would be no need for a decision about the moral good or evil in stealing if difficulties as a result of stealing and affecting other people's property had never arisen in society. But when problems did arise, then a solution was reached. The prohibition against stealing resulted in the removal of a perplexing and troublesome situation. Furthermore, there is no inherent reason to prevent stealing, under certain conditions and in certain situations, from being regarded as acceptable behavior. In a similar manner divorce is not right or wrong because some natural or divine law decrees it to be such. Rather, some societies have considered it wrong and others right in light of the different social consequences divorce had for them. Thus both those who consider divorce right and those who consider it wrong have arrived at valid ethical judgments.

Note the importance which Dewey placed on the social nature of judgments of good and evil. Rousseau and Spencer had not taken account of the social consequences of actions. Fundamentally, the difference is not a great one since all agree that it is the "experimentally gained knowledge of natural consequences which determines right and wrong.

What Dewey seems to be affirming is that since most human actions affect others the consequences of each action must be viewed with this in mind-"the moral and social quality of conduct are in the last analysis,

---

[27]Dewey, *Reconstruction in Philosophy, op. cit.*, pp. 161f; J. Dewey and J. Tufts, *Ethics* (New York: Henry Holt & Co., 1936), Chs. V-VIII.

identical with each other."[28] Dewey's answer to our question "What is good?" is: Those actions which society approves are good (i.e., the consequences have been judged good for and by society).

Reconstructionists, recognizing the significance of the social criterion of good, are quite specific in pointing up the necessity of achieving a consensus in matters involving moral choices. They argue that the only way to validate moral choices is by a "common persuasion," or a social consensus.[29] If the people involved in the moral issue do not agree that the consequences are good for them, there is not much sense in introducing the notion of social consequences at all.

The reader has detected, no doubt, the democratic flavor of Dewey's and the reconstructionist' view of morality. In reality, their views would be wholly inoperative in an autocratic or totalitarian system. Without free communication between individuals and groups it would be impossible to apply the social criterion of good or to arrive at a social consensus. Without the freedom to interact with fellow human beings no truly ethical judgments could be formulated.

This democratic emphasis also points up the need for the expansion of educational opportunity to include all the children of all the people. Intelligent and critical participation in the affairs of the family, community, state, nation, and world requires much more than elementary schooling in the basic skills. Education for democratic living cannot be accomplished in a few years. Also implied is the extension of the democratic process beyond the purely political domain. All phases of human living, in the family, the church, the school, and the like, should be characterized by democratic attitudes.[30]

Dewey's notion of what is good is easily understood by the modern American since so many moral decisions are made according to his principles. At the level of national and international politics decisions have been pragmatic. Solutions which resolve an issue are considered the right ones

---

[28]Dewey, *Democracy and Education, op. cit.*, p. 415; J. Dewey, *The Quest for Certainty* (New York: Minton, Balch & Co., 1929), p. 27; J. Dewey, *Human Nature and Conduct* (New York: Modern Library, 1930), p.75.

[29]See Raup *et al. op. cit.*, pp. 205f; K. D. Benne, "Educating for Wisdom in Value Judgments," *Progressive Education*, XXVII (April, 1950), 184; Brameld, *op. cit.*, p. 114.

[30]See B. Bode, *Democracy as a Way of Life* (New York: The Macmillan Co., 1950); J. Dewey "Democracy & Educational Administration," *School and Society*, XLV (April 3, 1937), 457-62.

even if they are new ones. Drastic changes are constantly being noted in the standards governing community life, family living, labor-management relations, and standards of dress. To paraphrase Boyd A. Bode, Dewey's disciple, in a democracy there are no absolutes.

It is not so simple, however, to explain value statements about beauty within his theory. As Harold Dunkel points out in his treatise on Dewey and the Fine Arts, it is difficult to see the relationship between the solving of real-life problems and such activities as painting, sculpture, dancing, dramatics and literature.[31] Spencer had put such activities on the bottom of the educator's priority list under the heading of leisure-time activities. Thus, when man had completed all the essential functions of living and had a little time remaining, he might wish to devote himself to such pastimes.[32] Although Dewey himself was quite interested in the fine arts, some interpreters of his views maintain that he agreed with Spencer in giving only a minor role to developing artistic taste.

Other interpreters feel that Dewey ceased to be a Deweyite when he talked about art. But settling that controversy cannot be attempted here.[33] The general impression garnered from Dewey's *Art as Experience* and *Art and Education* is that artistic experiences are just like any other human experience-there is nothing "special" about them.[34] As such they begin in a "perplexed and confused state" and culminate in a "harmonious, unified and resolved one."

This view suggests that Dewey's theory of art does not focus on the concept of beauty as do most theories. Thus Dewey held that the aesthetic experience which is a unified and harmonious one will contain an equilibrium of form and matter. Before such a judgment can be made, one must first attempt to grasp the meaning of a poem, a painting, or a symphony. An art work, then, is not something which contains an inherent

---

[31]H. B. Dunkel, "Dewey and the Fine Arts," *The School Review*, LXVII (Summer 1959), 229-46.

[32]See pp.139f. of this volume.

[33]See R. Rusk, *The Philosophical Bases of Education* (Boston: Houghton Mifflin Co., 1956), pp. 95ff.; S.C. Petter, "Some Questions on Dewey's Aesthetics," *The Philosophy of John Dewey*, ed. P.A. Schilpp (2nd ed.; New York: Tudor Publishing Co., 1951); H. Aiken "American Pragmatism Reconsidered," *Commentary*, XXXIV, 4 (October, 1962), 343.

[34]For a similar analysis of art as ordinary experience, see S.M. Eames, "Dewey's Views of Truth, Beauty, and Goodness," *Educational Theory*, XI (July, 1961), 174-86.

beauty merely to be subjectively enjoyed by all who behold it; one must experience a reaction to it that causes both emotional and cognitive commotion, turmoil, and tension. This is the confused and perplexed state which is an essential ingredient of all experience. The harmonious and resolved situation will be achieved when the observer, after sufficient reflection, recognizes the equilibrium of form and matter in the work of art.

This rather difficult transition from a state of perplexity to one of harmony requires both instruction and experience. Art production and appreciation like any other field of human activity demands rigorous training; it is not a facility which can be achieved by a nodding acquaintance with artists and art works. Dewey warned, however, that one's personal preferences and educational and cultural background should not bias his view of the art works of other times and cultures. Each of these must be understood and appreciated in their own temporal and social framework.

This warning suggests that Dewey rejected absolute standards in art just as he rejected them in other fields of human activity. Art, as well as those who view it, must adjust to changing times and altered circumstances. The critic who compares modern art unfavorably with Renaissance art is missing the whole function of art itself.[35]

Some educational adaptations of Dewey's aesthetic theory have been used on the belief that art must be functional. By functional it is usually meant that the student should be able to use his art training in home decorating, in making his choice of clothing and hairstyles, in community beautification projects, and in the worthy use of leisure time. Dewey recognized this utilitarian aspect of art education but felt that more intimate acquaintance with the fine arts will enhance these ordinary functions of art and make the experience more intensified and intrinsically more enjoyable. In the long run this attitude will also serve a useful purpose, namely, that of dissatisfaction with the drab and ugly and the desire to replace it with the beautiful.[36]

In summarizing this section on the nature of the good and the beautiful the following characteristics seem to be most prominent: (1) There can be no absolute or changeless standards for making choices; both the standards and the choices derived from them are relative and changing (evolutionary ethics). (2) All decisions about good and evil are rooted in experience; that is, they are empirical. For Spencer, the criterion of individual satisfaction

---

[35]For an illustration of relativity of art standards, see T. Shaw, *Precious Rubbish* (Boston: Stuart Art Gallery, 1956).

[36]Dewey, *Democracy and Education, op. cit.*, pp. 238-41, 278ff.

seemed to be dominant; for Dewey and his followers, satisfaction of the total situation was viewed as the most adequate criterion. In both instances, however, the consequences of the decisions or acts determine their goodness. (3) Social consensus or agreement regarding the acceptability of certain ways of acting or living will yield, according to social reconstructionist, the safest answers to questions of morality. (4) The democratic ethic is based upon the notion that those behavior patterns which produce the greatest good for the greatest number but yet safeguard the welfare of the minority are morally valid.

WHAT IS THE PURPOSE OF THE SCHOOL?

The early liberal was very outspoken in his rejection of the narrow intellectualistic goal of the conservative school. He pointed out that the conservative's dedication to character education was merely a verbal one since all classroom activities were designed to develop intellectual powers. To combat this narrow intellectualism, the liberal proposed the introduction of vocational, health, and physical education, moral training and the like. To use the jargon, he argued that the school is responsible for the growth or development of the whole child.

However, the early liberal, at least in practice, tended to view the school as an institution whose educational goals were quite distinct from those of the family or community. The nineteenth- and twentieth-century liberal, on the other hand, fused the educational functions of all agencies involved in the education of the young. For example, Herbart's educational treatises were designed to show that the intellectualistic goals of the schools of his time were not in harmony with sound psychology. He proposed that the school devote its efforts to developing moral living. Spencer, also, maintained that the school should assume the responsibility (presented in Spencer's order of their importance) for (1) healthful living and other aspects of human living that are essential for self-preservation; (2) vocational training and other practical arts which the person needs in order to Survive; (3) preparation for family living, i.e., begetting and rearing of children; (4) worthy citizenship; and (5) worthy use of leisure time. Ideally, the school should attempt to achieve all of these goals and thus develop the whole person. Limitations of time may force certain priorities upon educators.

Spencer's recommendations regarding the purpose of the school did not go unnoticed. In reality they were to become the basis for the *Seven Cardinal Principles* of secondary education published by the National

Education Association in 1918. These principles committed the school to achieve the goals of (1) health, (2) command of the fundamental processes, (3) worthy home membership, (4) vocational efficiency, (5) citizenship, (6) worthy use of leisure time, and (7) ethical character. These were developed later by the Educational Policies Commission of the N.E.A. as *The Purposes of Education in American Democracy* (1938). This statement updated Spencer's purposes of the school under the headings of (1) self-realization, (2) human relationships, (3) economic efficiency, and (4) civic responsibility.

The progressive education movement in America accepted Spencer's view of the goal of the school, at least in its broad outlines. The early leaders of this movement argued that the narrow intellectualism of the traditional school was wholly inadequate for a young, pioneering, and democratic nation. Francis Parker's experimental school at Cook County Normal introduced nature study, art, and social activities as an integral part of the elementary school life. Attention was given to the total development of the children. This movement which began before the turn of the century continued to stress the importance of such broad aims for the school.

But it was Dewey who synthesized all of the liberal, progressive thought just mentioned. It is clear from one of his early works, *My Pedagogic Creed*, that he rejected the notion that the school is an institution existing apart from the home and the community. In other words, the school is the continuation of the pupil's social life and cannot be isolated from the processes of daily living. "The school must represent life-life as real and vital to the child as that which he carries on in the home, in the neighborhood, or on the playground. . . . Education, therefore, is a process of living and not a preparation for future living."[37]

Throughout the Pedagogic Creed and his later works, Dewey emphasized the principle that the school is a form of community life. The learning of lessons in isolation from social living is miseducative-that is why conservative education was a failure. Like Spencer, he felt that the domestic sciences and manual arts are truly educative since they represent fundamental forms of social activity. Other subjects are educative only insofar as they are related to the social living of the pupil. Thus the school, as a social enterprise, has no final or ultimate goal and no goal outside itself. Since its activities are continuous with the social living of its clientele, "there is nothing to which education is subordinate save more education," and "to set up any end outside education, as furnishing its goal and standard,

---

[37]Dewey, *My Pedagogic Creed, op. cit.*, p. 6.

is to deprive the educational process of much of its meaning. . . ."[38]

Even if the school has no goals outside itself, it does not follow that there will be no change in the school's perception of its purpose. Obviously, as society changes, the goals of the school will change. In fact, Dewey considered flexibility an essential criterion of any workable goal. Only when goals lie within the educational process itself and are flexible is the group free to set forth other goals and the means of achieving them.[39] Goals and the means of achieving them are inseparable.

In Dewey's system the determination of educational goals both presumes the democratic way of life and proposes to strengthen this outlook. It is clear from his work that education is a social process and, as such, is directed to the development of social efficiency. Social efficiency is, therefore, both a means and an end. As an end, it implies the "cultivation of the power to join freely and fully in shared or common activities"; as a means, it enables groups of pupils to solve common problems which arise in the environment.

The emphasis which Dewey placed on the social nature of the educational process and on social efficiency as a goal of the school appears to be the starting point for some of his followers who argued that the school must take an active role in changing the social order. This group of "social frontiersmen" argued that the school not only *could* but *should* influence the direction of human affairs in a democracy.[40] In order to accomplish this feat, the schools need a clearly defined purpose. Activity for activity's sake will get one nowhere. To recognize that the individual's outlook is socially built and then do nothing about reconstructing society is refusing to face the fundamental issue, "What kind of social order do we want?" To indulge in adoration of the individual child is to do a disservice to him, since the world of reality is a complex social world.

George Counts, among others, asked the crucial question: "Dare the school build a new social order?" He answered the question in the affirmative. The schools must be given the vision of social democracy and through the powerful means at their disposal set about to reconstruct the social order. If youth are given this as a goal while they are in school and commit themselves to its realization, then, and only then, will the new social

---

[38]Dewey, *Democracy and Education, op. cit.*, pp. 60, 117, Ch. II; Dewey, *My Pedagogic Creed, op. cit.*, pp.6-11.

[39]Dewey, *Democracy and Education, op. cit.*, pp.121-24.

[40]See H. Rugg, *Foundations of American Education* (New York: World Book Co., 1947), pp. 577-82.

order be achieved.[41]

As the reader will recall, the times in which Counts was writing were trying ones. The Great Depression had brought widespread unemployment, suffering, and frustration to millions of Americans. It seemed evident to some economists that the capitalism of the nineteenth and early twentieth century was wholly outdated. Private enterprise with its laissez faire approach to social and economic matters would never be able to keep the country (and the entire world) from the scourge of economic catastrophes. People in an industrial society, it was argued, were too interdependent to be left at the mercy of an uncontrolled production and competition. The laborer had as much right to economic security as his employer. That these views rapidly gained popularity is noted in the massive support given the policies of the Franklin Roosevelt administration and the New Deal for all the people. Consequently many educators of the times believed that the school should cease being the stronghold of conservatism and become the beachhead of economic, political, and social reform.

More recently the thesis that the school should be the vanguard of social change and should devise the means of applying it in the classroom has received serious attention. The social frontiersmen of the depression era had brought the issue to the attention of liberal educators and had given them the challenge of doing something about it. One response to this challenge was the development of the method of group problem solving, which has already been discussed. The authors of *The Improvement of Practical Intelligence* (see p. 125) recognize that the schools must have some very specific goals and that everyone concerned should participate in deciding what these goals should be. Further application of the same principles to curriculum making as it relates to the goals of the school also has been made. Educators began discussing the issue of democratic authority and responsibility for establishing educational goals.[42]

In conclusion, it can be said that the nineteenth- and twentieth century liberals built upon their predecessors' view that the goals of the school should be to develop the "whole child." Spencer specified exactly what this total development implied in his famous five objectives of education. Dewey synthesized all liberal thought in his theory of "education as its own

---

[41] G. Counts, *Dare the School Build a New Social Order?* (New York: John Day Co., 1932). In this work Counts argues that the school should participate in the task of changing the United States from a capitalistic to a socialistic society.

[42] Brameld, *op. cit.*, Ch. VI. See pp. 152-54 in this volume.

end." The social aspects of Dewey's view of educational goals were selected by some of his followers for special emphasis in determining the goals of the schools. From this group came the school as social vanguard theory of educational goals.

WHAT SHOULD BE TAUGHT?

Early liberals, such as Comenius and Basedow, had argued that what was taught in the humanistic schools was wholly inadequate since it was so impractical and useless for most students. They demanded that useful subjects should not Only be introduced into the curriculum but should also become the heart of it. In addition, other liberals of the same period, such as Rousseau and Pestalozzi, gave theoretical and practical formulations of what later is called the activity curriculum, For them the curriculum is defined in terms of what a student *does* rather than what he is taught.

Among nineteenth- and twentieth-century liberals (who also rejected the validity of the intellectualistic, classical curriculum), the same two points of View can be noted. For example, Spencer recommended that the curriculum should contain subjects needed in or useful for preparing the pupils for the necessary activities of life. His most important category of studies, those needed for self-preservation, includes the areas which gave the student knowledge about health, physiology, preventive hygiene, physical culture, or, as Spencer said, "any knowledge which subserves direct self-preservation by preventing this loss of health."[43]

The second category, "knowledge which aids indirect self-preservation by facilitating the gaining of a livelihood," includes the skills of reading, writing, and arithmetic, which are essential for holding a job in an industrial society. Boys need knowledge of machinery and the skills necessary to run it. Girls need knowledge of the equipment in a modem home and training in its use. Any youth who plans on working in modern agriculture needs specific knowledge and training for that vocation. Under this second category Spencer also included the sciences of biology, physics, and chemistry, since many of their principles are basic in modern medicine and industry. Economics, marketing, business, and the like are also included here.[44]

The third category of studies, preparation for family living, is, according to Spencer, the most neglected area, The classical curriculum, he said, was

---

[43]Spencer, *op. cit.*, pp. 20-25.
[44]*Ibid.*, pp. 25-33.

designed for celibates and monks, for not one word was said about the all-important job of bringing up children. Young people receive all the information about family life from ignorant nurses and prejudiced grandmothers. Because of this lack of training, thousands of infants are either killed each year or survive with feeble constitutions. Instead of blaming such misfortunes on Providence, he said, people should insist that schools offer specific preparation for childbearing and child rearing. This training would enable the new generation of parents to raise healthy, happy, and cultured children. Spencer believed that this kind of training could be given in an easily understandable form through the use of illustrations and examples.[45]

The fourth category in Spencer's curriculum is "that which prepares for citizenship." The conservative curriculum touched upon this area only indirectly in history courses. According to Spencer, these courses consisted of a meaningless, disconnected accumulation of historical facts which were absolutely useless to the pupil; what possible use could young people make of the names of kings, ecclesiastics, or generals of bygone days. In place of such useless materials Spencer recommended the study of the political, social, and ecclesiastical structures under which the pupils are living. Let them see how the food, clothing, customs, and mores of one social class compare with those of another. Give them insight into labor-management relations, interculturation, and the role of science in society. Spencer chose to call this study descriptive sociology. In this area, too, the sciences, especially biology and psychology, must be considered foundational.[46]

The remaining division of the curriculum is devoted to preparing the student for "relaxations, pleasures, and amusements filling leisure hours." Spencer insisted that this area of human activity should not be slighted, even though it is the least important of the curricular divisions. He predicted, however, that it would become more important as industrialization made it possible for even the worker to have a great amount of leisure time. But it should always remain subsidiary to the first four areas. The first point Spencer made in connection with the teaching of fine arts and literature is that the presentation of these subjects must be related to science. The principles of mathematics, physics, psychology, biology, and linguistics underlie any subject worthy of the title Fine Arts. Consequently, *if* there is sufficient time for such subjects as literature, music, poetry, sculpture,

---

[45]*Ibid.*, pp. 40-51.
[46]*Ibid.*, pp. 51-59

painting, and drama, they should be included in the curriculum.[47]

It should be noted that Spencer insisted that the most important criterion for selecting curricular content is usefulness. The second criterion for selection of content is the disciplinary value of the subject. For Spencer, however, there was no opposition between the two criteria, since the subjects which are useful are also the ones with disciplinary value.

That the curriculum of the American schools of the twentieth century was influenced by Spencer's views is quite apparent. The subjects taught may not bear the same titles, but the same general areas are covered. What elementary or secondary school graduate has not heard about "how useful" a subject is, or will be, for him. Even Spencer's notion of what is useful is disciplinary creeps into educational theory and practice from time to time.

Spencer was fairly representative of those liberal educators who argued that useful subjects should make up the curriculum. The other view, namely, that the curriculum consists in what the student does (activity), was developed by Dewey and his followers, It is not implied, however, that the criterion of usefulness was not employed by them, as will be brought out in the succeeding discussion.

In keeping with his statement that the goal of the school or education is more education, Dewey could not list specific subjects as Spencer did.[48] Spencer stated quite clearly that certain subjects, depending upon their usefulness, must be in a well-balanced curriculum designed to promote full living. Dewey maintained, on the contrary, that the teacher should not begin with a completed subject, but proposed as the starting point for curriculum construction the social living of the child. In his *Pedagogic Creed* he stated that the pupils' social activities must be the center of correlation in the curriculum, rather than science or any other subject.

A more exhaustive treatment of the relationship of social activity to subject matter is found in *Democracy and Education*. In this work Dewey rejected the notion that learning subject matter is an end in itself, and he argued that the teacher cannot begin with the perfected form of any subject matter. Thus even though the science of biology, for example, contains a large body of facts and principles which are well validated, the teacher should not begin with the conviction that this material is to be "covered" at the particular level of the student (elementary, secondary, or college). If the

---

[47]*Ibid.*, pp. 59-73.
[48]Dewey felt Spencer's reliance on science as the center of correlation was based on a false assumption about the nature of scientific knowledge. See Dewey, *Democracy and Education, op. cit.*, p. 258.

coverage procedure is followed, the student simply masters the vocabulary and the learning is isolated from everyday experience. But when the student begins with a real problem, one rooted in daily living, whatever facts or principles he learns will be meaningful to him.

Dewey admitted that the student may not cover all of the material that the expert in the field knows, but such coverage is not important. Also, he granted that it may take the student much more time to learn what the teacher or the textbooks could do in less time. But, what the pupil finds out on his own he understands. Moreover, by following the step-by-step procedure in solving the problems which arise in daily living, he gains "independent power to deal with material within his range."[49]

The important point which Dewey was making is that education cannot start with a cut-and-dried curriculum containing specific subjects for each educational level. Rather, the curriculum should consist of integrated activities of real pupils engaged in the solution of real problems (experience units). Their search for solutions will lead them to some of the traditional subjects, but these will never be studied as isolated bodies of knowledge or as skills (such as reading or writing) independent of the activities of life. Thus whatever meaningful activities take place in school constitute the curriculum.[50]

Does this view of the curriculum imply that the school should cease to teach reading, writing, spelling, science, industrial arts, home economics, and the like? If the reference is to these areas as independent subjects, the answer is the school should not do so. But, if these subjects are viewed as skills to be learned or material to be used in connection with living and solving problems, then they are considered legitimate curricular content.

To illustrate this point, Dewey contrasted the subject-matter approach to history with his own view. If the student studies history as a record of the past, he sees little value for its inclusion in the curriculum. "The past is past, and the dead may be safely left to bury its dead," since there are too many current problems to be solved. But, he argued, if history is approached as an account of the forces affecting social life today, it has relevance. When

---

[49]Dewey, *Democracy and Education, op. cit.*, pp. 257-61. Dewey expressed the same view in an earlier work *The child and the Curriculum* (Chicago: Univ. of Chicago Press, 1903).

[50]See W. H. Kilpatrick, "The Experimentalist Outlook," *Philosophies of Education*, 41st N.S.S.E. Yearbook, Part I (Chicago: Univ. of Chicago Press, 1942), pp. 75ff.; Boyd H. Bode, *Modern Educational Theories* (new York: The Macmillan Co., 1927), Chs. II-VII.

viewed as a study of society it will enable the child to appreciate the values of social life and to see the forces which engender or hinder cooperation among men. Such an approach to history can be closely integrated with geography and nature study since these, too, are entwined in the social life of the child. The social life of the child will give meaning to the inclusion of history as well as geography and science in the curriculum.[51]

In practice, the schools which tried to follow Dewey's concept of the curriculum introduced general-area or broad-field courses, especially at the secondary level. The experience-centered "core curriculum," used in the junior high school, represents an attempt to apply the new principles to curriculum making.[52] At the elementary level, the basic skill subjects are integrated in activity programs built around the social life of the student. As the student climbs the educational ladder more and more elective courses are available to meet special needs and interests. But at all levels, curricular content will always change as society itself changes. The term emerging curriculum seems to express this view most adequately.[53]

Dewey's belief that "the child's own social activities should be the true center of correlation" in the curriculum led him to reject the early progressive notion that the interests of the individual child should be the sole criterion for selecting the content and activities. The child does not exist in isolation from various social groups but is an integral part of them.[54] Some of Dewey's followers, recognizing the importance of social experience, proposed a method of curriculum construction which might account for the major facets of social experience and at the same time involve the school in the reconstruction of society itself.[55] The traditional distinction between general education and specialized (vocational)

---

[51] J. Dewey, *The Child and the Curriculum; School and Society* (Phoenix Books ed.; Chicago: Univ. of Chicago Press, 1956), pp. 151-59.

[52] See N. Bossing and R. Faunce, *Developing the Core Curriculum* (New York: Prentice-Hall, 1951), Chs. I, IV, VI-IX; J. M. Gwynn, *Curriculum Principles and Social Trends* (New York: The Macmillan Co., 1960), Chs. X-XV; F. R. Zeran, *Life Adjustment Education in Action* (New York: Chartwell House, 1953).

[53] For a comprehensive explanation of these curricular patterns, see B. Smith *et al.*, *Fundamentals of Curriculum Development* (New York: World Book Co., 1960), Part IV.

[54] Dewey, *The Child and the Curriculum, op. cit.*, pp. 15-18.

[55] Smith, *et al., op. cit.*, pp. 2f.; Brameld, *op. cit.*, Chs. VIII, IX; Raup, *et al.*, *op. cit.*, pp. 275-79.

education is retained with some reservations (e.g., when specialized education is meant for a privileged class). Specialized curricula will, of course, be designed for a specific job and will be taken by those who wish to enter a certain profession or trade. But the building of the general curriculum designed for all the children of all the people is of the greatest concern to these philosophers. It is the general curriculum which will both reflect the social realities of the times and contain the elements for improvement of society.

Generally speaking, the activity curriculum of the "progressive" elementary school, which provides an integrated approach to learning skills and acquiring useful knowledge, would be acceptable to these theorists. They would, however, insist that experience in group planning and participation in cooperative programs of action at the young child's level be the predominant activities. A curriculum which emphasizes social objectives can never be wholly child-centered; it must be group-centered.

At the secondary level, which most educators seem to consider the crucial level for general education, a rather specific content is suggested. The first year of the secondary school curriculum should contain study of and practice in the group problem-solving process, or the methods of practical intelligence. A thorough study of the local community, its political and economic structure, and its plans for improvement should be followed by a study of the wider community. This might be considered a social science survey.

A science survey, emphasizing the meaning of science, its social function, and the role it plays in human welfare is placed in the second year. Also, a survey of art, its meaning, its social function, and the role it must play in human welfare should have a place in the course of study in the second year. In the third year, a study of education, its meaning, and how it is to be supported and controlled is included in the curriculum, but most of the activity and study of the third year should be devoted to human relations. This broad category covers personal and family relations, sex education, and the problems of race, nationality, socioeconomic classes, and religion.

The last year of the secondary school is devoted to mastering techniques and strategies for attaining goals (solving common problems and preparing youth for aggressive leadership in social reconstruction. The students are helped in the all-important task of formulating a set of values which will guide their personal and social conduct.[56]

---

[56]This four-year general education program is proposed by Brameld, *op. cit.*, pp. 218-50. It is not an official statement of any large body of

This curriculum, and others designed for social living, has several significant features. First, it will vary somewhat from community to community depending upon geographic location and socioeconomic factors. For example, a rural secondary school might emphasize the role of science in agriculture, whereas a metropolitan center might be more concerned with science in industry. Second, the curriculum is constantly being reconstructed to suit social changes which are taking place. Third, the task of curriculum construction is a cooperative effort on the part of administrators, community representatives, teachers, parents, pupils, and outside experts. Finally, the curriculum of general education is designed to assist the individual to become an efficient member of the social groups to which he belongs; it is not a program for personal aggrandizement or self-satisfaction.[57]

In summary, it can be noted that two somewhat different, but not completely opposing, views of the curriculum are found among nineteenth- and twentieth-century liberals: (1) One group defines the curriculum as an organized and integrated sequence of useful subjects; (2) the other group regards the curriculum as a meaningful sequence of activities growing out of the pupils' social life. Those concerned with the reconstruction of the social order propose the democratic methodology of curriculum building and suggest content and activities which will effect such a reconstruction.

HOW SHOULD ONE TEACH?

The nineteenth and twentieth centuries are by far the most productive in the entire history of education in the area of educational methodology. As mentioned before, conservative educators generally paid little attention to "how to teach" since their major concern was for "what to teach" and how this content could be employed to achieve the goal of cultivation of the intellect. The early liberals of the seventeenth and eighteenth centuries initiated the movement to improve the methods of teaching when they

---

educational theorists.

[57]To some theorists interested in the reconstruction of the social order, the methodology of curriculum construction is of major concern, i.e., they consider the means of arriving at decisions about the curriculum more important than its particular structure and content. See Smith, *et al.*, *op. cit.*; K. Benne and B. Muntyan, *Human Relations in Curriculum Change* (New York: Dryden, Press, 1951).

proposed and applied the natural method in opposition to the formalized methods of the conservatives.

Herbart, who had observed Pestalozzi's experimental school and was very much impressed by the natural method employed, devised an approach to teaching which he felt incorporated Pestalozzi's principles. He proposed four steps in the teaching process: (1) *Preparation*: This initial step, which is especially important in introducing new topics, consists in recalling to the students' minds anything they know from past experience about the topic. This is done by showing them pictures objects, and the like which are familiar. The teacher encourages the students to discuss what they know about the subject thus stirring up their interest in it. In other words, the teacher should always begin with that which is familiar to the students and of real interest to them. (2) *Association*: At this phase the students and teacher proceed from the specifics of experience and observation to the formulation of generalizations. For example, the pupils have experienced the results of cold temperatures, such as rain turning to snow and water, to ice. The teacher shows them pictures of Alpine peaks in summer covered with snow. From such specific knowledge pupils and teacher formulate generalizations about temperature and altitude. (3) *Presentation* (teaching): During this stage of the process the teacher furnishes information which the pupils could not discover for themselves and systematizes and synthesizes all related material into a unitary whole. Although the teacher is more active than the pupils at this stage, Herbart admonished him not to lose sight of the pupils' experience and knowledge and to relate these constantly to his presentation. (4) *Application*: At this stage the student is expected to demonstrate that he understands the material by applying his knowledge to novel situations, by working problems, or by doing projects calling for application of the principles learned.

Whether or not Herbart's teaching method is psychologically sound is not at issue here. The significant point is that he believed it represents the natural way pupils learn. Herbart claimed that the method is based on the findings of empirical psychology rather than the logic of the subject matter.[58] Dewey later clarified this distinction between the logical and the psychological approaches to teaching.

Spencer, too, contended that all teaching must begin with the specific experiences of the pupil. He complained that teachers violate the psychological approach when they begin by stating principles, laws,

---

[58]See J. Herbart, *The Science of Education* (Boston: D. C. Heath & Co., 1895); Dewey, *Democracy and Education, op. cit.*, pp.256-61.

definitions, and rules instead of basing their instruction upon the knowledge which the pupil possesses from experience. Consequently, pupils acquire a dislike for learning, whereas, by nature, it should be pleasant. Such miseducation can be avoided only if the teacher leads the student from the known to the unknown, from the simple to the complex, from the concrete to the abstract. Furthermore, the pupils must be the active participants in the process; the teacher is not to give knowledge but must permit and assist students to *discover* it. Spencer also believed that the natural method can and should be applied at all educational levels-elementary through higher education.[59]

The progressive education movement which incorporated the varied ideas of Rousseau, Pestalozzi, Herbart, Spencer, and Froebel also concentrated on the improvement of teaching methods. It is, perhaps, because of the progressive emphasis on method that many critics characterized the movement as fostering the notion that "as long as you know how to teach you do not have to be concerned with what to teach." However, the early progressive educators are remembered more for the specific teaching techniques they developed rather than for proposing a new philosophy of method. In fact, they accepted the general validity of the natural method and devised new ways of employing it.

It was Dewey, however, who made the first complete analysis of the teaching-learning process from the point of view of methodology. He was the first educational philosopher whose answer to the question "How should one teach (learn)?" harmonizes with the answer to the question "How do we know?" The work of Herbart and Spencer demonstrated the close relationship between theory of knowledge and method of teaching, but neither had succeeded in achieving the unity between the theoretical (philosophical) and the practical as Dewey did.

Although methods texts used in teacher education vary somewhat in their application of Dewey's method, they do follow the general lines of problem solving proposed in *How We Think* and others of Dewey's works.[60] As practiced in the classroom, the problem-solving method generally coincides with Dewey's original analysis.

The initial motivation for learning, according to Dewey, is sparked by some difficulty which the student experiences in the ordinary course of

---

[59]*op. cit.*, pp. 47ff., 115-61.

[60]See pp. 122-26 in this volume. Some texts in educational psychology maintain that Dewey's theory does not represent a psychologically accurate description of what takes place in the teaching-learning process.

events. He had no ready answer for, or way out of, the situation. Note that it is the felt difficulty of the student, not an artificial one set up by the teacher, which initiates the process; only when the student feels the difficulty will he be prodded to further observation and reflection.[61] The second step in problem solving consists in identifying and defining the problem in order that ensuing activities in the search for a solution will be properly directed. Such cannot be the case unless the learner can state quite specifically what the problem is. Very often this is the most difficult step in the process, since the student might not be able to proceed easily from the rather hazy state of "feeling a difficulty" to that of recognizing its real nature.

The next natural and logical step involves the systematic search for data about the problem as it is now defined. This search might take the student to various sources, such as his own or the teacher's experience books, an expert authority, and other community resources. Furthermore the search will take the student to all fields of knowledge related to the problem. Thus the student conceivably might have to consult many fields, such as history, political science, biology, and literature. One of the lessons the student learns from this activity is that the various fields of human knowledge are closely interrelated. A form of natural integration of subject matter takes place since the learner realizes that subject matter is simply information and knowledge needed to solve a specific problem.[62]

When the student has acquired sufficient data about the problem, he is prepared to take the next step in the method, i.e., to formulate possible solutions to the problem. Each possible solution or hypothesis must be judged in terms of its *anticipated consequences*. Since, in most cases at least, not all hypotheses can be tested simultaneously, one (or several) that appears most likely to resolve the difficulty in terms of its anticipated results is selected for initial testing.

The final step is, of course, the test of experience followed by acceptance or rejection of the hypothesis. If the anticipated results and the actual results are identical (or nearly so), the original felt difficulty disappears and the problem is solved. If not, the hypothesis is rejected and another must be tested.

Throughout the description of the method, the term student appears almost exclusively. This deliberate mention of the student's role was

---

[61] See W. H. Kilpatrick, *Foundations of Method* (New York: The Macmillan Co., 1926), p. 246; Dewey, *Democracy and Education, op. cit.*, pp. 258ff.
[62] See pp. 140-42 of this volume. Dewey's rejection of the dualism of subject matter and method is evident in this step of problem solving.

designed to emphasize the pupil-centeredness of the method. It is not implied, however, that the teacher is passive. On the contrary, he is very active; he is a guide in the learning process, even though he does not dominate it. He works with the students in locating and defining their problem, searching for relevant data, proposing hypotheses, and putting the hypotheses to the test of experience. The teaching-learning environment might have to be teacher-arranged; the teacher under certain conditions might be one of the sources of data; the teacher as an experienced adult will help in determining whether a satisfactory solution has been achieved or not. Indeed, the teacher's role is very important in all the methods proposed by the liberals.

Various adaptations of Dewey's problem-solving method were proposed by his followers. One of the most popular of these, the "project method" of W. H. Kilpatrick, is based upon the problem-solving philosophy of method.[63] The reconstructionist method of practical intelligence is problem solving applied to groups. Dewey himself had implied such an application but had not provided the analysis of the factors of social consensus, the role of utopian ideals, and the moods of those involved in the process.

Whether the liberal is using the problem-solving method or projects, he attempts to give the student as much direct experience as possible with the objects and situations being studied. Field trips to the local community are commonly used in the study of government and industry in action. When direct experience with the objects of study is not readily available, movies, pictures, recordings, and radio and television programs provide vicarious experience.

One characteristic of the methodology of the liberals is the importance which is placed upon student interest in the teaching-learning process. Only a few conservative educators, such as Quintilian, Saint Augustine and the Jesuits, showed much concern for the interests of the learner. Early liberals, like Pestalozzi and Rousseau, recognized the value of basing learning activities on the natural interests of the pupils. Herbart, however, developed a unitary doctrine of interest which encompassed the activity of both teacher and pupil. He recognized that interest is generated naturally in pupils and should not be squelched. It is the teacher's job to keep alive this spontaneous interest of the pupils but he must also constantly stir up additional interest in the topics being studied. Thus awakening interest is not only necessary in the initial steps of the teaching process, but it is just as essential to sustain interest throughout the learning activity. Herbart

---

[63]Kilpatrick, *op. cit.*, pp. 241, 345-61.

emphasized the notion that interest must be sustained because most teachers, who cared about pupil interest at all, used it only as a motivational device for introducing a lesson. In such cases, interest is an artificial adjunct to the teaching process rather than an integral part of it. When this limited view of interest is applied to the educational process, Herbart felt it would stifle the pupil's interest for learning in general.[64]

Dewey, also, discussed the effects of interest on methodology. He, too, rejected the notion that interest is something external to the teaching act. For him "interest, concern, mean that self and the world are engaged with each other in a developing situation." In other words, when a pupil has a problem he is already interested, and he does not have to be motivated to learn. Thus if a teacher has to *make* the material interesting there is something wrong-he has failed to perceive or show the connection between the learning activity and the ongoing activities and purposes of the learner.[65]

Dewey's objection to the artificial use of interest in teaching is reiterated in his refusal to separate interest and effort in the teaching-learning process. The tendency of conservatives and even some early liberals to view interest and effort as different aspects of the educative process is one of the dualism which Dewey felt destroyed the unity and continuity of the process. Whereas the conservative and some liberals had considered interest as a means of producing effort, Dewey considered them as coterminous. Thus a child at play is not employing interest in the game to produce the effort required to play the game; for all practical purposes they are one and the same.

To summarize this section on education methodology the following points seem central: (1) The nineteenth- and twentieth-century liberals accept the validity of the natural method employed by their seventeenth-and eighteenth-century predecessors. (2) Herbart devised a teaching method which he believed was solidly rooted in scientific psychology. (3) For Dewey, the natural method of learning and teaching was problem solving, i.e., proceeding from a perplexed, confused situation to a unitary, harmonious one. (4) Dewey's method was adapted by the reconstructionist to solve group problems since these are of primary concern to twentieth-century man. (5) The role of interest, though interpreted variously by Spencer, Herbart, and Dewey, is considered essential in all modern liberal theories of teaching.

---

[64]J. Herbart, *Outlines of Educational Doctrine*, A. F. Lange (trans.) (New York: The Macmillan Co., 1901), pp.44-66, 126.
[65]Dewey, *Democracy and Education, op. cit.*, pp. 146-50.

HOW SHOULD PUPILS BE EVALUATED?

Throughout this book, it has been noted that all educators, conservative and liberal, recognize that pupils must be evaluated. Conservatives limited their evaluation chiefly to mastery of subject matter. Essay and oral examinations serve this purpose quite adequately. Early liberals, on the other hand, broadened the purposes of evaluation to include the factors of total growth-mental, physical, emotional, and social. Self-evaluation by pupils is not only encouraged but becomes an integral part of appraisal. Absolute and external standards are abandoned in favor of measures of relative change in pupil behavior and achievement.

Thus the foundation for a new philosophy of evaluation had been laid by the early liberals. But progress in measurement of all the factors mentioned in the preceding paragraph did not begin until the twentieth century. Even nineteenth-century educators, such as Spencer and Herbart, made no significant contribution to the measurement of the factors they considered important. In spite of all their emphasis on science, they did not develop scientifically sound measuring instruments,

The works of Galton, Cattell, and Wundt represent the first attempts at scientific measurement of factors which are of concern to the school. Since the liberal is interested in the development of the whole child, academic achievement is only one factor to be evaluated. Galton and Binet were among the first to propose measures for assessing personality traits of pupils. Binet's pioneering work in the testing of intelligence enabled teachers to determine the individual differences among pupils and adjust their teaching to them. The objective testing of achievement received great impetus from the work of Rice, enabling teachers to eliminate the subjectivity and unreliability of the oral and essay examinations used in the conservative school.

Viewed in the light of highly developed techniques of the twentieth century, these late nineteenth- and early twentieth-century measuring instruments might appear quite crude, but this is not the significant point for the philosophy of education. What is important is that measurement is expanded to encompass the broadened goals of the school and that measurement must be done in a scientific manner.

Perhaps the most important figure in the modernization of educational measurement is E. L. Thorndike. Thorndike's tests were based upon the principles of his experimental psychology and statistical analysis. In addition to employing this scientific foundation for his tests, Thorndike was the first to standardize his measuring instruments by trying them out on a large norm group, by administering them under controlled conditions, and by providing the statistical data necessary for the interpretation of the test results.

Yet another important outgrowth of Thorndike's work was the measurement of special aptitudes, such as musical, artistic, secretarial, mechanical, and others. The liberal was able to put these to good use since he recognized abilities other than those associated with purely verbal factors. (The conservative had limited evaluation almost exclusively to verbal and abstract factors.) Even for the appraisal of intelligence, performance or nonverbal tests were constructed. These tests were built on the belief that intelligence consists in what one does or can do rather than what words one knows.

The heyday of the measurement era included the years from the close of World War I to 1930. But, like most reform movements, it tended to overemphasize certain aspects of measurement. For instance, in their enthusiasm for objectivity, the experts overlooked the necessity of making certain judgments about the value, or nonvalue, of objective testing itself. Perhaps some of these factors were just as significant as those which could be measured objectively. Skill in problem solving, work on special projects, use of resource materials, critical analysis of results, emotional stability in the face of difficulties, appreciation of values, skill in applying what is learned to novel situations are facets of the educational process which the liberal felt should be of great concern to the teacher. Because of these serious shortcomings in the field of measurement, many liberals, including Dewey, registered opposition to the exclusive use of, and reliance upon, objective tests as means of appraisal of student behavior. They were, however, not opposed to the application of the principles of scientific psychology and measurement to the determination of student aptitudes, interests and achievement. They were demanding that measurement be "liberalized."

The recognition of the importance of these neglected areas brought about the shift from the narrow concept of measurement to the broader concept, evaluation. A good example of the new approach to evaluation is found in the Eight-Year Study of the Progressive Education Association. Achievement tests, attitude and rating scales, anecdotal records, and the like were employed to determine the extent to which students had progressed on such factors as reasoning (problem solving), social sensitivity and beliefs, civic responsibility, appreciation of literature and art, personal and social development. In other words, an attempt was made to determine the extent to which the school achieved all of its objectives.[66]

This broader concept, evaluation, was soon applied to reporting pupil progress. In many progressive schools the traditional report card was abandoned in favor of a progress report to the parents covering all of the areas just mentioned. Even when report cards were not eliminated another part was added covering interests, attitudes, appreciation, social adjustment, and the like. Evaluation of the development of the whole child is not only recognized as essential but is actually implemented in schools.

This period in educational history has undoubtedly been the most productive in the fields of measurement and evaluation. It witnessed the beginning and the development of reliable, valid, and adequate measures of achievement, interests, personality, intelligence, special aptitudes, health, skills, and social adjustment. The somewhat narrow conception of measurement gave way to the broader notion of evaluation which encompassed factors which could not be measured by objective paper and pencil tests.

HOW ARE FREEDOM AND DISCIPLINE TO BE HARMONIZED?

The critics of educational liberalism frequently attack the lack of discipline and the presence of too much pupil freedom in the progressive school. It is true that the early liberals, especially Rousseau, wished to free the student from the autocratic rule of the conservative teacher and give him the opportunity to discipline himself. The natural consequences of his behavior were considered the best form of discipline for the pupil - the painful results of certain actions constituted their own punishment. This attitude toward freedom and discipline produced a lunatic fringe group of teachers who allowed even very young children to do just as they pleased.

But the liberals of the nineteenth and twentieth centuries never preached absolute freedom or complete absence of discipline. Spencer, for instance, suggested a gradual freeing of the child from parental and teacher control.

---

[66]E.R. Smith and R.W. Tyler *et al.*, *Appraising and Recording School Progress* (New York: Harper and Brothers, 1942). See also, E. Bayles, *Democratic Educational Theory* (New York: Harper and Brothers, 1960), Ch. XIV.

As the child matures he should be granted more freedom of choice and action; give him the opportunity to make mistakes and learn from them. But self-discipline is an achievement of the mature person, not the little child.[67]

Dewey, too, definitely rejected the notion that freedom consists in the absence of all restrictions. He maintained that one is free to the degree to which one acts in harmony with the knowledge one possesses; freedom implies an understanding and mastery of the situations. [68] Thus freeing the student *from* external autocratic authority is only the first step in the educational process. The second step must follow - freeing the student *for* the intelligent solution of real problems.

For another significant reason, Dewey could never accept the laissez faire conception of freedom. Since education is "social living," obviously no one can do just as he pleases. Education fails, he said, when "it neglects the fundamental principle of the school as a form of community life." Since freedom is a concern of moral education, "the best and deepest moral training is precisely that which one gets through having to enter into proper relationships with others in a unity of work and thought."[69]

Dewey expounded this same view of freedom in his other works, and it is the only view which is consistent with his general philosophy. The very existence of an organic society limits the freedom of the individual members of that society. The pupil is free to interact with other members of the class in conducting the social life of their own little community and in solving the problems at hand. Dewey also pointed out that the teacher cannot abrogate his responsibility to the immature children in his class. In reality, he argued, the democratic classroom where freedom and responsibility are properly harmonized calls for more, rather than less, guidance by the teachers.[70]

Thus for Dewey, discipline is not a concept to be separated from freedom. He rejected the traditional dualism of freedom and discipline on the grounds that these two aspects of teaching were essentially the same. For the conservative teacher, discipline was a means for checking youth's unbridled striving for freedom from external control; discipline was

---

[67]Spencer, *op.cit...*, Ch. III.

[68]Dewey, *The Quest for Certainty, op.cit..*, pp.249f.

[69]Dewey, *My Pedagogic Creed, op.cit..*, pp. 6, 8.

[70]J. Dewey, *Education and the Social Order* (New York: League for Industrial Democracy, 1943), p.3.

designed to tend the pupil to be obedient to the authority of his elders and to control his evil tendencies. Such an approach to behavior, according to Dewey, results in conformity, not true self-discipline. The truly self-disciplined person is one who deliberately considers the consequences of his actions and follows through on a chosen course of action in spite of obstacles, confusion, and hardships. The disciplined person or class has the mastery of the resources necessary to carry out a plan of action; to use the proper means to achieve desired ends is to be disciplined. Thus without freedom to work toward chosen ends there can be no discipline, and without discipline there can be no freedom.

Those who argue that the school should participate in the reconstruction of society are even more emphatic in their rejection of the laissez faire conception of freedom and discipline. They, too, believe that the authoritarianism of the conservative school must be abandoned. But, by repudiating authoritarianism, they do not imply that there is no authority in society, the school, or the classroom; that is anarchy, not democracy. Democratic society as well as the democratic classroom must have rules and regulations and persons or experts with authority. The essential difference between authoritarianism and democratic authority is that the former locates power to rule in some external force or group such as God, a sacred code, a social class, or a person; the latter, however, places final authority in all matters in the enlightened and informed judgment of all the people.[71]

According to the reconstructionists, then, there must be law and order in every classroom, but the members of the class including the teacher must participate in making the decisions and rules which will affect the group. Truly democratic decisions will incorporate the valid insights of all the participants. Only when pupils are free to make decisions in cooperative enterprises can it be said that they are disciplined for democracy.

Clearly, then, pupils are not to be given absolute freedom from all restraint. The fact that they are members of a class, are enrolled in a certain school, and live in a community entails limitations on their personal freedom. These very real social restrictions demand discipline. Indeed, disciplining for democratic social living is a necessary goal of all school activities.[72]

---

[71] See K.D. Benne, *A Conception of Authority* (New York: Bureau of Publications, Teachers College, Columbia Univ., 1945).

[72] A great deal has been written about the proper harmony between freedom and discipline by the advocates of this point of view; e.g. see Raup *et al. op.*

Before closing this chapter it might be well to note the extent to which twentieth-century educational liberalism has influenced education in countries outside the United States. In the early essays of the Bolshevik revolution liberal ideas were quite popular in Russian educational circles. Dewey's philosophy was incorporated into the educational reforms of such influential leaders as A. P. Pinkevitch, P. B. Blonski, A. Lunacharski, and, to some extent, A. S. Makarenko. In the 1930's, however, Dewey fell into disrepute among Soviet Communists because of his defense of Trotsky. Since that time Dewey has been the *bete noire* in Russian educational literature.[73]

In spite of this attack on liberalism, Russian education retained some features which might be considered liberal. Most notably, the classical curriculum of pre-revolution schools was replaced by one with physical education, vocational subjects, the arts, and concentrated training for Soviet citizenship. Also, educational opportunity was expanded to include all youth and adults not only for the years of elementary education but for post-elementary education of various kinds.

Italy, Spain, and most South American countries still retain the general outlines of conservative classical education with some minor modifications due to advances in science and technology.

During World War II, the French government in exile formed the Langevin commission to review the entire structure of French education. This group recommended sweeping changes in French schools, among them that equal educational opportunity be extended to the secondary schools thereby giving more students the opportunity to enter institutions of higher learning; the classical curriculum *(culture generale)* be de-emphasized, and one designed to meet the needs and interests of all students be introduced. Some of these recommendations have affected education at mid-century, but French education still cannot be considered liberal in the sense that we have been using the term in this text, especially at the

---

cit.; W. Stanley, *Education and Social Integration* (New York: Bureau of Publications, Teachers College, Columbia Univ., 1953);
B. Smith, "Squaring the Curriculum with Social realities," *Educational Leadership*, IX (January, 1952), 215-19; Brameld, *op. cit.*, Chs. Vii, X, XI; Smith et al., *op.cit.*, Ch. V.

[73]See W. Brickman and S. Lehrer, *John Dewey: Master Educator* (New York: Society for the Advancement of Education, 1959), pp. 101-4.

secondary and higher levels.[74]

Of the modern school systems which prior to World War II were very conservative, that of the Federal Republic of Germany adopted the most liberal policy after the war. This change might be due, in part, to the influence of the American occupation and assistance. Great strides have been made toward equalizing educational opportunity; methods where the teacher dominates and the pupils are purely passive have almost disappeared; learning has been brought in touch with everyday life, especially in the area of social studies; teacher and pupil freedom is recognized and respected; faculty and student participation in school self-government is widespread; the harsh discipline of the traditional German school is generally not found; officially, at least, the vocational curriculum is given equal status with the academic; modern methods of measurement and evaluation are used widely.[75]

In Great Britain a "reluctant revolution" is taking place in education. The coexistence of a hereditary monarchy, titled nobility, and democratic socialism has its parallel in education. Conservative education has a strong grip on British schools, yet there are some liberal aspects in the system. Perhaps most significant of all is the relatively recent provision for free education through the secondary level. Although cultivation of the intellect is still the goal of the prestige schools, health and physical education, vocational competence, and recreational pursuits are considered an integral part of the school program, especially during the first seven or eight years of schooling. The newer progressive secondary schools might be compared to the American comprehensive high school, insofar as they are designed to meet the needs of all youth of that particular age. There is, however, strong opposition to this type of school, even from the liberal socialists.[76]

Other European countries have introduced liberal elements into their educational systems, especially at the elementary school level. The secondary schools, however, tend to retain the essential pattern of

---

[74]See E. J. King, *Other Schools and Ours* (New York: Rinehart and Co., 1958), Ch. III.

[75]See *Meet Germany* (Hamburg: Atlantic-Brucke, 1963), pp. 103-10; W. Stahl, *Education for Democracy in West Germany* (New York: Frederick A. Praeger, 1961).

[76]See King, *op.cit.*., Ch. IV.

conservative education. It is, of course, too early to predict the direction that education will take in the dozens of new African and Asian nations. At present, indications are that they will abandon much of the educational conservatism of their former colonial rulers. This might be explained in terms of a general reaction against all that is associated with colonialism rather than as simply a reaction against conservative education.

CHAPTER SUMMARY

Although the nineteenth- and twentieth-century educational liberals built upon the theories of the early liberals, many important modifications and innovations are to be noted. Evolutionary theories about the origin of man are widely accepted and applied to educational theory. Mind-body dualism is emphatically rejected; mind is viewed as a function of the human organism. The social origin of human behavior is considered central in the redefinition of freedom, authority, and responsibility. The role of experience and science as valid modes of knowing are more clearly delineated. Problem solving is proposed as a mode of knowing encompassing both everyday experience and the more technical methods of the empirical sciences. Group problem solving is presented as the best means of arriving at knowledge or solutions considered necessary for group living. Truth is derived from individual or group experience and the empirical sciences. The consequences of an idea or theory and social consensus are proposed as criteria for truth. Values are rooted in the natural behavior patterns of man. The resolution of moral and social problems arising in the day-to-day affairs of man gives rise to moral standards and codes. Since man and his environment are in a state of flux, all values are relative. The consensus of the group or society is the final authority in value decisions.

Educational theory during this period witnessed the greatest development in the history of education. The following appear to be the most significant changes. Educational theory relies greatly upon the findings of the behavioral sciences, especially psychology and sociology. The purpose of the school is clearly defined in terms of the development of the whole child. Additional responsibility is placed upon the school for the reconstruction of the social order. A curriculum designed to achieve the broadened objectives of the school contains activities to develop physical fitness, vocational competence, family living, civic responsibility, and the worthy use of leisure time. The natural method is expanded to include problem solving, the project method, the socialized class, and a host of auxiliary teaching techniques. Oral and essay tests fall into disrepute and are replaced by scientifically constructed measuring instruments. The broader concept, evaluation, is employed to determine the total growth of the educand in all phases of human development. Freedom and discipline are viewed as correlative aspects of the same educational process. Social conditions in the modern world demand that both freedom and discipline be redefined in democratic terms.

BIBLIOGRAPHY

Bayles, Ernest. *Democratic Educational Theory.* New York: Harper and Brothers, 1960.

Benne, K. D. *A Conception of Authority.* New York: Bureau of Publications, Teachers College, Columbia Univ., 1945.

Benne, K. D. "Education for Wisdom in Value Judgments," *Progressive Education,* XXVII (April, 1950), 181-84.

Benne, K. D., and Muntyan, B. (eds.). *Human Relations and Curriculum Change.* New York: Dryden Press, 1951.

Blewett, John. *John Dewey: His Thought and Influence.* New York: Fordham Univ. Press, 1960.

Bode, Boyd. *Democracy as a Way of Life.* New York: The Macmillan Co., 1950.

Brameld, Theodore. *Toward a Reconstructed Philosophy of Education.* New York: Dryden Press, 1956.

Brulsman, W., and Lehrer, S. *John Dewey: Master Educator.* New York: Society for the Advancement of Education, 1959.

Brumbaugh, R. S., and Lawrence, N. M. *Philosophers on Education.* Boston: Houghton Mifflin Co., 1963. Ch. VI.

Burton, W. H. *The Guidance of Learning Activities.* 2nd ed. New York: Appleton-Century- Crofts , 1 952 .

Childs, John. *American Pragmatism b Education.* New York: Henry Holt & Co., 1956.

Comte, Auguste. *Positive Philosophy.* Translated by H. Martineau. New York: C. Blanchard Co., 1855.

Counts, George. *Dare The School Build A New Social Order?* New York:

John   Day Co., 1932.

Cremin, L. A. *The Transformation of the School.* New York: Vintage Books, 1964.

Dewey, John. "My Pedagogic Creed," *The School Journal,* LIV, No. 3 (January   16, 1897), 77-80.

Dewey, John. *The Child and The Curriculum.* Chicago: Univ. of Chicago Press, 1902.

Dewey, John. *Democracy and Education.* New York: The Macmillan Co., 1916.

Dewey, John. *Creative Intelligence.* New York: Henry Holt & Co., 1917.

Dewey, John. Human Nature and Conduct. New York: Henry Holt & Co. 1922.

Dewey, John. *Experience and Nature.* Chicago: Open Court Publishing

Dewey, John. *The Public and Its Problems.* New York: Henry Holt & Co. 1927.

Dewey, John. *The Quest for Certainty.* New York: Minton, Balch & Co.,

Dewey, John. *How We Think.* Boston: D. C. Heath & Co., 1910 rev. ed., 1933.

Dewey, John. *Art as Experience.* New York: Minton, Balch & Co., 1934.

Dewey, John. "Democracy and Educational Administration," *School And Society,*   XLV (April, 1937), 457-62.

Dewey, John. *Education and the Social Order.* New York: League for Industrial Democracy, 1943.

Dewey, John. *Reconstruction in Philosophy.* Enlarged ed. Boston: Beacon Press, 1948.

Dewey, John, and Tufts, J. *Ethics.* New York: Henry Holt & Co., 1936.

Dewey, John, *et al. Creative Intelligence.* New York: Henry Holt & Co.,

Dewey, John. *Experience and Education.* New York: The Macmillan Co. 1949.

Dunkel, H. B. "Dewey and The Fine Arts," *The School Review,* LXVII (Summer,   1959), 229-46.

Faunce, R., and Bossing, N. *Developing the Core Curriculum.* Englewood Cliffs,   N.J.: Prentice-Hall, 1951.

Geiger, G. R. "An Experimentalist Approach to Education," *Modern Philosophies   and Education,* 54th N.S.S.E. Yearbook. Chicago: Univ. of Chicago Press,   1955. Ch. V.

Gwynn, J. M. *Curriculum Principles and Social Trends.* New York: The

Macmillan Co., 1960.

Herbart, J. *The Science of Education*. Boston: D. C. Heath & Co., 1895.

Herbart, J. *Outline of Educational Doctrine*. Translated by A. F. Lange. New York: The Macmillan Co., 1901.

Herbst, J. "Herbert Spencer & the Genteel Tradition in American Education," *Educational Theory, XI* (April, 1901), 99-111.

Kilpatrick, W. H. *The Project Method*. New York: Bureau of Publications Teachers College, Columbia Univ., 1921.

Kilpatrick, W. H. *Foundations of Method*. New York: The Macmillan Co., 1926.

Kilpatrick, W. H. "The Experimentalist Outlook," *Philosophies of Education*. 41st N.S.S.E. Yearbook. Chicago: Univ. of Chicago Press, 1942.

Ratner, Joseph (Ed). *Intelligence in the Modern World-John Dewey's Philosophy*. New York: Modern Library, 1939.

Raup, R. Bruce, *et al*. *The Improvement of Practical Intelligence*. New York: Harper and Brothers, 1950.

Roth, R. J. *John Dewey and Self-Realization*. Englewood Cliffs, N. J.: Prentice-Hall, 1962.

Rugg, Harold. *Foundations of Modern Education*. New York: World Book Co., 1947.

Schilpp, Paul A. (ed.). *The Philosophy of John Dewey*. 2nd ed. New York: Tudor Publishing Co., 1951.

Shaw, Theodore. *Precious Rubbish*. Boston: Stuart Art Gallery, 1956.

Smith, B. Othanel, *et al*. *Fundamentals of Curriculum Development*. New York: World Book Co., 1960.

Somjee, A. H. *The Political Theory of John Dewey*. New York: Teachers College Press, 1968.

Spencer, Herbert. *Education: Intellectual, Moral and Physical*. New York: D. Appleton Century, 1866.

Spencer, Herbert. *First Principles of a New System of Philosophy*. New York: D. Appleton Co., 1896.

Zeran, F. R. *Life Adjustment Education in Action*. New York: Chartwell House, 1953.

Chapter VII

The Neo-Conservative Reaction

That the liberal philosophy of Dewey and his followers achieved great popularity in the United States is granted by friend and foe alike. In the colleges of education throughout the country, the liberals by far outnumbered the conservatives. Columbia University, at which Dewey spent most of his professional life, became the heart of the American liberal educational movement. From this institution came the influential leaders of the late progressive movement and the "social frontiersmen" who were to dominate the field of philosophy of education for several decades to come. Since the liberals also staffed the methods courses and other professional education courses in teacher's colleges, most teachers tended to accept their views and put them to work in the classroom.

The elementary schools of the country witnessed the greatest effect of the liberal movement whereas high schools and colleges tended to be more conservative. But even at the high school level, the influence of liberal thought was quite evident. In fact, some high schools turned completely to the new education, while others made only a few concessions to the liberal ideas. The large comprehensive high schools in urban areas developing at about the same time were more apt to adopt the liberal curriculum and methodology than were the smaller rural schools. Many colleges, too, joined the trend toward liberalism. The demise of the classical curriculum and the appearance of the free elective system are but two instances of the rise of liberalism in higher education.

As one might expect, opposition to liberalism often took the form of anti-Deweyism. Some of the critics were nothing more than anti-Dewey. Others, though, constructed systematic philosophies of education which they believed might counteract the dominance of liberalism in American educational theory. The differences between these two kinds of neo-conservatives are, of course, very great. The latter category consists of philosophers and philosophers of education, such as Lodge, Harne, Butler, Maritain (and many Thomists), Adler, Broudy, who are conversant with the philosophical issues as well as the educational disputes flowing from them. Various labels are used to designate these thinkers such as neo-humanists, idealists, classical-realists, neo-realists, essentialists, and neo-Thomists. The thinking of these neo-conservatives is most important at least from the point of view of the philosopher of education.

However, the other group of neo-conservatives should not be overlooked in an introductory text, if for no other reason than that they cause a stir in the public press and legislative halls of the nation. In this latter category one finds highly influential people such as Bestor, Jr., Lynd, Mortimer Smith, Kirk; Molnar, Admiral Rickover, Max Rafferty, and a host of other critics of American education. Very often it is the thinking of these lay critics which the average teacher and layman must deal with rather than the theories of the bona fide philosopher of education.

Also, it is worth noting that at least some of the new conservatives incorporate many of the findings of modern psychology and sociology in their educational theories. Then, too, most of them work within the democratic framework of the twentieth-century America which moderates, to some extent, the elitism of the old conservatives. Some conservatives even admit that Dewey made some significant contributions to educational theory and practice.[1]

One of the first systematic reactions against the liberal philosophy of Dewey came from the idealist, H. H. Horne, a professor at New York University. He had used Dewey's *Democracy and Education* as a text for his courses in philosophy of education since its appearance. Horne disagreed with Dewey's basic philosophical position, although he did grant that Dewey proposed the most significant change in educational theory since Plato. In order that students might have some basis for contrasting Dewey's educational philosophy with another system, Horne (with Dewey's blessing) published a book entitled *The Democratic Philosophy of Education-Companion to Dewey's Democracy and Education*. In this volume Horne contrasted his philosophy of idealism, point by point, with the philosophy of Dewey. Thus Horne's philosophy might be considered the first systematic rebuttal of the liberalism of Dewey and his followers.

To be sure, there had been others before him, such as Morris, Superintendent of St. Louis Schools and United States Commissioner of Education, who had espoused idealism in education. Other contemporaries

---

[1]See e.g., M. Smith, *And Madly Teach* (Chicago: Henry Regnery Co., 1949), pp. 20ff.

of Horne, such as Lodge and Rusk, lent their support to this anti-Dewey movement. At mid-century, Butler appears to have become the spokesman for the neo-idealists in the area of philosophy of education.[2]

Idealism is a complex philosophy, perhaps one of the most complex treated in this text. Also, there are many varieties of it, such as objective and subjective idealism, personal and absolute idealism. It will not be necessary, however, for our purposes to distinguish these many variations since substantial agreement can be found in the answers to the basic questions which are asked about the nature of man, theory of knowledge, and the like. After a discussion of idealism, the philosophical and educational beliefs of all other neo-conservatives will be presented as responses to our questions.

IDEALISM

What Is Man?

Idealism generally is classified as a philosophy of spirit. It is not surprising, then, that man is viewed as a spiritual being with specific qualities that distinguish him essentially from all lower animal forms. It is true that man is a part of nature if, in nature, you include the spiritual. But man is not merely a lost molecule in the vast world of spirit or a product of biological evolution; he is a *person* with his own individual traits, characteristics, abilities, likes, and dislikes. In this sense, he is an independent entity - an individual mind.

The fact of the existence of the individual mind is the heart of the idealist philosophy of man. It is the mind that thinks, raises problems, and solves them. Mind not only interprets what is observed, but nothing can be observed unless there is a mind to observe it. Man, as a knowing being, is mind. This is man's starting point - the consciousness of his own mind. Thus the twentieth century idealist, like his classical forebears, Plato and St. Augustine, defines man chiefly in terms of mental activity.

But what is the nature of the mind? What powers does it possess? Mind

---

[2]J. D. Butler, *Four Philosophies and Their Practice in Education and Religion* (New York: Harper and Brothers, 1951, 1957); J. D. Butler, *Idealism in Education* (New York:Harper & Row, 1966).

is not material; that is, it is spiritual.[3] It must be such since it does not occupy space, has no weight, and has no dimension. The mind contains only ideas which themselves are immaterial. Further, mind cannot come from matter since matter cannot produce a form of being higher than itself. Consequently, mind must be derived from mind. The individual mind which each person possesses must be the product of an infinite spirit (God or the Absolute). The material body might well be a product of evolution, but the mind cannot be evolved from matter. In fact, the process of evolution is guided by the infinite mind since matter itself cannot be the cause of the purposiveness detected in evolving organisms.

Does the idealist equate the mind of each person with the mind of God? It seems not. God is infinite spirit; man's mind is finite spirit. Thus both are spiritual beings, but one is infinitely superior to the other.

What powers does mind possess? Its most important power is thought since, as Butler maintains, Descartes' dictum "I think therefore I am" is the first step toward all knowledge.[4] It is the mind that knows - not the body. Like Plato, Aristotle, and all conservatives, the idealist holds that the student's intellect is of the greatest concern to the teacher. All activities worthy of the name education somehow must be associated with the intellectual powers of the educand, rather than with purely biological functions.

Free will is a second power of mind. The idealist insists that freedom of choice is a sine qua non of being human. Man makes choices during his conscious moments. Some men even make the choice to deny the freedom of their will But this choice itself is a free choice. Thus those schools of modern psychology which explain human choice in terms of environmental or hereditary forces are flouting their own experience. Also, the presence of evil in the world demands that man have the power to choose between good and evil. Without freedom of choice there is no rational grounds for reward and punishment, no argument for personal responsibility. How can one be held accountable for actions which are determined by forces outside oneself? For the idealist, human existence makes no sense without freedom of the will.

---

[3]*Contemporary Idealism in America*, ed. C. T. Barrette (New York: The Macmillan Co., 1932), p. 36.

[4]Butler, *Four Philosophies, op.cit*, p.536.

Finally, if man is a spiritual self, he must possess the prerogative of immortality. Man's own reason tells him that death cannot be the end of his existence. The idea of personal immortality is intuitive (some say/ innate). Only matter is destructible since it is a creation of mind; but mind cannot destroy itself since spirit cannot perish. It makes no sense to the idealist to say that a spirit can die and all that the mind has accomplished will pass out of existence when the body dies.[5]

Horne provided a summary answer to our question "What is man?" when he said that "The learner is a finite person, growing, when properly educated, into the image of an infinite person, that his real origin is deity, that his nature is freedom and that his destiny is immortality.[6]

One final question remains which has been hotly debated between conservatives and liberals. It relates to the aristocratic versus egalitarian position taken by the advocates of each side. Indications are that the idealists align themselves with the conservatives on this issue. They argue that, although all men possess a certain basic equality by the very fact that they are human, it seems obvious that their minds are not all of equal stature. Some possess much more native ability than others; some have achieved far greater heights of creativity in areas of human endeavor; some names are worth remembering whereas others might better be forgotten. In the difficult task of education, it must be remembered that some pupils can pursue intellectual studies whereas others must be content to work with their hands. This does not mean that a democracy should not provide the opportunity for each pupil to develop his talents to their fullest extent. But it does mean that there is a hierarchy of minds, talents, artistic productions, school subjects, and occupations; one is not as noble or good as the other. There seems to be little doubt that the idealist has restated the conservative position of Plato in modern terms.[7]

---

[5]See *ibid.*, pp. 226-32; H. Horne, "An Idealistic Philosophy of Education," *Philosophies of Education*, 41st N.S.S.E. Yearbook, Part I (Chicago: Univ. Of Chicago Press, 1942), pp. 141-49.

[6]Horne, *op.cit.*, p. 155.

[7]See J. Royce, *Lectures on Modern Idealism* (New York: University Press, 1919),

How Do We Know?

The first objection the idealist raises to the liberal's answer to the question of how we arrive at knowledge is in making experience the primary mode of knowing. Since the idealist defines man in terms of mental activity, he must recognize a mode of knowing other than experience. Horne insisted that the mind goes beyond experience in many instances. For example, when the mind studies or examines the conditions of experience itself, it is going beyond experience. In fact, man would not even know that he "is experiencing" unless he had mental consciousness of it. Man constructs his view of the world outside himself. Thus experience does not determine what the mind knows. [8]

Other instances of knowledge, acquired prior to experience, are found in the work of early astronomers, who formulated theories about the origin of the earth, stars, and planets long before they were able to observe or experience the phenomena. By the use of reason, mathematicians, logicians, and metaphysicians have created ideas and systems of thought which transcend experience. The idealist points out that, in reality, even some of the speculative theories of the liberals go beyond ordinary experience. [9]

The idealist seems to go one step farther than merely asserting that reason is a way of acquiring knowledge or a mode of knowing; he considers it the primary mode of knowing. His views on the subject matter of the school and the methods of teaching (discussed on pp. 172f.) show the idealist's preference for the rational modes of knowing. To be sure, direct experience and learning by doing are admitted and even encouraged, but they do not hold the central position they did in Rousseau's and Dewey's theories of teaching and learning.

---

p. 325ff; H. Horne,*The Democratic Philosophy of Education*(New York: The Macmillan Co., 1932),Chs. XIX, XX; R. Lodge,*Philosophy of Education*(New York: Harper and Bros., 1947,) p. 125; T. Greene, "A Liberal Idealist Christian Philosophy of Education,'*Modern Philosophies and Education*, 54th N.S.S.E. Yearbook, Part I (Chicago: Univ. of Chicago Press, 1955), pp. 128-30.

[8]Butler,*Four philosophies, op.cit*, p.195.

[9]Horne, *The Democraici Philosophy of Education, op.cit* pp. 184-86.

Yet another mode of knowing, recognized by some idealists, is called intuition. Some thinkers regard intuition as a power of reason and therefore do not consider it a special mode. Others look upon it as a special power of the mind to acquire knowledge by immediate insight or awareness.

Since most idealists hold some belief in God or an Absolute Spirit, faith, or revelation, also is admitted as a mode of knowing. Included in this way of knowing are the revelations of the Bible and other source books of faith and any immediate revelations which the Infinite Spirit might wish to convey to an individual mind or a group of people. One common form of this belief in direct revelation of God to man is found in Christian mysticism as well as in many Oriental religions. This latter kind of knowledge is called infused and is therefore different from the revelation of the Bible.

It was noted in Chapter VI that Dewey held that all knowledge-seeking activities were initiated by a problematic situation which arose to disrupt the organism's harmony with itself or its surroundings. In other words, if there were no difficulties there would be no thinking and knowing. The idealist admits that difficulties do cause the mind to seek knowledge which will resolve them. But they insist that mind also has an innate desire to know and learn. Thus learning can take place without the motivation of immediate problems. As a result of this view the idealist curriculum contains many subjects and activities not directly related to the daily-life activities of the student or his problems. They might be highly academic in nature, calling for purely mental activity with no pragmatic purpose.

In summary, it should be noted that the idealist relies on similar modes of knowing proposed by the ancient, medieval, and humanistic conservatives. Reason, since it is rooted in mental activity, is the primary way of arriving at knowledge. Experience, faith, and intuition also are recognized as legitimate avenues to knowledge.

What Is Truth?

From the foregoing section, it is evident that the idealist must reject the liberal's notion that truth is a result of experience alone, even if that experience is consciously reflected upon by the knower. But, before stating just which truths are acceptable to the idealist, it might be well to explain his criterion for truth. Dewey had proposed that the consequences or results of a certain hypothesis, theory, or idea determine its truth. Thus, if one suggests that a shorter work week will solve the problem of unemployment and the test of experience shows that it does solve the problem, then this hypothesis is true or acceptable. The idealist does not deny that consequences or results affect the notion of truth. But, he proposes a higher criterion which goes beyond the consequence theory. The idealist calls this the coherence theory of truth. According to this notion, "truth is orderly and systematic, a web of closely intertwined relationships.[10]

Perhaps the best way of explaining the coherence theory is to apply it to a subject matter which all readers know, mathematics. In order to construct a system of geometry, for example, one must begin with certain undefined elements (terms), such as line or point, whose fundamental properties are described by the postulates (axioms - assumptions). A well-known postulate in geometry, the parallel postulate, affirms that through a point not on a line one and only one line parallel to the line can be drawn. A mathematical system also uses definitions based on the undefined elements and non-technical terms to describe further elements of the system. From the undefined elements, postulates, and definitions many theorems are proved. If a proposition contradicts either one of the postulates, a definition, or some theorem, the proposition cannot be a theorem in the system. The presence of the inconsistency indicates that an error has occurred and that particular proposition does not fit the system.

The idealist applies the coherence theory of truth to all knowledge which can be acquired about the physical, social, and transempirical universe. Every experience. every problem must be viewed in terms of the unitary whole. Knowledge arrived at in piecemeal fashion is likely to be false because it is not acquired in relation to other knowledge. For example, one might make certain statements about morals which, when taken singly, appear to be true, reasonable, and sound, but, when put together, reveal inconsistencies. Obviously, then, some of the statements are false. Or one's moral insight might provide the answer to questions of right and wrong, which perceives the unity or consistency in human behavior. Similarly, in judging a piece of art one will apply the intuitive (rational) criteria of harmony and unity to determine the aesthetic quality of the work.[11]

Underlying the idealist theory of truth, is the well-known principle of contradiction, which has been accepted as "self-evident" by conservative philosophers throughout the ages. For the idealist, the principle of contradiction not only is the basis for logical reasoning, but it is a

---

[10]Butler,*Four Philosophies, op.cit*, p. 198.

[11]See pp. 169-71 in this volume.

characteristic of reality.[12] Clearly then, deductive reasoning plays a central role in the idealistic theory of truth. The reader w will recall that deductive reasoning results in necessary truths. Conservative philosophers have attached the note of certainty, immutability, and absoluteness to such truths. So, too, the idealist affirms that the truths of reason have the characteristic of immutability.

Are all forms of knowledge changeless or are there some "relative truths" in the idealist system of thought? It appears that this philosophy admits the possibility of both relative and immutable truths First of all, the world is not viewed by most idealists as finished or closed. Changes are taking place in both the physical and social realms. Therefore, much of our knowledge about the world is incomplete and tentative. The history of science provides ample evidence for the mutability of many truths. Furthermore, as the human race acquires greater understanding of itself and the world it will modify many of its beliefs. [13]

One point must be kept in mind, however, in order to understand the idealist notion of truth. The truths of reason, revelation, experience, and intuition cannot contradict one another. The truths arrived at by these various means must form a coherent thought system. The idealist's penchant for consistency does not permit him to countenance the idea that a truth from revelation might contradict one from reason or experience and that both will be true. His convictions about the non-contradictory construction of the universe would, of course, prevent this.

In summary, the idealist believes that coherence is the criterion of truth; that some truths are absolute and immutable while other and lesser truths are relative and changing that revelation, reason, experience, and intuition provide truths of concern to human existence; that truths constitute a thought system free from internal contradictions.

What Is Good?

The idealist's answer to the question of what is good is implicit in the preceding discussion. Since the idealist rejects the consequence theory of

---

[12]In its rudimentary form it asserts that something cannot be and not be at the same time. For example, it is inconsistent to claim that you exist and do not exist.

[13]See Greene, *op.cit.*, pp 108-10; Horne, *The Democratic Philosophy of Education, op.cit*, pp. 483-90.

truth (because he makes a distinction between the circumstances of a moral action and the moral value of the action), he must reject the natural consequence theory of morality. The pragmatic view which holds that human behavior is to be judged in terms of its consequences can never satisfy the idealist's demand for consistency. He cannot brook the notion that the criteria for good and beauty are so flexible that the values of one generation might become "evils" for succeeding generations - there must be something permanent from which values can be derived and to which they can be anchored in a changing world. This meeting point, for the idealist, is human nature itself since man's mind enables him to determine what these values are. Horne looked upon certain values as fundamental - health, character, social justice, skill, art, love, knowledge, philosophy, and religion. These do not have to be tested in experience, they are rooted in human existence. Whether man finds them useful or not is beside the point. Man *accepts* these values because his rational powers locate them in his own nature; they are not considered values simply because they are acceptable to man. The idealist does not affirm that the values just mentioned exist in a world apart from the activities of man. On the contrary, if there were no minds, selves, or persons to possess and enjoy values, one could not speak of values at all, but since persons do exist there are values.[14]

Why do men hold the same fundamental goods if they do not exist independent of him? Kant, speaking for many idealists, affirmed that there is an inborn moral sense in man's mind (expressed in the categorical imperative) which commands him to do what is right and avoid what is evil. This moral sense for doing good and avoiding evil is just as much a part of man's makeup as seeing, feeling, or thinking - without it one would not be human. Man can rely on this internal power to tell him what is right and wrong just as he can rely on his senses to tell him that the sun is shining or that ice is cold. There are instances, however, in which the choice between right and wrong is difficult to determine. When in doubt, ask yourself if under similar circumstances you would want every other person to act in the same manner as you are acting (or proposing to act). Follow the rule of conduct which you want every other person to follow. Grant to others the same rights and privileges which you desire for yourself. If you follow this maxim you cannot treat the other persons as means to an end, especially not

[14]See Horne, "An Idealistic Philosophy of Education," *op.cit.*, pp. 182ff.; Butler, *FourPhilosophies, op.cit*, pp. 206-9.

as means to one's own selfish ends. Generally stated, then, Kant's fundamental criterion of good and evil is "So act that the maxim of your deed may stand as universal moral law." Kant believed the Ten Commandments of the Hebrew-Christian tradition contained the guide to moral behavior since they expressed the content of the categorical imperative.[15] That Kant and other idealists point to the Decalogue as the best expression of the categorical imperative also indicates their feeling that all human values are but temporal manifestations of an eternal order. These eternal values, are rooted in the existence of a changeless Supreme Being.

Such a code of morality does not allow for changes in the fundamental guides to behavior - these are immutable. Minor adaptations which are made to meet changing social situations do not involve a change in the principles. Thus the application of the principles of social justice in primitive societies will vary somewhat from their application in complex industrial societies, but the principles applying to both groups are the same.

The educational import of this view of morality is evident in the conservative curriculum and aims advocated by the idealist. The cultural heritage is transmitted to students simply because it contains the eternal values which are not to be abandoned in spite of changing times.

Although the idealist places great emphasis on the moral powers of man, aesthetic intuition and perception are not slighted. In fact the fine arts (aesthetic values) have a prominent place in his philosophical and educational systems. He disagrees with Spencer's hierarchy of educational aims which places the study and appreciation of art at the bottom of the list and also Dewey's failure to give the arts a more significant role in his educational scheme.

What does art portray for the idealist? Is the art work supposed to be a replica or representation of an object? Artistic productions should be the portrayal of an idea, not an object. The person who paints a tree that looks exactly like the tree in his back yard might do better by taking a photograph of the tree. The true artist, on the other hand, will place the abstract idea of tree on his canvas. The painting will contain the essential elements of what the mind conceives of as a tree. The same should be true of sculpture; that is, it is more important that an ideas is conveyed than that a statue represents an object.

---

[15]See A. E. Avey, *Handbook of History of Philosophy* (New York: Barnes & Noble, 1954), pp. 168ff.

idealistic conception of art since they are idea-centered. It is not the physical movements of the dancer which make his actions artistic, rather, it is the ideas which the movements convey that make the dance an artistic activity. Likewise, literary masterpieces are not mere collections of words that make sense, but consist in harmonious language which convey the loftiest ideas of the mind. Drama combines the elements of literature and an overt action in an attempt to convey abstract ideas.

Finally, music is the art form which divorces itself completely from the world of things. Although some musical compositions have words, these are not essential to the art form. One listening to Mendelssohn's *Spring Song* can conjure up the ideas of blossoming trees, babbling brooks, blue skies dotted with fluffy clouds, and a host of other ideas. Many emotional responses, such as sadness, joy, loneliness, and a feeling of fresh life, might come from the same selection. There is no limit to the ideas and emotional responses which music can bring to the artist and the listener. But none of these are tied to any specific object in nature.[16]

It might appear that the idealist could consider any drawing or painting, any writing or drama, or any musical composition a piece of art. Such is not the case. Recall that the idealist insists that the touchstone of truth is coherence and consistency. Thus any product of the human mind which lays claim to being artistic must possess unity or coherence, it must be free of internal contradictions. For example, a drama in which the minor characters dominate the stage would represent an internal inconsistency, or a poem which is inconsistent in its use of meter violates the same principle. A corollary of this first criterion is that of harmony. The necessity for harmony is obvious in music, but it also must be characteristic of all other art forms. A short story or poem which lacks harmony is just as deficient in artistic quality as a musical selection which is not harmonious.

Art work, then must meet at least two criteria: unity and harmony. Other criteria are proposed by idealists, but they, too, are rational criteria - they are the conditions which the mind imposes upon its own products. In other words, the criteria for art do not come from the world of objects and things but from the mind. Obviously, not every work which claims to be artistic can be considered such. Also implied is a hierarchy of art works. For example, Shakespeare's plays are better than Albee's *American Dream*. In Albee's drama absurdity constitutes the very form of the production. There is no connection between scenes and at times no connection between the

---

[16]See Butler, *Four Philosophies, op.cit*, pp. 212ff.

lines of the actors who speak in sequence. It is the school's responsibility to instruct the learner, not only in the production and appreciation of fine art, but also in discrimination between the better and lesser art. The ideal school cannot content itself with presenting everything to the student which claims to be artistic; it must present the best exemplars of the fine arts, the best products of the human mind. Some art works are eternal, others are temporary and not worthy of the pupil's time.

In summary, the essential points in the idealist's answer to the question "What is good?" are as follows: (1) All values are rooted in man's spiritual nature and are derived ultimately from eternal values. (2) The fundamental values by which man lives are immutable. (3) The command to do good and avoid evil is just as innate in man as thinking or reasoning. (4) The Ten Commandments of the Hebrew-Christian tradition offer the best expression of human and eternal values. (5) Art is a portrayal of the world of ideas rather than the world of things. (6) Unity and harmony are the two most fundamental criteria for judging art. (7) The school bears the responsibility for giving the student a harmonious set of values for guiding his moral, spiritual, and aesthetic life.

What Is the Purpose of the School?

Idealists speak of self-realization as the ultimate aim of education. But achievement of this aim is the work of a lifetime and a result of the combined efforts of the home, church, school, and other educational agencies. Also, for the Christian idealist this aim includes ultimate union with God. Since the individual cannot achieve self-realization without being joined in some social unity, certain social purposes are implied in the aim of education in general. Certainly, no idealist expects the school to be all things to all men. He does believe, however, that the school has more responsibility in some areas than in others in achieving the twin aims of individual and social betterment. Theodore Greene clarifies this priority of functions when he affirms that some overlapping of purposes is bound to happen between the various educational agencies. But he insists that the school must never become an arm of government, it must never assume the family's role in meeting the physical, emotional, and spiritual needs of the child. Rather he demands that the school concentrate on what it is qualified to do, "the preservation, dissemination and extension of man's knowledge of himself and his total environment .... the school is the only institution whose *primary* responsibility is scholarship and education, the pursuit of knowledge and the *cultivation of the mind.*" [17]

Greene and other idealists contend that even though the school's primary responsibility is cultivation of mind and pursuit of knowledge, they cannot agree with the narrow intellectualism of some conservatives. Simply because man forms an organic unit, the school cannot overlook the senses, imagination, will, and emotions - these are part of man's total being. Cultivation of mind and scholarly activities cannot be carried on effectively without proper attention being given to the total behavioral pattern of the educand. It appears that the idealist does not object to the school's attempting to develop physical fitness, social efficiency, and vocational competence as long as these endeavors do not displace the primary objectives of the school. So to some extent, at least, the idealist is in considerable agreement with the liberals. On one point, however, Horne was critical of the liberalism of Rousseau, Herbart, Spencer, and Dewey. Each of these theorists, he claimed, slighted the highest element in man, the spiritual mind.[18]

The succeeding sections on What should be taught?" and "How should one teach?" will show how the idealist achieves the primary and secondary purposes of the school and how he modifies the intellectualism of some conservative educational theorists.

What Should Be Taught?

The idealist qualifies his answer to this question by asserting that the learner and the teacher are more important in the educative process than the curriculum. But, both the learner and the teacher need a curriculum - the learner must have something to learn and the teacher, something to teach.

How does one determine what is worth learning and teaching? Horne suggests that the criteria for selection of curricular content should be (1) the abilities and needs of the learner, (2) the requirements of society, and (3) the nature of the universe in which we live. Meeting the student's needs calls for work in the sciences (knowing), arts (feeling), and the practical arts (doing or willing). Physics, chemistry, biology, sociology, and similar courses give the student the knowledge he needs about himself and the universe. Knowledge and appreciation of music, drama, literature, and the

---

[17]Greene, *op.cit.*, pp. 116ff.

[18]Horne, "An Idealistic Philosophy of Education," *op.cit.*, pp. 186-91.

like assist man to make a proper emotional adjustment to the world around him. Finally, vocational education provides him with the skills necessary to maintain his own life as well as to become a productive member of society.[19]

Even though this curriculum is heavily weighted with traditional subject matter and the fine arts, the idealist has made at least one concession to the liberals, namely, granting vocational education some place in the course of study. But Horne disagrees with Dewey and other liberals who equated practical and intellectual studies. For the idealist the intellectual studies are primary because they are concerned with changeless essences, universals, and concepts. The world of pure thought characterized by timelessness is more worthy of study than that of practical activities.[20] Greene, who also argues for the inclusion of vocational training, athletics, club activities, and the like in the curriculum does not place them on an equal footing with the intellectual disciplines; they are necessary to bring balance into a well-rounded education. On the other hand he insists that the intellectual disciplines are not to be considered impractical or designed for the leisure class. On the contrary, he feels that the intellectual subjects are most useful, not only for the future scientist, leader, and scholar, but for every citizen of a democracy.

The disciplines or subject-matter areas which Greene feels all men should have to live a full life are the (1) formal, (2) factual, (3) normative, and (4) synoptic disciplines. The formal disciplines include the study of correct thinking, logic and mathematics, and the vernacular and foreign languages. The natural, social, and behavioral sciences constitute the core subjects of the factual disciplines. The normative disciplines include the study of morals, the fine arts, and religion. History, theology, and philosophy are classified as the synoptic disciplines since they unify all of man's knowledge and experience. [21] Of course, these subjects will be spread out over the years of formal education, and some adjustment must be made to meet differences in ability levels among students. Not all students will be able to cover each and every subject to its culmination. Some will never be able to go beyond the elementary level of any subject; others will attain the heights of scholarship in one or several of the areas.

---

[19]See *ibid.*, pp. 158-64; Greene *op.cit.*, pp. 118-20.

[20]Horne, *The Democratic Philosophy of education op.cit.*, pp. 366-68.

[21]Greene, *op.cit.*, pp. 118-19, 121-23.

It is worth noting that unlike the curriculum of Spencer and Dewey, the general education program of Horne and Greene is not *immediately* useful or aimed at producing social efficiency or preparation for citizenship. The idealist may argue that these latter areas are integral parts of the educational whole. However, some parts are of smaller and lesser importance than others. There seems to be little doubt that in the idealist curriculum, the intellectual disciplines (formal, factual, and synoptic) make up the largest segment. Even the normative disciplines, ethics, aesthetics, and religion, are approached chiefly as cognitive activities.[22]

In most respects, then, the idealistic curriculum follows the lines of pre-Deweyan conservatism. As in the Platonic and humanistic curriculum, character formation, personality development, physical fitness, and the like are integrated into the curriculum as necessary but *secondary* elements.

How Should One Teach?

The idealist agrees with the conservatives when he asserts that method is a way of doing things and is something different from the things to be done. Dewey objected to this dualism of method versus subject matter and argued for the identity of the two. The idealist, then, is always willing to try "new" methods, if he feels they will enable him better to teach the pupils the subject matter. Therefore, he makes no special plea for the methods of the conservative school. Horne feels that it is not whether a method is traditional or progressive that makes it good. Rather the age, maturity, and interest of the pupils, class size, subject matter, and purpose of the lesson will determine the choice of method.

One consideration, however, does seem very important in the idealist choice of method, namely, the extent to which the method assists the student in cultivating his own mental powers. Socratic method (questioning and discussion) is one of the oldest and most esteemed teaching methods, with its origin in idealism. In fact, the Socratic method affords the key to selection of method according to the idealist. All good teaching methods will actively engage the mental powers of the student; any method or technique which fails to activate the student's mind defeats the primary aim of education.[23]

---

[22]See Butler, *Four Philosophies, op.cit.,* pp. 254-58; Horne, "An Idealistic Philosophy of Education,"*op.cit.,* pp. 186ff.

[23]Horne, "An Idealistic Philosophy of Education," *op.cit.,* pp. 164-72; Butler, *Four*

Like the great idealist of early Christianity, St. Augustine, the modern idealist is more concerned with the role of the teacher as a person in the educative process than he is with teaching methods or techniques. (One of St. Augustine's outstanding educational treatises is The Teacher.) Butler, summarizing the thinking of the idealists, lists the following characteristics of the ideal teacher.

(1) The teacher should personify the world of ideas and ideals for his students.

(2) The teacher must possess a thorough understanding of the nature of his pupils. Unless he recognizes the central function of mind in the total personality of the educand, the teacher cannot perform the duties proper to his position.

(3) The teacher must be fully trained in the professional aspects of his job. The idealist does not accept the dictum that "teachers are born, not made." He needs professional training just as the doctor, lawyer, and clergyman need it.

(4) The teacher must be a model to his pupils. He must be worthy of their admiration and respect. A teacher who has to force his pupils to respect him by using threats and punishment lacks the personality traits of the good teacher.

(5) It follows, then, that the pupil-teacher relationship should be characterized by friendliness rather than by a master-slave relationship.

(6) The personality traits and the professional training of the teacher should enable him to enkindle in the student an ardent desire to learn. students to live the full life of the spirit. In this aspect of the educative process, the teacher cooperates with God in perfecting his charges' spiritual faculties and achieving final union with the Infinite.

(8) The teacher must know and appreciate the subject matter which he teaches; he must continue learning more about his subject; he must be able to communicate his subject to his students, or, better, he should be the expert intermediary between the learner's mind and the subject matter.

(9) The teacher should be an advocate of democratic living and the general progress of the people. He must do more than preach democracy and progress; he must exemplify both in the classroom. (Other idealists believe that forms of government other than democracy are compatible with Idealism.)

(10) Finally, a good teacher gradually will de-emphasize his own role in

---

*Philosophies, op.cit.*pp. 258-61; Lodge, *op. cit.,*pp. 256-62.

the learning process. He will rejoice in the student's gradual assumption of responsibility for learning. As the student develops the abilities within him toward their complete fulfillment, the teacher will decrease his direct influence on the student. Negatively stated, this means that the teacher will not interfere with the student's drive toward self-realization.[24]

Other aspects of the teacher's role in the educative process such as maintaining discipline will be discussed in succeeding sections of this chapter.

How Should Pupils Be Evaluated?

Even though the idealist's primary concern is with mental functions and ideas, he does not limit evaluation of pupil progress exclusively to testing for knowledge of subject matter. In fact, some idealists, such as Lodge, assert that this objective of evaluation has been overemphasized. He suggests techniques of evaluation which will measure the subjective aspects of the development of mental power. He argues that "things are as they are perceived by the knower" and, consequently, factual items of the purely objective type fail to take this important factor into consideration. Thus the testing procedures which Thorndike and other advocates of the "science of measurement" proposed actually violate the nature of the learner.

In place of objective measures of achievement, the idealist recommends measuring instruments which will bring out the rational elements of the student's mental processes, such as ability to organize, logical consistency, and deductive power. Thus when a teacher gives an examination he will pose questions which will demand the use of all the resources at the student's disposal. Obviously, test items with a simple true or false answer, or those which call for a single word or phrase response, are worthless, simply because they do not test the student's full mental powers. Unless the student can use such piecemeal knowledge within the context of the discussion of a whole situation or problem, it is meaningless.

Perhaps an example will clarify this notion of evaluation in terms of rational *wholes* rather than of isolated facts or parts. A student may be able to respond correctly to dozens of specific objective items about Shakespeare's Hamlet. He may know all the names, places, and sequence of events within the play. He may be able to give a definition of every word used. But all of this specific knowledge of the play gives the teacher

---

[24]Butler, *Four Philosophies, op.cit.,*pp. 240-43.

absolutely no insight into the student's grasp of the momentous ideas which this masterpiece purports to convey.

It seems there can be no purely objective criterion in this approach to evaluation in spite of the idealist's contention that there are authentic truths and values. The student should be able to incorporate these truths and values into his responses to general questions of the "discuss" or "explain and evaluate" type. These will be judged in terms of originality of expression, completeness, clarity, unity, profundity, and vitality. Only an essay or oral examination will provide the opportunity for the student to display these mental qualities. Objective, short-answer examinations can be used, at best, as auxiliary devices with a very limited function upon which only minor emphasis can be placed.

If one objects to the lack of objectivity of such examination procedures and the resultant subjectivity in grading by the examiner, the idealist will admit that his evaluation is truly subjective. But, he counters that this is as it should be since the examiner is trying to gain insight into the workings of the student's mind. An essay by a student will give the examiner the opportunity to judge the student's total mental powers as evidenced by vigorous expression, penetrating insight, mental creativity and total mental growth. Admittedly, these are subjective, both on the part of the examiner and the examinee.

The idealist will agree that there may be a relatively high correlation between the results of the standardized and teacher-made objective and short-answer tests currently in use and his own subjective tests. But he warns that such "objective" measures can never reach the heart of true mental power.

Even though the idealist is concerned primarily with determining the mental development of the educand, he avers that other factors are to be considered in the overall evaluation of the pupil. Thus, physical and moral growth are to be assessed by the means available to the educator. Reports to parents and students on these aspects of the educative process are important to the success of any school program.[25]

How Are Freedom and Discipline to Be Harmonized?

In answering this question, the idealist is cognizant of the fact that

---

[25]See Lodge, *op. cit., pp.* 275-79.

existing political and social conditions will have a significant effect on the relationship of freedom and discipline. Thus one can expect to find less pupil freedom and more teacher-centered discipline in an autocratic society. The converse will be noted in democratic societies. Nevertheless, the idealist maintains that one's view of the nature of man and society will suggest certain guidelines for harmonizing these two factors.

For the idealist, man's spiritual nature is free; i.e., he possesses freedom of the will. On the other hand, man is an integral part of society. As are all other aspects of reality, an ideal society is characterized by unity or cohesion. Clearly, then, the individual is not free in the absolute sense. So long as he is with others (and this is generally the case in school) his freedom is limited by their very presence. Consequently, one of the responsibilities which the educator cannot shirk is disciplining the immature mind for living harmoniously in society. the idealist grants that this adjustment of the individual to society could take place by granting the young all the freedom they want. Eventually the hard knock of live would "socialize' them. But, since insufficient time to achieve this end is available in the years of compulsory education, the external control of the teacher and other authorities, is the most practicable means of attaining and maintaining discipline in the classroom Horne, for example. points to the educational value of obedience, self-denial, and recognition of authority as essentials in the discipline of youth.[26]

Greene also contends that discipline can be maintained without violating the individual's innate spontaneity. Therefore, he distinguishes regimentation, which produces robots, from discipline, which is necessary to prevent social and personal anarchy. Proper discipline will lead the young from a state if immaturity where external control is necessary, to one of maturity where internal control by the person becomes the guide.[27]

Butler adds yet another consideration to the problem of discipline, viz., its relationship to interest and effort. He views interest as the natural attraction of the learner for a certain subject or activity. Thus no external motivation by the teacher, or even by the student, is necessary to concentrate on the task at hand. Effort implies some conscious endeavor on the student's part to perform a task in which he has insufficient interest. Discipline involves action by an external authority to prod the pupil to learn

---

[26]Horne, *The Democratic Philosophy of Education* p. 174.

[27]Greene, *op.cit.*, pp. 130ff.

the assigned materials. And, Butler concludes, all three are necessary to maintain a proper learning atmosphere in the school.[28]

OTHER NEO-CONSERVATIVES

The idealistic reaction against Dewey's liberalism is readily recognized as deriving from a single philosophical point of view. Furthermore, the advocates of this position usually identify themselves as idealists, which is most helpful in predicting their stand on the issues discussed in this text. But the critics of liberalism we are about to consider cannot be as easily categorized as they belong to various groups. First, as mentioned in the introductory paragraphs of this chapter, some of them are merely critics of Dewey and his followers. These critics, who often are representatives of the academic disciplines in universities and colleges, usually are not schooled in philosophy or philosophy of education. Others are not associated with educational institutions at all, but enter the arena of educational debate from other fields such as business, the military, and journalism. Usually, these people do not treat the questions from a philosophical base at all, but are content to concentrate their fire on certain educational practices which they dislike.

Second, some of the thinkers discussed in this section, such as Broudy, Wild, Adler, Bell, and Hutchins, have developed systematic philosophies of education. From these thinkers one can expect answers, grounded in philosophy, to the fundamental questions which have been posed throughout this book.

Third, to complicate the puzzle even more, some of the neo-conservatives are representatives of various religious groups, whereas others are secularists, or at least do not bring religious issues into the educational debate.

In spite of these many differences in the background of the new conservatives, some common beliefs can be detected. These basic agreements will be pointed up, and, where it seems necessary, fundamental differences in their points of view will be noted.

---

[28]Butler, *Four Philosophies, op.cit.,*pp. 247-50.

What Is Man?

The new conservatives censure the liberals for neglecting intellectual training and supplanting it with social development and vocational training. Thus one point upon which they are in fundamental agreement about man's nature is that, for educational purposes at least, man possesses an intellect, or mind, distinguishable from his body. Rationality is the essential property of mind and the one to which educators must devote their major efforts. Therefore, although not all the neo-conservatives are Aristotelians, they accept his definition of man as a "rational animal." For them, rationality is not defined in terms of the human organism's adaptation to environment but rather as the use of intellectual powers.

Clifton Fadiman, in his plea for a return to the conservative education of the pre-Dewey era, views this issue as the crucial one in the conflict. He says the conservative's case for basic education in the intellectual disciplines clearly rests upon the assumption that man is both rational and animal. The liberal on the other hand, he says, who defines man solely in terms of biological and social adaptation, must defend the value of physical, social, and vocational education. [29]

Admiral Rickover, in his testimony before the House Appropriations Committee, appeals to the authority of Plato, Aristotle, and Whitehead and insists that the mind, or intellect, not the body, or emotions, is the school's central concern. Clearly, he is convinced that the school can concern itself with a mind which is distinguishable (for educational purposes) from the body and its functions. [30] He argues further that the possession of reasoning power is a universal characteristic of man. Primitive man and contemporary savages also have such powers of mind, albeit in less developed degrees. Nevertheless, it is the possession of reason which makes them human.

This explicit (or implicit) espousal of traditional mind-body dualism will be the key factor in determining the purpose of the school, the curriculum, and teaching methods. Adler, Hutchins, Maritain, M. Smith,

---

[29] See *The Case for Basic Education*, ed. J.D. Koerner (Boston: Little, Brown & Co., 1959), pp. 3ff; R. M. Hutchins, *Conflict in Education* (New York: Harper and Brothers, 1953), pp. 79ff.

[30] H. G. Rickover, *American Education - A National Failure* (New York: E. P. Dutton & Co., 1963), pp. 306-8. See also, M. Adler, *Paideia Proposal*, N.Y. Macmillan Co., 1982, pp. 42ff.

and many others base their criticisms of educational liberalism upon the belief that man's reason is the sole characteristic which distinguishes him from other animals.

A belief closely allied to that of the existence of man's mind is found in the notion that the human mind tends by nature to seek knowledge; that is, it has an innate drive and capacity to learn. The conservative will grant that indeterminate situations or problems do stimulate the mind to seek resolutions of difficulties. But, such stimulation is not essential since man, by nature, is a "knower - he will learn and come to know whether or not there are indeterminate situations.[31]

Not every learner, however, possesses the same capacity for learning or the same desire to learn. Conservatives agree that the existence of individual differences is a harsh reality which educators, students, and parents must recognize. All men are essentially equal since all are human beings. But not all are equally educable since some have the capacity and desire for learning whereas others do not. R. M. Hutchins states this position very bluntly when he says that education as *development of the mind* and education *for all* are incompatible.[32]

Liberal ideals such as those expressed in *Education for All American Youth* are doomed to failure since education is adjusted to youth rather than youth to being educated. Max Rafferty is even more thoroughgoing in his rejection of the liberal notion that all youth should be in school for twelve or more years. Such an egalitarian view of man, he avers, only encourages the "cult of the slob." Those who have neither the desire nor the ability to profit from a rigid mental diet, he says, should be "booted out." [33]

Arthur Bestor, although he favors free public education for all, demands that the intellectual elite be given special attention in the educational program. Like Plato, he believes that there are intellectual classes and that only the gifted class should be afforded the benefits of higher education. The average student should not be accommodated in the name of democracy.[34]

---

[31]*Ibid.*, p. 4.

[32]R. M. Hutchins, *Some Observations on American Education* (London: Cambridge Univ. Press, 1956), ppIXf.

[33]Max *Rafferty, Suffer Little Children* (New York: Devin-Adair Co., Signet Book, 1962),Ch. V; seeHutchins,*Conflict in education,op.cit.*,Ch. I.

[34]A. Bestor, "Educating the Gifted Child," *The New Republic* CXXXVI (March 4,

Along with the rejection of liberal egalitarianism, the conservative generally pleads for more recognition for freedom of individual choice. As just noted students must demonstrate the will to learn or they will not profit from the intellectual training offered in educational institutions. Broudy presents the arguments for human freedom of choice very succinctly by showing that, in spite of environmental (external) forces and basic (internal) drives, man still can select among possibilities - he possesses freedom of the will.[35] Individuals are the direct cause of some events; theirs is not merely a freedom to interact with others in the redirection of the course of events, but actually to be the cause of certain events.

Yet another belief which allies some of the neo-conservatives to the ancient, medieval, and Renaissance thinkers is their belief in a spiritual soul in man. This view is held by those with a religious orientation and encompasses many different creeds. Bell, John Wild, Adler, Hutchins, Molnar, Smith, some members of the Council for Basic Education, and a host of Catholic and Protestant educators comprise this group. For these philosophers, the activities of mind or intellect are rooted in man's immortal soul. Because of the Hebrew-Christian background of these theorists, generally they recognize that man's nature is tainted by evil tendencies. One of the purposes of school discipline is to assist youth in gaining control over their inclinations to idleness, mischief, and disobedience to authority. True freedom, it is argued, can never be achieved unless man has achieved control over the lower inclinations of his nature. [36]

The group under consideration thus seems to hold many of the same views about the nature of man as the conservatives of bygone days. It should be noted, however, that a number of today's neo-conservatives have incorporated the findings of the behavioral sciences into their educational theories. This is especially true of those who are associated with the areas of professional education. Harry Broudy, a "classical realist," and Breed, a "new realist" might be cited as examples of neo-conservatives who have

---

1957), 12-16; see H.G. Rickover, *Education and Freedom* (New York: E. P. Dutton & Co., 1959),Ch. VII.

[35]H. Broudy, *Building a Philosophy of education* (Englewood Cliffs, N.J.: Prentice-Hall, 1961), pp. 54-61.

[36]See, for example, J. Maritain, *Education at the Crossroads* (paperback ed.; New Haven, Conn.: Yale Univ. Press, 1960), p.95.

achieved an integration of conservative philosophy of education with modern behavioral science. [37]

The major objection of the new conservatism to the liberal doctrines about man lies in the latter's denial or neglect of the intellectual, rational capacity of human beings. Russell Kirk and Thomas Molnar cite this debunking of the intellect by the progressive liberals as the basic cause for the ills of modern education. [38]

How Do We Know?

A partial response to this question can be derived from the neo-conservative's criticism of what he dislikes in the liberal's answer. The point which he attacks most vehemently is the liberal's reliance on experience and science as the sole means of arriving at knowledge. When this belief is translated into the educational equivalent of learning by doing, most of the traditional disciplines no longer are relevant. Therefore, the conservative demands that reason be reinstated in its former place as the highest mode of knowing. For example, Hutchins says that since man is a rational being he can attain his highest perfection only through the exercise of his reason. Maritain, Mortimer Smith, Fadiman, and others express the same view when they demand a return to the solid intellectual disciplines which will take the student far above the level of experience proposed by the liberal as the center of the educational process. [39]

Which disciplines are truly intellectual? Those which entail abstraction from experience and activities beyond the range of ordinary experience. Thus, while agreeing to the inclusion in educational institutions of some nonacademic activities (physical and vocational education and social development), twentieth-century conservatives insist that these be given a subordinate place in the school program. Further, they insist that such

---

[37]See Broudy, *op.cit.,*; and R. Breed, "Education and the Realistic Outlook,"
Philosophies of Education, 41st N.S.S.E. Yearbook, Part I (Chicago: Univ.of Chicago Press, 1941),Ch. III.

[38]T. Molnar, *The Future of education* (New York: Fleet Publishing Co., 1961), pp.9-33.

[39]Maritain, *op.cit.*, pp. 91ff; Smith, *op.cit.,*p. 8f; Hutchins, *Conflict in education, op.cit.,*pp. 80f.;Koerner,*op.cit.,* pp. 9f.;Adler,*op.cit.,* pp. 236f.

activities be recognized for what they are and be classified as training or recreation, not education.[40]

It was previously noted that many conservatives also object to preeminence given to science as abode of knowing.[41] Does it follow that they do not recognize the empirical sciences or the scientific mode of knowing? On the contrary, most of them view the sciences as truly intellectual disciplines. Their objection to the liberal's view lies in the latter's refusal to admit the validity of other, chiefly the rational, modes of knowing. As long as the sciences do not displace classical and modern languages, literature, history, and other humanistic studies, the conservative has no objection to their presence in the curriculum. In fact, some of the twentieth-century opponents of educational liberalism, such as Rickover, Bestor, and Fuller, seem to consider the sciences the primary intellectual disciplines. So long as these disciplines are given systematic treatment in the classroom, they exercise the mental faculties of the students just as thoroughly as the literary studies of old.

Finally, those conservatives with a religious orientation also recognize the theological mode of knowing. In this respect, they follow the path of the medieval and early Christian thinkers and place their trust in the various sources of religious faith. Also, they argue that apparent conflicts between the empirical, rational, and theological modes of knowing can be resolved.[42]

The neo-conservative, then, recognizes the rational mode of knowing and places great emphasis upon it in the educative process. For some, the sciences are viewed as intellectual disciplines, abstract in nature, and calling for the exercise of reasoning power. Faith, too, is acknowledged by some modern conservatives as a means of acquiring knowledge.

What Is Truth?

Since the new conservatives recognize various ways of acquiring

---

[40]See Smith,*op.cit.*, pp. 8f.

[41]Hutchins,*Conflict in Education,* *op.cit.*,p. 71.

[42]See Maritain, *op.cit.*, p. 6; B. I. Bell, *Crises in Education* (New York: McGraw-Hill Book Co., 1949); Smith, *op.cit.*, Ch. IV; W. McGucken, "The Philosophy of Catholic Education,*Philosophies of education,* pp. 251-87.

knowledge, one can look for some distinctions in, or clarifications of, the term truth. Rational truths, for example, are viewed as universal. They possess immutability and finality which render them valid for all times and in all places. Hutchins and Adler argue that the universality of such truths is founded directly on the nature of the world and on the rational nature of man which itself is universal. [43]

The truths of reason for most conservatives are rooted in the first principles of metaphysics, such as the principles of contradiction and identity. From these first principles one can deduce a logically coherent set of beliefs about man and the universe which will remain constant despite the changes of time and place. Change itself can be interpreted in terms of changeless principles. Even the results of the empirical sciences which are admittedly mutable are attained by a logic that is itself changeless.

Molnar points out that a school program based on the liberal's philosophy of education, especially Dewey's, must degenerate into meaningless activities if for no other reason than its denial of any permanence to truth and values. If there are no permanent truths or values, then there is nothing to transmit to the young and education has no reason for existence.[44]

Even those conservatives with a scientific orientation oppose the liberal notion that truth is purely relative. Breed, for example, in his defense of modern conservatism, contends that there are quite permanent elements of experience and empirical science which are worth knowing. Also, he argues for the immutability of "facts" and the necessity for the student to learn at least those facts basic to an understanding of the physical and social universe.[45]

Conservatives admit, however, that man's mind is capable of discovering new truths. But, before the immature mind can launch out in search of new truths, it must master the essential ones contained in the cultural heritage. As Hutchins says all youth "should know how to read, write and figure and . . . they should understand the great philosophers, historians, scientists and artists." [46]

---

[43]Hutchins,*Conflict in Education, op.cit.*pp. 69-72;Adler,*op.cit.,*pp. 197-99.

[44]Molnasr,*op.cit.,*Ch. IV.

[45]Breed,*op.cit.,*pp. 96, 108-14, 116-18.

[46]Hutchins,*Conflict in Education, op.cit.*p. 88.

One might argue that Rickover is assuming the same point when he demands the establishment of a national curriculum and national standards for all pupils in all elementary and secondary schools. This universal curriculum will contain the basic truths upon which the future scientist, engineer, or politician will build his professional career as well as his personal and civic life.[47] Only when he has laid a solid foundation in school can he be expected to add to the edifice of knowledge as a mature adult.

Finally, those conservatives who accept faith and revelation as valid modes of knowing also regard the knowledge derived from these sources as truths worthy of man's highest concern. These truths take precedence over those of reason and experience in the educational process since they constitute the guide for man's attainment of his final end. Further, it is argued, there should be no contradiction between the truths derived from faith, reason, and science since all come from the Author of all truth. But, should there be some *apparent* conflict the truths of divine origin are to be trusted rather than those of unaided reason and science.[48]

What Is Good?

The critics of Dewey's liberalism are almost unanimous in their complaint that traditional values have been abandoned in favor of transitory and shallow ones. Russell Kirk points out that the twentieth-century liberal's goal of social efficiency or life-adjustment implies the denial of the value of the individual personality and the concomitant "goods" which accrue from the development of the mind of each child. He says, also, that Dewey detested the idea of perfecting the "inner personality" of the student because it implies social division or lack of communication with others. He attacks Dewey's contention that "spiritual culture is rotten" because it is conceived as something internal and exclusive for the individual.[49] For Kirk and other conservatives, the development of the individual as a spiritual, personal inner self is one of the highest goods to be sought in the educational process.

---

[47]Rickover,*American Education, op.cit.*,pp. 306-19.
[48]See Mc Gucken, *op.cit.,* pp. 252-58; Maritain, *op.cit.,* pp. 73f.; Bell, *op.cit.,*
     passim.

[49]See R. Kirk's Foreward to Molnar, *op.cit.,* pp. 11f. Kirk quotes from Dewey's
     Democracy and Education in this instance.

What are the other fundamental values or goods which the conservative wishes the school to promote? Like traditional philosophers he considers happiness as the final good for man. Also, as just mentioned, the development of the individual is an educational good which can be subsumed under the general notion of happiness. Justice, benevolence, temperance, fortitude, patriotism, and wisdom are fundamental goods acceptable to the twentieth-century conservative just as they were to his ancient and medieval forebears. But as will be noted in "What is the purpose of the school?" the conservative educator does not place the responsibility for students' living a virtuous life on the school; its primary responsibility is to transmit to the young a *Knowledge* and *understanding* of the traditional values by which man has lived throughout the ages.[50]

An important consideration for philosophy of education relates to the method the conservative uses for arriving at value. As previously indicated, reason is recognized as a primary mode of knowing, so too reason plays an important role in determining what is good. But whereas the function of reason in acquiring knowledge abstracts from particular cases to arrive at the universal or general, it never completely abstracts from concrete situations when it is concerned with deciding what is good. Thus the traditionalist holds that ethics (the science of the good) is a practical science whose aim is to lead man to the good life under the direction of reason or the intellect. But it is the same intellect which directs man's search for the good as well as his search for abstract knowledge. And in the final analysis it is reason which proposes that one course of action is good and another evil or that one is better than another.[51]

In addition to the natural goods which human beings grasp by reason and which are considered acceptable to most conservatives, those with a theological orientation hold many goods derived from faith and revelation. It is true that various religions may espouse different moral codes. Some, for example, consider dancing and drinking alcoholic beverages evil; others hold these as morally acceptable provided temperance is exercised. Some believe divorce to be evil; others find it acceptable under certain conditions. But, in spite of these differences in moral codes, all religious minded conservatives hold that faith and revelation provide positive guides for

---

[50]See V. Smith, *The School Examined* (Milwaukee: Bruce Publishing Co., 1960), pp. 186-96; Rickover,*Education and Freedom, op.cit.,* pp. 183ff.

[51]See V. Smith,*op.cit.,* pp. 183ff.

behavior.

As noted earlier, the conservative objects to the liberal's belief that good and evil are relative to time, place, and changing social conditions. Conservatives contend that the *fundamental values* by which man lives are immutable. This is so because man's nature does not change. Folkways and customs, they admit, will undergo changes, but those goods apprehended by reason as basic to man's nature will not change. Thus as long as man is man, the moral virtues of justice, temperance and the like will be good. Murder, stealing, fornication, lying, and similar behaviors will always be evil.

In summary, the conservative believes that happiness is the most basic good. But, in order to achieve happiness man must do good and avoid evil. To do good means to be just, temperate, benevolent, patriotic, and so forth. To avoid evil man must shun certain acts which are contrary to his rational nature. Further, the fundamental values by which man lives are immutable and absolute. Adaptations or reinterpretation might be made in fundamental values to suit social changes, but the principles of morality will remain constant. In other words, social customs and folkways will evolve, essential morality will not. [52]

Most neo-conservatives reveal little interest in aesthetics, and relating the beautiful to the good has not been a central concern for many of them. For example, the Council for Basic Education places art and music in the category of curriculum electives. Literature seems to be considered the chief medium in the educational program for developing aesthetic perception. More important to the conservative, perhaps, is the belief that the classics of literature contain the best of the cultural heritage. Rafferty defines a classic as a literary work which has stood the test of time and has been widely accepted by cultured people. The classics, he argues, should serve as the foundational materials for a literary program; contemporary works should be studied only after the classics have been examined. Further, contemporary literary works are to be evaluated as to their artistic value on the basis of traditional literary standards exemplified in the classics. [53]

The views expressed by Rafferty are similar to those of the founders of the Great Books movement in American education. These educators believe

---

[52]See *ibid.*, pp. 186-202; Broudy, *op.cit.,* pp. 254f; M. Adler, *A Dialectic of Morals* (Notre Dame, Ind.:Notre Dame Univ. Press, 1941);Maritain,*op.cit.,* pp. 93f.

[53]See "Interview of Max Rafferty," *Scholastic Teacher,* LXXXIII (September, 1963), 5-7f.

that certain great masterpieces of literature contain the basic knowledge of the cultural heritage which will serve as materials for cultivating the intellectual powers of the student.

Apart from this rather tangential approach to aesthetics most modern educational conservatives do little by way of proposing a theory of art. A notable exception to this general rule is found in the work of H. S. Broudy.[54] He argues that art actually provides different types of knowledge. For example, the artist who writes a novel or paints a picture about South American Indians has to know something about these people so that he can incorporate such knowledge in his art work. Also, he has to know the various techniques of presenting his subject even though his own technique may prove to be different from any of those he has studied. Then, there is the area of art history which contains knowledge in the same sense that American history does.

However, the crucial point for educational philosophy is whether art works themselves convey any knowledge. Broudy maintains they do, since (in his theory) the fine arts are classified as *areas of knowledge* to be included in the curriculum.[55] In what ways, then, do art works convey knowledge? In realistic literature, for example, the author may give a description of how people live although he uses fictional heroes and villains. Thus Pasternak's *Doctor Zhivago* portrays, in a very moving way, the trials and tribulations of the Russian people during and after the Communist revolution. In the same way a poem might give the reader a vivid picture of the coming of spring in Dixie. Or a musical selection might majestically convey the notion of a severe thunderstorm. In these examples the arts are systems of communication which can be learned just as the symbols of ordinary communication or those of mathematics can be learned. It is true that the learner may have to acquire some background knowledge about the setting of the art work in order to grasp its meaning. Thus to understand religious art one must know something about the "root metaphors" which undergird the art work.

A second sense in which art can be viewed as an area of knowledge suitable for inclusion in the curriculum lies in the treatment of the various aesthetic theories. These might be considered the legitimate subject matter

---

[54]H. Broudy, "The Structure of Knowledge in the Arts," *Education and the Structure of Knowledge*, ed. S.Elam (Chicago:Rand McNally & Co., 1964),Ch.III.

[55]See pp. 192f. in this volume.

of the philosophy of art.

A final way in which the arts are related to knowledge lies in the aesthetic experience. In this instance, perception rather than memory or reason is the significant factor; the symbols used give the meaning rather than simply referring to an object; the personal pleasure experienced is derived from the sensory qualities, the form, and the expressive properties rather than from the factual or systematic content of the work.[56]

The role of art criticism is not neglected in this theory of art since it is a very important aspect of art appreciation courses. This area involves all the other types of knowledge *about* art just mentioned, including aesthetic theory. One cannot be critical of art works if one knows little or nothing about them. Thus the kinds of knowledge one gets from works of art criticism are descriptions of the content and structure of the work under consideration, an evaluation of the artist's adherence to the principles of art to which he subscribes and a pointing up of failures on the part of the artist to achieve a certain effect.[57]

As intimated, education can play a very important role by assisting the young to get experience in appreciating art works as well as in trying their hand at producing them. Children can learn the various artistic media such as color, sound, word arrangement, or rhythm. They can master the principles of pattern, order, and design and apply the criteria of unity, contrast, harmony, form, and balance to their own art productions and those of others. The great masters of all ages can be presented both as models and as motivation for art appreciation and production.

Although Broudy holds that aesthetic experience is rooted in human nature, not all people can be artists. The majority of students will not get much beyond the stage of appreciating art. Nevertheless, the person who can never become an outstanding artist but yet appreciates art will transfer much of this artistic taste to his everyday living. His home, classroom, office, and wearing apparel will reflect "good taste." Without this aesthetic sense man is a little less human than he should be. Thus Broudy attempts to

---

[56]Broudy, "The Structure of Knowledge in the Arts," *op.cit.,* pp. 80-88. Broudy recognizes the problem of subjectivity in aesthetic experience and resolves it within his theory.

[57]*Ibid.,* p. 95. A similar classical realist view is found in V. Hamm, *The Pattern of Criticism* (Milwaukee: Bruce Publishing CO., 1960), Chs. I, IV, VI, VIII; V. Hamm, *Language, Truth, and Poetry*(Milwaukee: Marquette Univ. Press, 1960).

place art education in perspective in the entire school program. And while he does not demand for art the first place in the curriculum, he does insist that it have a place. [58]

What Is the Purpose of the School?

The new conservatives are in accord with their liberal opponents that the "whole child" needs developing. But, they counter, the school is only one of the agencies involved in the process. American education, they aver, is a national failure because of the liberal's insistence that the school must educate the whole child. How, for example, asks Mortimer Smith, can one possibly expect the school to develop salable skills, physical fitness, democratic citizenship qualities, habits for future family living, knowledge and skill as a consumer, and a host of other aims? Most of these tasks should be returned to their rightful place in the family or some community organization. But instead of doing this, each new re-evaluation of the school system finds the liberals saying that the school must do more for youth.[59]

R. M. Hutchins also wishes to relieve the school of its many non-educational tasks so it can concentrate on the development of the intellectual powers of the students. The moral, spiritual, social, and emotional aspects of man's behavior certainly are important, but the school has neither the time nor the right to involve itself in such matters. Physical fitness, social adjustment, and the like are worthy aims, indeed, but they cannot be achieved by the school without watering down the intellectual curriculum. In fact, Hutchins and other conservatives contend that the person who has undergone a rigid intellectual discipline - that is, one who has been taught at school to respect facts, reason, and logic, who feels at home in the world of ideas and abstract concepts - is the one who is best prepared to handle family, job, and civic responsibilities. [60]

What is the conservative's reaction to making the reform of society the

---

[58]Broudy, *Building A Philosophy of Education, op.cit.*Ch. IX.

[59]M. Smith, *op.cit.,* pp. 26-31; M. Smith, *The Diminished Mind* (Chicago: Henry Regnery Co., 1954),Chs. II, III.

[60]Hutchins, *Conflict in Education, op.cit.,* pp. 70-73. See Rickover, *American Education, op.cit.,* p. 23; McGucken, *op.cit.,* pp. 268f. Adler, *Paideia Proposal,* pp.15-36.

goal of the school? He seems solidly opposed to this reconstructionist goal for several reasons. First, he contends that it is the responsibility of adults, not children, to change the social order. Therefore, adult education, not the schooling of children, might be a legitimate means of achieving such a goal. Second, children would be the easy victims of propaganda because of their intellectual and emotional immaturity and inexperience. Third, the school would have no proper function or goal once the change in the social order had been achieved. Thus, if the goal was to change society from an individualistic, capitalistic one to a social democracy, the school would have no reason for existing once this goal had been realized. Finally, the school can do its part for the improvement of society by giving its clientele the intellectual training and knowledge they will need to solve social problems when they become adults. [61]

There seems to be little doubt, then, that for the neo-conservative the cultivation of the intellect by teaching the teachable subjects (cultural heritage) is the primary and almost exclusive purpose of the school. He concedes that emergencies might arise when the school is expected to assist other agencies. Thus the breakdown in the family structure which is evident in contemporary society might call for giving the school some responsibility for personal counseling until the family itself or some social agency can dispense this function. But educators must never permit parents or the community to saddle them with the myriad duties necessary to bring children to adulthood. The school can be successful only when it concentrates all its resources on its primary goal, the development of intellectual power, or, in Bestor's words, intellectual discipline.

What Should Be Taught?

It might be well to begin this section by pointing up the criticisms advanced by many neo-conservatives against what they consider the inadequacies of the liberal or progressive curriculum. First, they complain about the displacement of solids by adjustment courses and demand that all these frills either be eliminated from the curriculum or relegated to the extracurricular domain. By frills they usually mean such courses as driver training, child care, interior decorating, social grooming, and the like. Even if the student does not spend all his time on such activities, they distract him

---

[61]See Hutchins, *Conflict in education*, op. cit., CH.III; A. Bestor, Restoration of Learning (New York: Alfred AKnoopf, 1955), pp. 146-38.

from concentrating on the important subjects. [62]

A second objection voiced against the liberal curriculum is its excessive emphasis on current interests and problems. The conservative argues that the discussion of current political, social, and economic problems is only incidental to an understanding of these basic disciplines. Using contemporary problems as the central focus in subject matter tends to confuse the student as well as to flout the logical order of the subject matter. Also, this emphasis on contemporaneity fails to give the student a knowledge of what events preceded the present problem or what principles underlie the issue, which are essential to an understanding of it. Further, students' personal problems too often become the central focus of the problem-centered curriculum. As Bestor says, the purpose of the school is not to debate the controversial issues of the day or solve students' problem, but to present wideranging systematic knowledge. [63]

A third charge leveled against the program of the liberals is "vocationalism." Generally, conservatives believe that the inroads of vocationalism have destroyed the traditional notion of the school as an institution devoted to transmitting knowledge and developing the minds of the pupils. The major danger resulting from making vocational courses an integral part of the curriculum is that they might be viewed as the central or essential part of the school program.[64] Thus even those moderate conservatives who feel that specialized training should not be eliminated warn that it can never be "regarded as a substitute for general education." In other words, so long as vocational education is kept in proper perspective - subsidiary to the academic subjects - it may be given a place in the curriculum.[65]

---

[62]See M. Smith, *And Madly Teach, op.cit.,* pp. 29ff; Hutchins, *Some Observations on American Education, op.cit.,* p. 42; A. Lynd, *Quackery in the Public Schools* (Boston:Liile, Brown & Co., 1953), pp. 33-35.

[63]Bestor, *The Restoration of Learning, op.cit.,* pp. 125-38. Hutchins also rejects the notion of "immediate needs" as the criterion for selections of curricular content, see *Conflict in Education, op.ci*Ch. II.

[64]V. Smith,*op.cit.,* p. 90. Adler,*Paideia Proposal,* p. 35.

[65]W. C. Bagley, "Essentialism in Education," *N.E.A. Journal,* XXX (October, 19941), pp. 201-2; Broudy, Building a Philosophy of Education, op.ci*pp. 330f.*

Finally, many neo-conservatives are critical of the modern combinations of traditional subjects into packages such as language arts, social studies, and core curricula. Social studies and language arts, some say, "should be relegated to the scrap heap reserved for outworn clichés. . ." The core curriculum, too, is viewed as a "dissolved" curriculum which is bound to result in a neglect of all subjects umbrellaed under it. [67] Perhaps the fundamental reason for opposition to the broad areas approach is that the logical (or chronological for historical studies) order of each discipline is lost. Thus the student not only fails to learn the important content of each subject but also does not grasp the internal order of each.

To ensure the proper treatment of each subject, many new conservatives are appealing to the scholars from university departments in each subject-matter area to establish the content and sequence of their specialty for inclusion in the elementary and secondary curriculum. Quite a number of such programs are now in use in mathematics and the sciences. History, English, and other subject-matter fields are providing similar guidance to the elementary and secondary school curriculum-makers. In general none of these programs of study are determined by student needs and interests. Rather, they constitute a systematic presentation of each basic intellectual discipline.

It is not necessary for our purposes to list all the curricular patterns suggested by different conservatives. A few examples should suffice. On one end of the spectrum, the Council for Basic Education recommends going back to the pre-Deweyan curriculum. Thus the elementary school should teach reading (phonics), writing, arithmetic, spelling, grammar, elementary science, and the like. These should be taught and mastered as separate subjects, not as language arts, social studies, or adventures in living.

The secondary school curriculum should contain the following subjects as essential to a good high school curriculum: citizenship, American history, European and world history, geography, English composition and literature, mathematics   (algebra, geometry, trigonometry), biology, chemistry, physics, classical and modern languages. Art, music, speech, and other electives can be taken provided the student is able to handle them over and above the basic courses. [68] This is essentially the college preparatory

---

[67] Rafferty, *op. cit.*, pp. 26-44; W.C.Bagley, "An Essentialist Platform for the Advancement of American Education," *Educational Administration and Supervision*, XXIV (April, 1938), 244f.

[68] Koerner, *op.cit., passim.*

curriculum found in most preprogressive high schools and retained by many conservative high schools to this day. Notably absent from this listing are courses with a vocational orientation or those meeting the needs and interests of students and the adjustment aspects of living in modern society. Rather, the primary concern of such a curriculum is the transmission of knowledge and, indirectly, the development of intellectual power.

On the other end of the conservative spectrum one finds curricular proposals which do not simply go back to pre-Deweyan days but are grounded in a thoroughly reasoned philosophy of education. One such proposal is found in the work of Broudy and contains those areas of knowledge and those skills and habits necessary for all youth. Under areas of knowledge (for general education) are included such fields as (1) the symbolic tools of learning and thinking and communication-language (native and foreign), mathematics, and the fine arts; (2) the sciences-physics, chemistry, astronomy, geology, biology, psychology, and sociology, (3) the study of the past-historical and biographical materials; (4) the knowledge needed to cope with the future-the role of the applied sciences (e.g., medicine) in the modern world, the regulative fields of knowledge (political science, economics), and also such areas as education, journalism, and mass media; (5) integration of knowledge-ethical and aesthetic systems, giving the student knowledge and understanding of the different value systems which have guided men throughout the ages.

Undoubtedly this is a big order even when one views it in terms of twelve years of compulsory education. To encompass all of this knowledge in a program of general education not only calls for great organizational and methodological skill but also wise selection of the most important elements of each area and their proper placement at each grade level. Obviously, not all these areas can be covered to the satisfaction of specialists in each field or can all be treated at every grade level. Thus it is admitted that some areas cannot be taught as separate subjects but must be combined into general courses. Simply because separate subjects are combined does not mean that the treatment of the various bodies of knowledge will be unorderly or unsystematic. Finally, Broudy's curriculum for general education allows for problems courses in each of the areas of knowledge. Such courses can be effective, however, only when the student is relatively well-versed in the subject matter of that area, that is, near the end of the sequence of content courses.[69]

From this brief description of Broudy's curriculum for general education

---

[69] Broudy, *Building a Philosophy of Education, op. cit* Chs. XII, XIII

several points should be noted. The first, and perhaps the most important, is that its primary concern is the transmission of knowledge; second, wherever possible the logical, systematic presentation of each subject is to be preferred to other modes of giving knowledge. Third, vocational or specialized training must never take precedence over general education. In other words, the basic skills and knowledge (academic subjects) remain at the top in the hierarchy of curricular offerings. Finally, all other activities under school auspices such as clubs, social activities, hobby hours, and the like are considered extracurricular.

How Should One Teach?

The conservatives are generally quite critical of the natural method of teaching inaugurated by Rousseau and Pestalozzi and developed by Dewey and his followers. A few will admit that relating thought and action, as exemplified in the problem-solving and project methods, marks a forward step in teaching methodology.[70] But, they contend, the real value has been vitiated because liberals have regarded it as the sole criterion for judging the effectiveness of teaching-learning methods.

One aspect of modern methodology which is attacked quite vehemently is the liberal's devotion to learning by doing. Many conservatives see no sense whatsoever in having children spend endless hours reinventing things which could be learned in half an hour's reading. Furthermore, a child or young adult does not have to do or experience something to understand it. He can learn the meaning and implications of democratic government without having elections, and so forth, in the classroom. He can learn the essential ideas conveyed in Shakespeare's works without building model stages or acting out certain portions of his plays.

What the conservative is demanding is that teaching-learning methodology be freed from the philosophy of activism. Learning from systematic presentation by teachers and books not only will save the student untold hours of fruitless searching, but will give him an understanding of the logic of the subject matter itself. Learning by doing has its place, especially in laboratory courses, but it is by no means the best or the only method. Problems and projects should be introduced only after the student has mastered the fundamentals of the subject matter at hand.[71]

---

[70] See M. Smith, *And Madly Teach*, op. cit., p. 20.
[71] See Broudy, *Building a Philosophy of Education*, op. cit, pp. 326ff.; Rickover,
[71] *American Education, op. cit*, p. 100; Bestor, *op. cit*, pp. 125f.

Other aspects of progressive methodology also are criticized by the conservative. The democratic permissiveness of many pupil- or group-centered classrooms is censured frequently. Similar contempt is shown for the emphasis the liberal teacher places on pupil interaction as an essential ingredient of good classroom procedure. More will be said about these topics on following pages in the discussion of freedom and discipline.

Since the conservative disputes the efficacy of the "natural method" and other progressive methods, what does he suggest by way of teaching methods? In most instances, he demands a return to the methods used in the preprogressive schools. Thus lecture (or teacher) presentation and recitation by students on the material covered by the teacher or the assigned textbooks is often recommended. However, most conservatives are more concerned with the students learning the subject matter than they are with the methods and techniques the teacher uses to achieve this goal.

Broudy suggests several approaches a teacher might use to enable the learner to perceive, relate, and classify knowledge (achieve insight and mastery) in any given field. Socratic method, which relies on the question-answer technique, has been a very successful method for more than twenty centuries. The disputation, which gained prominence in the medieval schools, lends itself well to developing the deductive powers of the learner. Drill and memorization serve as means for mastering basic facts and skills needed to progress through any subject matter. The lecture method has a long history of success in conservative schools as a means of conveying information, insights, and understandings to students. Also mentioned is the prelection method of the Jesuits discussed in Chapter IV. Finally, Broudy suggests possible adaptations which the conservatives might make of the activity method.[72]

In general, the conservative demands more teacher control and dominance in the teaching-learning process. He might grant that modern scientific psychology (or even educational research) can be of assistance to the educator in improving older teaching methods and devising new ones.[73] But method should never take precedence over content. For this reason he is very critical of the emphasis placed on methods courses in teacher education institutions.

---

[72]See Broudy, *Building a Philosophy of Education, op. cit,* Ch. XIV.
[73]Bestor, *Restoration of Learning, op. cit,* p. 143.

How Should Pupils Be Evaluated?

The neo-conservative's answer to the question of pupil evaluation is quite simple: The pupil must be evaluated *rigorously* on the basis of what he knows and how he handles this knowledge.[74] It is high time, he contends, to put a halt to attempting to determine a student's social adjustment and the many other nonintellectual factors which have been of so much concern to the liberal. Since it is not the school's business to develop the whole child, educators should devote their evaluation efforts to academic achievement. As Rickover says, we cannot deny the importance of "high moral standards, of good character, of kindness, of humaneness, of ability to get along with fellow citizens," but first and foremost we must determine standards of intellectual excellence to be achieved by pupils in elementary and secondary schools.[75]

The conservative demands the reinstatement of high standards of achievement. Teachers and administrators must abandon the practice of continuous promotion and insist that students master the subject matter and intellectual skills of each grade before they are promoted.[76] Some conservatives even recommend that national standards be set up by scholars in each subject-matter area and that comprehensive examinations be administered on a nationwide basis. Such a testing program would enable educational authorities to grant diplomas according to the type of examination passed. In this way, a high school diploma, which today is absolutely meaningless, would come to have real significance. Whereas today the same high school diploma is granted to the student who has taken a solid academic course and to the one who has taken driver-training, wood shop, coeducational cooking, and a few watered-down academics, the new diplomas would differentiate the type of program completed and the level of achievement.

In order to determine whether the school is achieving its objectives or whether the student is progressing, conservatives argue that all examinations, whether designed for a single course in a subject or for comprehensive evaluation of a whole field, should measure several things. First, mastery of the essential facts and principles of the subject must be determined. Second, evidence must be secured about the student's mastery of the

---

[74] See Bagley, *op. cit*, pp. 244f.

[75] Rickover, *American Education, op. cit*, pp. 307f.

[76] Molnar, *op. cit*, pp. 93f.; Hutchins, *Some Observations on American Education, op. cit*, Ch. IV. Adler, *Paideira Proposal*, pp. 42-43.

intellectual skills and logic needed for understanding the discipline. Third, means must be devised for evaluating the overall mental development of the pupil as evidenced by his ability to analyze, organize, and synthesize. Symbolic skill will play an important part in this last phase of measurement. Therefore, a combination of objective and essay examinations (sometimes supplemented by oral tests) perhaps would be the best means of evaluating achievement.

From the point of view of philosophy of education, the significant aspect of the neo-conservative recommendations about evaluation consists in limiting it to academic achievement. Evaluation of achievement in the basic disciplines will yield the best measure of the pupil's intellectual development. The school should not be expected to determine the student's social efficiency, moral development, or physical fitness.

It should be noted, before closing this section on evaluation, that most twentieth-century conservatives do not offer specific models of examinations. They are content to advise that these examinations should be constructed by scholars and experts in the various academic disciplines rather than by "educationists" who know little or nothing about the fields. They contend that it is precisely because the educationists have taken over the measurement field that true standards have disappeared.

How Are Freedom and Discipline to Be Harmonized?

It should be mentioned at the outset that few conservatives demand that schools return to the harsh and inhumane discipline of the pre-liberal era. Mortimer Smith, for example, commends Rousseau, Pestalozzi, and Dewey for introducing humaneness in education, for recognizing the child as a human being who has every right to a happy and expressive life, even in school. But Smith and other conservatives believe that the liberals have gone too far in their worship of permissiveness and freedom.[77] However, later liberals, such as the reconstructionist, also reject the permissiveness of the child-centered school of the 1920's and 30's. In its place, they established the doctrine of democratic group control, which is just as unacceptable to the conservative as extreme permissiveness.

What the conservative is demanding in regard to pupil freedom and discipline is an educational environment where the pupil is under the

---

[77]M. Smith,*And Madly Teach, op. cit*, pp. 20, 49ff.;Maritain,*op. cit*, p. 33; Rafferty,*op. cit*, Ch. V; Rickover,*American Education, op. cit*, p. 103;Molnar, *op. cit*, pp. 13f., 143 note 3.

authority of his teachers rather than his own or that of his classmates. He objects to such practices as pupil-teaching planning, which gives the immature and uninformed pupils a voice in the choice of what is to be studied as well as in the control of their own classroom behavior.[78]

Another facet of the liberal's emphasis on pupil freedom to which the conservative objects is permitting the young to select those studies which are of interest to them. It is argued that children and adolescents are too immature to know what is best for their intellectual development. If left to their own devices they will take the easiest courses. Youngsters need the discipline of hard work and difficult subjects. Since they will not choose these freely, educators must require the basic subjects and, as Rickover says, use discipline to get the knowledge into their resistant little heads.[79]

Bernard I. Bell suggested another reason for the need for strict discipline in the classroom. He said that the naive liberal view that the child is innately good (or at least not inclined to evil) is false. Children, especially adolescents, are not little angels who can do no wrong. On the contrary, they will cause as much trouble as they can get away with. Since they are not disciplined at home, they resent any discipline at school. As one teacher told him, she left teaching because she could take it no longer; she could not bear being insulted every day by a pack of "impudent and unlicked cubs" whom she was not permitted to discipline because the progressive school administrators did not believe in discipline.[80]

In summary, the new conservatives are asking for enough external control or discipline so that students may be free from innate laziness and external distractions in their pursuit of knowledge. Second, only when the student has disciplined himself by the rigorous study of academic subjects will his mind be freed from error, emotionalism, and prejudice; only then will his mind be free to seek the truth. Third, overemphasis on cooperation and group consensus, even though they might achieve harmony in the classroom, is unacceptable as a means of discipline.

---

[78]This objection to the liberal view of freedom was voiced by W. Bagley in the 1930's and has been repeated often since that time. SBagley, *op. cit*, p. 251; Molnar, *op. cit*, Ch. VII; M. Smith *And Madly Teach, op. cit*, pp. 49-55.
[79]Rickover, *American Education, op. cit*, p. 120.
[80]Bell, *op. cit*, pp. 216ff.

CHAPTER SUMMARY

Twentieth-century educational conservatism is represented by two somewhat different, although not necessarily exclusive, approaches. The most publicized approach is one of criticism, chiefly of John Dewey and progressive education. The other consists in reasoned systems of educational philosophy most of which include an updating of conservatism in order to adapt it to modern times and incorporate the insights of the behavioral sciences. In many cases, the latter approach also contains a critical evaluation of liberal philosophical and educational doctrines.

The following points reflect the philosophical beliefs of the neoconservatives. Although man's activities cannot be divided into completely disconnected functions, such as those of the body, the mind (intellect), or the emotions, educational activities can and should concentrate on the mental or intellectual functions. Thus man not only possesses mental functions, but they are considered the highest functions of his nature. "It is the mind that matters." For the religion-oriented conservative the mental activities of man are rooted in a spiritual, immortal soul. Man's rational capacities distinguish him from animals. The possession of reason, albeit in different degrees, constitutes man's universal nature. Thus all men, by the very fact that they are human, possess the same common nature in spite of differences in environmental and hereditary background. Freedom of the will is a characteristic of human nature. Environmental forces might affect freedom, but they do not destroy it. The conservatives of the Hebrew-Christian persuasion (as well as some nontheists) insist that youth are inclined to be lazy and display evil tendencies. Thus all human beings, but especially youth, need external guidance and discipline. Individual differences in intellectual ability are a harsh reality; some human beings are capable of great intellectual achievements, others are not. Some can profit only from fundamental education, whereas others will do well in higher studies.

The rational mode of knowing is most characteristically human. Experience and science are valid modes but are limited to knowledge of particulars. For the theistic conservative, faith and revelation also are valid sources of knowledge. Rational truths are characterized by universality and immutability, e.g., laws of nature and some general moral principles apprehended by reason. Empirical truths, since they involve particulars, are subject to change and modification.

Ethical values are rooted in nature and/or mind itself. The fundamental values by which man lives are not subject to the whims of individuals or social change. Folkways and customs may change, basic ethical norms are immutable. Certain rational standards such as harmony and unity determine aesthetic value. Not all art is good art. The school is responsible for giving its clientele an understanding and appreciation of good art by means of the masterpieces of the human mind.

In the realm of educational theory and practice the neo-conservatives demand the following reforms. The development of the whole person and the reform of society might be the purpose of education in the broadest sense of the term, but the school is only one of the agencies concerned with education. Its proper function is the development of the intellectual powers of man through the medium of the accumulated knowledge of mankind. The school might assist other agencies when necessary in providing moral, physical, and emotional education, but this always must be considered secondary. In general the curriculum should consist of the intellectual skills and the systematic study of the academic disciplines which challenge the mental capacity of the student. The frills of the progressive school should be relegated to the domain of extracurricular or post-school activities. Teaching-learning methods must be more formal than those of the progressive school. Learning by doing is not an effective method of covering the vast amount of knowledge students should be expected to learn. Problem solving and related methods should be employed only after the student has acquired an adequate background in the subject matter. The school should concern itself primarily with the evaluation of academic achievement and the development of mental capacity. Evaluation of personality traits, physical development, and the like might be used if these measures can assist the school in determining reasons for academic failure. Classroom discipline must be humane but firm. Authority should rest with the teacher, not with the pupils. Pupil freedom is limited by pupils' age and maturity, curricular requirements, and the need for an atmosphere conducive to learning.

BIBLIOGRAPHY

Adler, Mortimer*A Guide Book to Learning*. N.Y. Macmillan 1986.
Adler, Mortimer.*The Paideia Proposal*, New York: Macmillan Co. 1982.
Adler, Mortimer. *A Dialectic of Morals*. Notre Dame, Ind.: Univ. of Notre

Dame Press, 1941.

Adler, Mortimer, and Mayer, Milton. *The Revolution in Education*. Chicago: Univ. of Chicago Press, 1958.

Bagley, W. C. "AnEssentialist Platform for the Advancement of American Education," *Educational Administration and Supervision*, XXIV (April, 1938), 241 - 56.

Bell, B.I. *Crisis in Education*. New York: Whittlesey House, 1949.

Bestor, Arthur.*Educational Wastelands*. Urbana: Univ. of Illinois Press, 1953.

Bestor, Arthur.*The Restoration of Learning*. New York: Alfred A. Knopf, 1955.

Boyer, Ernest.*High School*. New York, Harper & Row, 1983.

Brameld, Theodore.*Philosophies of Education in Cultural Perspective*. New York:Holt-Dryden Co., 1955. Parts III, IV.

Broudy, Harry.*Building a Philosophy of Education*. 2nd ed. Englewood Cliffs,N.J.: Prentice-Hall 1961.

Butler, J. D.*Four Philosophies and Their Practice in Education and Religion*. Rev. ed. New York:Harper and Brothers, 1957. Parts III, IV.pgs. 187-218.

Butler, J.D. *Idealism in Education*. Harper & Row 1966.

Fine, Benjamin.*Our Children are Cheated*. New York: HenryHolt & Co., 1947.

Fowler, C. "Strong Arts, Strong Schools*Educational Leadership*. Nov., 1994. (4)

Greene, Theodore. "A Liberal Christian Idealist Philosophy Educa tion,"*Modern Philosophies and Education*. 54th N.S.S.E. Yeabook. Chicago: Univ. of Chicago Press, 1955Ch. IV.

Home, Herman H.*The Democratic Philosophy of Education*. New York: The Macmillan Co., 1932.

Home, Herman H. "An Idealistic Philosophy of Education*Philosophy of Education*, 41st N.S.S.E. Yearbook, Part I. Chicago: Univ. of Chicago Press, 1942.Ch. IV.

Hutchins, R.M.*A Conversation on Education*. New York: Fund for the Republic, 1963.

Hutchins, R. M.*Education for Freedom*. Baton Rouge: Louisiana State Univ. Press, 1944.

Hutchins, R. M.*Conflict in Education*. New York:Harper and Brothers, 1953.

Hutchins, R. M.*The University of Utopia*. Chicago: Univ. of Chicago

Press 1953.

Hutchins, R. M.*Some Observations on American Education.*
Cambridge: Cambridge Univ. Press, 1956.

Kneller, G. F.*Introduction to the Philosophy of Education.* John
Wiley & Son, 1964.pgs 8-10.

Koerner, J. D. (ed.)*The Case for Basic Education.* Boston: Little,
Brown & Co., 1959.

Lodge, R. C.*Philosophy of Education.* Rev. ed. New York:Harper and
Brothers, 1947.

Lynn, E.M., "The Education We Receive: Lessons in Reception
From Emerson andCauell."*Teachers College Record* Winter,
1994. pp. 241.

MacDonald, J.*A Philosophy of Education.* ScottForesman & Co.
1965

Mayer, Frederich.*Philosophy of Education for Our Time.* Odyssey
Press, 1958.

McGucken, William. "The Philosophy of Catholic Education,"
Philosophies of Education. 41st N.S.S.E. Yearbook. Chicago:
Univ. of Chicago Press, 1942Ch. VI.

Maritain, Jacques.*The Range of Reason.* New York: CharlesScribner's
Sons, 1942.

Maritain, Jacques.*True Humanism.* 6th ed. New York: CharleScrib
ner's Sons, 1954.

Maritain, Jacques. Thomist Views on Education,*Modern Philosophies
and Education.* 54th N.S.S.E. Yearbook. Chicago: Univ. of Chicago
Press, 1955.Ch. III.

Maritain, Jacques*Education at the Crossroads.* New Haven: Yale
Univ. Press 1960.

Molnar, Thomas.*The Future of Education.* New York: Fleet Publishing
Co., 1961.

Neff, Frederick C.*Philosophy and American Education.* The Center for
Applied Research in Education, 1966. pp. 10-34.

Phenix, Philip (ed.)*Philosophies of Education.* New York: JohnWiley
& Sons, 1961.Chs. II, IV, VII, VIII, X.

Rafferty, Max.*Suffer Little Children.* New York:Devin-Adair Co.,1963.

Rich, John Martin*Innovations in Education Performers and Their
Critics.* Boston:Allyn & Bacon, 1985.

Rickover, H. G.*American Education-A National Failure.* New York: E.
P.Dutton & Co., 1963.

Rusk, Robert R. *The Philosophical Bases of Education.* Re. ed. Boston:
Houghton Mifflin Co., 1956.Chs. III, VII.

Ryan, Kevin. Mining then values in the Curriculum.*Educational
Leadership.* Nov, 1993. (16)

Scott, W. C., Hill, C. N., and Burns, H. W.*The Great Debate.*
Englewood Cliffs,N.J.: Prentice Hall, 1959.

Smith, Mortimer.*And Madly Teach.* HenryRegnery Co., 1949.

Smith, Mortimer.*The Diminished Mind.* Chicago: HenryRegnery Co.,
1954.

Smith, Vincent.*The School Examined.* Milwaukee: Bruce Publishing Co.,
1960.

Wild, John. "Education and Society: A Realistic View.*Modern Philos
ophies and Education.* 54th N.S.S.E. Yearbook. Chicago: Univ. of
Chicago Press, 1955.Ch. II.

Chapter VIII

Educational Liberalism Redefined

The early liberals discussed in Chapter V represent the revolt against the authoritarian rigidity of monarchical political systems and ecclesiastical hierarchies as well as of the traditional school. Their concern with freeing the individual from unwarranted external control prompted Rousseau, Basedow, Pestalozzi, and Froebel to argue for releasing the child from the restrictions placed upon him by teachers and his elders. The early American progressive school with its child-centered classroom embodied these same beliefs. The one notion which unites all of these theorists and movements is that of *individual* freedom. Teachers and adults are to give assistance and guidance to the child in developing his abilities and meeting his needs; they are not viewed as absolute authorities in the education process.

Later liberals such as Dewey, experimentalists, and reconstructionists, contending that modern industrial society is most complex and its members wholly interdependent, shifted their emphasis from the individual to society or the group. Thus one of Dewey's earliest and perhaps most influential statements, *My Pedagogic Creed*, made the social life of the child the context for freedom. From this time on the individual is seldom treated in isolation from the social groups to which he belongs. Individual freedom, then, is limited by social patterns. Freedom consists in one's right to interact with others (in the group or society) for the public good.

A recent intellectual movement (almost exclusively a twentieth-century philosophy) calls for a redefinition of liberalism. This philosophy, it is maintained, represents a reaction against both old and new "isms" which submerge the individual in an impersonal social world. Many of its advocates witnessed the complete loss of individuality under Nazism, fascism, and communism; in the narrowly sectarian religions; and even in the social democracies. In truth, they say, the modern thought systems are just as illiberal as the older systems they oppose. Man, having hardly been liberated from the age-old restrictions of authoritarian philosophies, adopted new systems which gave him security but which took away his individual freedom. Even where individual freedom was not restricted by political means, certain social pressures led men to conform to an accepted mold. What is needed then to counteract the almost complete lack of freedom in the modern world is a totally new outlook on human existence, Thus no new philosophical system or substantive doctrine is called for, but in the words of George Kneller a new state of mind. This state of mind has been labeled existentialism,

What is existentialism? Perhaps the best answer to this question was given by Nicolas Berdyaev when he said "I am existentialism." Each thinker who espouses this outlook is his own master. This fact accounts for the vast differences among the thinkers who call themselves existentialists. Some, like Kierkegaard, Marcel, and Jaspers, are Christians (although nonconformist ones); others, like Sartre, Nietzsche, and Heidegger, are atheists; some are theologians, like Buber and Tillich; many are novelists, playwrights, and artists, like Camus, Berdyaev, Sartre, Kafka, Dostoevski, and a host of "moderns."

Since existentialism is not a philosophical system and since there is such great individuality and independence found among existentialists, it is difficult to find answers to the basic questions we have been asking throughout the text, For some questions, especially those involving educational practice, no answers are offered by existentialism. What is the purpose, the reader might ask, of discussing existentialism in a philosophy of education text if it appears to have little or no bearing on the field? In response to this query it might be said that it takes some time for a new philosophical outlook to be translated into educational practice. Also, it seems that existentialist thought is beginning to have some effect on both educational theory and practice especially as these apply to higher education. Finally, because of the interest expressed by many education students and teachers in existentialism, one can expect to see some of these ideas translated into classroom practice even at the elementary and secondary level.

WHAT DOES IT MEAN TO BE HUMAN?

The question has been posed in this form because the existentialist does not believe that man is born with a ready-made nature. As Sartre says, "If man as the existentialist sees him is not definable it is because to begin with he is nothing."[1] Rather, each person creates his own nature, But one cannot accomplish this unless he is free. Therefore, first and foremost, *to be human means to be free*. "Man is to freedom condemned."

The notion that man has no predetermined nature is the central reason for the existentialist doctrine that "existence is prior essence." It affirms that man exists first; then, because he is free, he creates his own essence. This view rejects the conservative definitions of man as a rational animal, or as spiritual being with definite powers and characteristics, or as Communist man, or even as an American or Frenchman. It also denies the liberal notion of man as a product of his physical or social environment. It asks man to cast aside the intellectual security he found in the traditional closed systems of thought which specified what he should be. It calls upon each person to abandon the economic security he might find in the many political, religious, and social "isms" of the twentieth century. It bids him to accept his condemnation to freedom with all the dire consequences accompanying it.

The consequences are dire indeed, since man cannot blame his fallen nature, his physical environment, or the social context in which he lives for what he is. Every individual must bear the responsibility for what he does and for what he becomes. For this reason one finds the literature of the existentialist laden with such terms as guilt, dread, anguish, anxiety, abandonment, fear, terror, loneliness, and death. Although these terms are not used univocally by all existentialists, they do convey the general notion that the person's task of bringing himself from the nothingness of which Sartre spoke to being something is a very serious business.

For example, the experience of existential anguish, involving a distinct set of emotional states, is extremely intense. It might be brought about by the realization of the terrible responsibility which absolute freedom places upon the person. It may be felt when one makes a decision with the full awareness that he cannot predict what the consequences of his choice might be for himself and for others. Finally, anguish is an experience from which no man who is willing to face the inevitability of death can escape.

Man can never escape feelings of anguish, despair, and so forth if he wishes to remain wholly a man. The person who achieves complete contentment ceases to be a man since he no longer makes choices of any moment; he ceases to be human and becomes like a cabbage or a contented pig. Thus man cannot build up his defenses against trials and tribulations by

---

[1]J.P. Sartre,*Existentialism and Humanism*(London: Methuen & Co., 1948), p. 28.

accepting the security offered him by the closed religious or political systems. When he does this he exchanges his freedom (his very humanity) for superficial contentment.

In fine, to be human means to be free. It means one must start from nothingness and create himself as he wishes to be. It means one must accept existential anguish, fear, dread, and the like and make his decisions to act in spite of all difficulties, including the inevitability of death.

It is this notion of absolute freedom which has the most meaning for education. As will be noted, it puts the whole educational enterprise in a new light.

WHAT IS KNOWLEDGE-SEEKING AND TRUTH?

As was noted, the existentialist is not a philosopher in the usual sense of the word. This statement applies especially in the search for answers to questions involving the knowing process and the definition of truth. Treatises on the theory of knowledge which make up such an important part of the literature of philosophical systems are not produced by existentialists. They do not concern themselves with the traditional debates on empiricism versus rationalism. The problems of inductive and deductive logic they leave to the mathematician and the scientist. They spend no time on the philosophy of science, since this area does not involve human choice. Let the scientists, they say, work out the philosophy of science; the philosopher has more important issues to face. Neither is cosmological speculation about the origin and nature of the physical universe of any concern to the existentialist philosopher.

If none of these matters (which have been so hotly debated by other theorists discussed in this text) are pursued by the existentialist, does it follow that he is not at all concerned with the knowing process or the nature of truth? Indeed, this area is important for him, but in a sense quite different from the manner in which most philosophers discuss it. It is as knowing and truth affect man in his choices and commitments that is of major moment to the existentialist. This mode of knowing and the truths derived from it bear no real likeness to empirical and rational modes. The acquisition of existential knowledge is not supervised by the canons of formal logic or the scientific method. Rather, it can he characterized as human, subjective, introspective, and intuitive.

In one sense the existential mode of knowing is experience-centered.

However, the existentialist notion of experience is not that of the objective world acting upon a passive knower. Rather, for him, experience implies a free person actively engaged in a struggle with cosmic and human forces. Before man can have any knowledge he must first have an intuitive understanding of his contacts with the world and people. This is a purely subjective process which is unique with each individual and does not yield universal knowledge.

When the person interprets these subjective experiences and expresses them in ordinary language or in the various art forms he has arrived at truth. Existential truth, then, is always subjective and dependent upon the free choice of each individual knower. An important element of existential truth is that it is always followed by action and commitment to the achievement of the individual's goals.

WHAT IS GOOD?

As noted, the existentialist does not look upon the philosopher's role as that of analyzing or determining the nature of scientific knowledge or of answering the usual epistemological questions which are so important for most modern philosophers (both conservative and liberal). But finding an answer to the question "What is good?" is of prime importance to the existentialist.[2] In reality, one might say, questions of value are the only truly philosophical questions. He has answers for such questions; he proposes a summum bonum and a hierarchy of values.

It is evident that the existentialist rejects the notion held by Plato, Aristotle, and many other conservatives that individual happiness is man's highest good. For the existentialist the attainment of perfect happiness is not only impossible for man but undesirable. It is impossible to attain it since man's absolute freedom militates against his ever accepting any particular state in which he finds himself. Existential anguish, dread, and the inevitability of crisis and death make happiness an unattainable goal. What is even more terrifying to the existentialist is what would become of man if he were able to achieve perfect happiness. The perfectly happy person would cease to be human; "he would be reduced to the state of unconscious brutes." Animals who are well-fed and have adequate shelter are perfectly content; some people who have all their needs and wants cared for from the

---

[2]D.E. Denton, "Albert Camus: Philosopher of Moral Concern"*Educaitonal Theory*, XIV (April, 1964), 99.

cradle to the grave are perfectly content. But they live like animals because they never make choices about serious matters or perform any truly human acts; they have ceased to be human because they no longer alter the course of their lives by personal choice or human commitment.[3]

The existentialist cannot accept individual happiness as the highest good, but neither can he resign himself to that kind of happiness which man finds in group solidarity aided by science and technology. Aldous Huxley's *Brave New World* depicts the dehumanization of man in a world characterized by group solidarity and freedom from want. If a person feels the urge to become human again by expressing his freedom, he is lulled back into his animal state by soma tablets. But, the existentialist feels that he does not have to use fictional situations to prove his point. There are countries today which provide cradle to grave security. The revolt of youth in these countries against the conformity engendered by complete security affords ample evidence that the human desire for freedom cannot be stifled.

From the discussion just completed, the reader has undoubtedly surmised what the highest value is for the existentialist. It is not happiness of the individual; it is not adjustment to and security in the group; it is not freedom from want and tribulation. *Freedom of choice* is the highest good since it gives each person the opportunities to create himself.[4] Other values with high rank in the existentialist list are personal love and commitment, individual dignity, and creative effort.[5] Many other values are mentioned in the literature, but they are proposed by a particular man, whereas those listed are held in common by most existentialists.

Other points about values on which existentialists agree should be mentioned. First, in order for any value to be experienced, the person must accept anguish, tribulation, and suffering. Thus a person who does not experience existential anguish or suffering in, for instance, human love is not experiencing a value at all. He is just going through the motions. Second, true existential anguish is not to be confused with scrupulosity, apathy, or cowardice. These states of mind keep man from action. Finally, true existential values make man more conscious of his responsibility, arouse those passions which will stir him to his innermost depths, and prod him to commit himself to a course of action engaging all his efforts.

It seems quite clear, then, that the existentialists agree, at least on the

---

[3]R.G. Olson, *An Introduction to Existentialism* (New York: Dover Publications, 1962), p. 19.

[4]N.Greene, *Jean-Paul Sartre, The Existentialist Ethic* (Ann Arbor: Univ. of Michigan Press, 1960) Ch. IV *passim.*

[5]Olson, *op. cit.,* p. 17.

general outlines, that freedom is the highest good. The common source of all values is the personal awareness of mental suffering intrinsic to being human. The common purpose of all true values is to free man from petty fears and impersonal philosophizing about life. Finally, all values are characterized by an intensity which moves their possessor to action.

Since the existentialists are so concerned with value theory, it is not surprising to find that they have great interest in the fine arts. In reality they are the only contemporary philosophers who use the arts as a means of conveying certain philosophical insights to their audience. It is not that they do not use the language of technical philosophy, but such language is not the only medium of communication. Sartre and Marcel, for example, have produced technical works as well as novels and plays. In both types of literature, the same existential themes are treated.

The various art forms, then, are vehicles for the expression of the human situation. The anguish, dread, fear, and abandonment of man in a hostile and uncertain world are portrayed in all their depth in the novels and plays of Camus and Sartre. The student is, perhaps, more familiar with the novels of Dostoevski, *The Brothers Karamazov* and *Crime and Punishment.* In these widely-read literary masterpieces the characters are in constant struggle with human and cosmic forces. Human anguish and despair are emphasized in every paragraph. There is no happy romantic ending; all that matters is that each man is personally involved in the battle of life and that he decides his own fate. Thus, for Dostoevski, personal freedom was the very heart of man's existence. His heroes are not contented, secure individuals but, instead, those such as Raskolnikov, in *Crime and Punishment,* who are making choices contrary to the accepted norms of the times. Far from bringing them happiness, their freedom plunges them into the writhing current of a turbulent stream. They experience no comfort and peace of mind, but yet they will not abandon their dreadful freedom. All well-meaning people who try to give advice on rational or scientific grounds are rejected by these lovers of freedom. Not even the security of organized religion with its fellowship and mutual assistance is viewed as a good exchange for freedom.

A French ballet, *The Young Man and Death,* by Jean Cocteau is another example depicting the existential anguish and melancholy of a youth in his futile flight from death. Music, painting, and sculpture, too, can emphasize the same existential themes. Of course, it is more difficult to achieve the same effect with these media than with literary works. Nevertheless, many composers, painters, and sculptors, especially in Europe, purportedly have been quite successful in conveying existential themes. Personal freedom also is accounted for, at least indirectly, by the complete disregard for the traditional canons of composition, structure, and design. Their music is often cacophonous; their painting and sculpture abstract and completely incomprehensible to the traditionalist or the man on the street.

This approach to the arts suggests another important aspect of existentialist aesthetic theory, namely, there are no external or rational criteria by which one can judge art works. Thus the conservative views of art criticism which demand adherence to a Christian ethic, a socialistic realism, or certain standards such as harmony and unity are incompatible with existentialist thought. Also, the notion that art must serve some practical need or portray nature as it is destroys artistic freedom.

What is art for the existentialist? It is one way (and perhaps the most important way), for man to describe his intuitive grasp of the things and events which present themselves to his consciousness; by this means he can express his innermost feelings, passions, fears, and, above all, his freedom. Therefore, art is not a servant of other human endeavors or is it their master. Art is, par excellence, the mode of understanding and expressing the human situation.

EXISTENTIALISM AND EDUCATIONAL THEORY

For the student who is accustomed to finding ready answers to educational questions involving philosophy, existentialist treatises are likely to leave him quite at sea. The well-known names of adherents of existentialism have not helped since they have given no systematic attention to the most perplexing problems of educational theory and practice. It is not uncommon, therefore, to read that the existentialist outlook constitutes a denial of education in the institutionalized form in which we know it.[6] This evaluation of existentialism regarding education (by outsiders looking in) is quite understandable. Both the conservatives of the Platonic, Christian, and humanistic bent and the liberals of the Dewey school view education as a social undertaking. In Communistic conservatism, this social orientation is even more marked than in the older conservative educational patterns. The educational programs of conservatives and liberals alike embody a preference for certain subject matter or activities and patterns of behavior. Practically all national educational systems consider compulsory education an essential social good. Certainly all of these characteristics of

---

[6]V. Morris, "Existentialism and Education,"*Educational Theory*, IV (October, 1954), 258.

institutionalized education violate the first principle of existentialism, personal freedom. Undoubtedly, the educational world would have a radically different appearance if the existentialists were to reconstruct it. If one were permitted a flight of fancy into that new world, certain features would strike the onlooker by their sharp contrast with existing patterns.

In the first place, the emphasis on universal, compulsory education as the prime requisite for a healthy society would be questioned.[7] Ideally, children and youth should attend school because they choose to do so. Second, the intellectualistic goals of conservative schools and the democratic social aims of the liberal schools would be out of place. The primary aim of the existential school would be to develop moral freedom. Third, the existentialist would hardly countenance the required, cut-and-dried curriculum of the conservative school whether it be nationally or locally prescribed, nor would he see any real value in the "adoration of science" so prevalent in modern schools. Likewise he would not agree with Dewey that the social life of the child should be the center of curricular activities. Man, as free agent, would constitute the only possible center of the curriculum.

Certainly, teaching methods, classroom discipline, and evaluation would be neither authoritarian and teacher-centered as they are in the conservative school nor group-centered (democratic) as found in the Dewey school. The learner would have to be his own master, the judge of his own actions, and the determiner of his own success.

However, it does not appear that the existentialist outlook will capture the educational stronghold to such an extent that it will create a new school-at least not in the near future. Even Dewey's comprehensive and highly influential system was unable to achieve such a victory. It might be well, however, to indicate how the present structure of education might be modified by applying the philosophical beliefs of existentialists to certain facets of educational theory and practice,

The first major change must be made in teacher education programs. At present, entirely too much time is devoted to the scientific study of man as an "object." Child and adolescent psychology work with the purely measurable and observable aspects of behavior. The learner is viewed as an organism who is determined by his heredity and environment to act in such and such a way. Freedom of choice, responsibility for action, and the psychology of human commitment are seldom mentioned simply because there are no statistical studies in these areas. The other behavioral sciences

---

[7]G. Kneller, "Education, Knowledge and the Problem of Existence," Proceedings of the Philosophy of Education Society (Lawrence: Univ. of Kansas, 1961), pp. 137f.

which the student pursues are dominated by the same determinism. Teachers are taught "how to manipulate individuals and groups" in a democratic manner. These courses in social engineering assist the teacher in bringing the nonconformist into cooperation with others.[8]

The second area of professional education which must undergo a drastic overhaul is that of teaching methods. One will search in vain in methods texts and course syllabi for reference to free choice, anguish, or any of the emotive states stressed by existentialists. The human element is wholly excluded from methodological considerations. The only concern of methods courses is how to organize subject matter, how to plan activities in the democratic classroom, and what are important teaching techniques and tricks of the trade.

Even in the area of philosophy of education the student is indoctrinated with one or the other "ism." Professors of philosophy of education tend to preach one system as being the best rather than to encourage the student to make a true existential choice and then to commit himself to his choice with all his energy.

Only when schools of education abandon their indoctrination of teachers can one expect to bring about a truly human education for children and youth. This change of heart will be noted, first and foremost, in the purpose of the school.

WHAT IS THE PURPOSE OF THE SCHOOL?

Simply stated, the purpose of the school according to the existentialist is to free the individual. The early liberals began with the same statement of purpose, but their belief soon succumbed to the doctrine of sociality espoused by Dewey and his followers. Since this doctrine emphasized the social nature of all experience, the absolute freedom of the individual, so dear to the existentialist, is drastically limited by the demand for enriching and improving corporate life. [9]

---

[8]See F.N.Kerlinger, "The Implications of the Permissiveness Doctrine in American Education,"*Educational Theory*, X (April, 1960), 120-28; RUlich's comments on RHarper's essay in*Modern Philosophies and Education*, 54th N.S.S.E. Yearbook (Chicago: Univ. of Chicago Press, 1955), pp. 254f.

[9]V. Morris, "Freedom and Choice in the Educative Process,"*Educational Theory*, VIII (October, 1958), 231-39. In this article, Professor Morris, who is a follower of Dewey, maintains that emphasis on the social nature of education in Deweyan philosophy constitutes a near rejection of individual liberty. See pp. 239f. of this

What, exactly, does the existentialist mean by freeing the individual? First, the individual must be freed from the notion that he must think and act as others do in order to be regarded as a good person. Second, to be free means to understand one's own situation in a world filled with uncertainty and sorrow. Third, the individual must be freed from anonymity in the lonely crowd. This will enable him to recognize and utilize his powers to create his own being. Finally, to free the individual means that the person is the starting point for all educational activities as well as for all life activities. Thus the school can justify its existence only if its goal is the development of the free individual-one who acknowledges his own freedom and accepts the awesome responsibility for his acts.[10]

WHAT SHOULD BE TAUGHT?

Let us see how this newly defined liberal goal might modify the current curricula of both the liberal (Deweyan) and conservative schools. The problem-centered curriculum is unacceptable because of its social (or group) orientation and its almost exclusive emphasis upon problems of immediate concern. Furthermore, a problem is not considered solved until a solution is agreed upon by the participants. For the existentialist, problems must be individually and freely chosen; they will be of more than immediate concern to the person and should reflect the persistent problems of the human situation. Finally, there are no solutions to many problems involving the human situation.

The existentialist also sees little human value in most programs of vocational education. Vocational subjects have pragmatic value insofar as they assist the student to earn a living. But vocational training without the addition of subjects which appeal to the human element in the pupil is not education at all-animals and robots can be trained.[11]

Neither would the curriculum of the conservative school satisfy the existentialist. For example, Nietzsche's criticism of the typical continental secondary school is most scathing. He said it rewards conformity and mediocrity and reproves and penalizes the expression of individuality and

---

volume; AWirth, "On Existentialism, The Emperor's New Clothes and Education,"*Educational Theory,* V (July, 1955), 152-58.

[10] R. Harper, "Significance of Existence and Recognition for Education," *Modern Philosophies and Education, op. cit.*pp. 226-29.

[11] G. Kneller,*Existentialism and Education*(New York: Philosophical Library, 1958), pp. 135-37.

freedom.[12] Even the subject of composition, he said, which should give the student the opportunity to express his individuality, is so hemmed in by rules and   regulations   that it serves only to kill initiative and free expression.

It might appear that the existentialist would eliminate all the subjects of the conservative school as well as the activities of the liberal school. On the contrary, it seems that the existentialist would not insist that traditional or progressive curricula be rejected.[13] Rather, he would prefer that an entirely different approach be taken to both the old and the new in the curriculum. Even vocational training can be carried on in the total context of the human situation. The role of free choice, human creativity, moral judgment, and aesthetic perception can be woven into teaching craftsmanship so that the student will be more human when he completes his training than he was when he began it.[14] The other subjects, such as mathematics, the sciences, history, music, and art, likewise can be approached from the existential outlook. Each of these has some bearing upon human existence. So long as the existence of the individual is the central focus of these subjects (and of any activities) they can be truly educative.[15]

Further, school subjects should be made the instruments for the realization of subjective feeling such as dread and anguish. Thus the important thing is not subject matter but the individual's reaction to it. When subjects are taught as cold and lifeless bodies of knowledge   with no relevance to the human situation they are miseducative.

One curricular area which the conservative school often neglected and the liberal school considered nonessential, the fine arts, would be given an important place in the existentialist program. The extensive use of the art forms by the existentialist as means of communicating philosophical beliefs suggests that literature, drama, the dance, painting, and music would enjoy a large share of school time. After all, these are the noblest and most personal instruments for expressing individual freedom and for describing the profoundest human emotions.

---

[12]F. Nietzsche,*The Future of Educational Institution*(London: T.N. Foulis, 1909), pp. 52-60.

[13] Harper,*op. cit*, p. 223.

[14]Kneller,*Existentialism and Education, op. cit* pp. 137f.

[15]Harper,*op. cit*, pp. 223f.

HOW SHOULD ONE TEACH?

What does the existentialist have to say about teaching methods? Obviously the formal methods of the conservative school with all their rigidity and pupil passivity are a contradiction to the existentialist penchant for personal freedom and commitment. The problem-solving method of the Deweyan liberals is also inadequate because of its social-centeredness. However, Morris believes that certain modifications in the problem-solving method might make it at least partially acceptable to the existentialist. The criterion of individual choice in proposing possible solutions and in accepting or rejecting a solution would have to be reinstated.

In teaching methodology, Kneller (the foremost expositor of existentialism in American education) says that there is no doubt that the Socratic method is favored over other approaches to teaching. For Socrates, the only truth worthy of man's consideration began and ended in the individual's subjective experience. The answers to all the perplexing questions of life must come from within the person. Socrates was most successful in motivating his students to question themselves about their own existence. He was able to get them to realize that the passive, uncritical way they were living constituted a denial of their personal freedom. Yet, he did not give them the truth but expected them to draw the truth from their own subjective experience. For this reason, Socrates was wont to give the student the impression that his teacher had no knowledge or answers to their questions. This technique forced the student to find his own answers and to commit himself to a certain way of life because of his own personal choice rather than upon the authority of the teacher. Finally, the method is not designed for finding cold, objective facts or universally valid conclusions of reason or socially acceptable norms of behavior. Its sole purpose is to convince the learner of his freedom and to motivate him to use all of his potentialities to understand himself and choose his own way of life.[16]

The mass education of the twentieth century renders the existentialist notion of teaching methodology nearly unattainable. Large lecture sections, teaching machines, and other devices depersonalize the teaching-learning process, But even when the teacher is compelled to resort to such devices, he must do his best to be more than an information-giver and above all he must resist the temptation of giving all the answers. Whether he is lecturing

---

[16] Kneller, "Education, Knowledge, and the Problem of Existence,"*op. cit*, pp. 133f.

in history, the fine arts, the humanities, or the sciences, the teacher can bring out the human side of the subject.

A recent lecture on the Civil War by a history teacher exemplified the existential approach. The lecturer selected a dozen or so names of combatants from the state of Wisconsin who had volunteered for service in that state's regiment. All but one were people not mentioned in history books. One was a young man in his teens, another a married man with children. He described the existential anguish which accompanied the free choice of each volunteer. The lecturer dwelt on the personal struggle of the father in making his decision to leave wife and children and plunge into a dangerous and uncertain future.

The correspondence of these men to their families back home was used to depict their fear, dread, struggles with the unknown, and daily encounters with death, The anguish of a woman who lost her husband and several sons to the cause was so movingly presented that each listener experienced her sorrow.

The lecture lasted far longer than the typical class, yet no one in the audience stirred. No one took notes to prepare for an examination. For the teacher and for his class history was not a recounting of the dead past; it was a human experience. All of the human passions-love, hate, dread, fear, anguish-which the actors on the stage of history experienced were relived by the audience. Each listener asked himself what choices he would make were he in the same human situation as the men who marched away.

Literature and art probably lend themselves more to the existentialist approach to teaching than do the less human disciplines such as mathematics or chemistry. But even in the latter subject-matter areas, the teacher should do his best to make the classroom activities a personal experience for the learner. In such subjects the logic of experience and commitment should take precedence over the logic of the subject matter.

What has been said about the curriculum and teaching methods applies with equal force to evaluation. Examinations, both objective and essay, which have little or no relevance to the human situation force the students to be grade hunters rather than learners, Also, social adjustment and civic and vocational competence which are so important to the social liberals can never serve as criteria of evaluation for the existentialist.[17]

Unfortunately, the existentialist does not offer specific suggestions for new evaluation techniques. He only admonishes the teacher to devise ways and means of determining whether the student has become personally involved in his studies and how this personal involvement has enabled him

[17] Wirth, *op. cit*, pp. 155f.

to grapple with truly human problems. Perhaps, even more important, is the extent to which the individual student has seriously begun (and continues) to develop his own freedom and to create his own being.

HOW ARE FREEDOM AND DISCIPLINE TO BE HARMONIZED?

In answering the question of how to harmonize freedom and discipline the existentialist faces an almost inescapable dilemma. On the one hand, he demands that each person be absolutely free. On the other, he admits the harsh reality that conflict between persons is inevitable because of absolute freedom. What is a teacher to do when the inevitable clash of free persons takes place in a classroom? Morris, in commenting on the existentialists' notion of discipline, says that they would advocate the same approach as conservative educators.[18] This is, perhaps, the only way open to the existentialist since he rejects the environmentalist belief that misbehavior is caused by a bad home, cultural deprivation, and the like. Therefore, the teacher might have to be arbitrary about maintaining at least enough order so that each student can be free to go about the serious business of building his own way of life.

There are many other ways, however, in which personal freedom can be exercised in an institutional setting such as that found in the school. For example, students might be given greater freedom of choice in selecting subjects, projects, topics for themes, and boundless freedom of creative expression in the arts. Less emphasis could be placed on group cooperation and conformity to accepted norms of behavior. In general, freedom can be enshrined in the school if only educators again place the individual at the center of the educative process. Much of the present administrative efficiency would be lost; there would be fewer well-adjusted, placid persons; there would be fewer organization men produced. But, in the long run, there would be more educated persons who would be willing to make the leap into uncertainty and bear the responsibility for their actions.

CHAPTER SUMMARY

The individualistic liberalism of Rousseau, Pestalozzi, and the early American progressives with its emphasis on personal freedom and the

---

[18]V. Morris *Philosophy and the American School* (Boston: Houghton Mifflin Co., 1961), p. 429.

rejection of external authority was replaced by the social liberalism of Dewey. In the latter school of thought the authority of the people or society replaces the authority of king, emperor, or pope. In either case (conservative or social liberal) the individual is not the master of his own destiny. But, even in the liberalism of Rousseau, man is not completely free; he is born good, but society corrupts him; man is a child of nature and, therefore, chooses according to it.

A group of thinkers, whose popularity has increased in the last few decades, has demanded a redefinition of liberalism. This new liberalism calls for a radically different approach to the problems of philosophy as well as to the concerns of every day living. It might be called a philosophy of radical individualism.

The philosophical beliefs which the new state of mind stresses are:

To be human means to be absolutely free. Man is not born with a ready-made human nature; rather, his freedom enables him to create his own nature. This awesome responsibility engenders in the person existential anguish, dread, abandonment, loneliness, and similar emotional states. The inevitability of death only augments the agony of the human situation.

Existential knowing is a purely subjective process by which the individual acquires an intuitive grasp of his experience with objects, events, and persons. These experiences, with all their subjective elements, are described in the language of philosophy, or through the medium of the fine arts. Existential truth is the result of all the subjective elements of human knowing and feeling. It implies free choice of ends and of means of achieving these ends; action and wholehearted commitment are essential ingredients of existential truth.

Ethical concerns constitute the most important part of existentialist philosophy. Neither individual happiness nor group solidarity are viewed as man's summum bonum. In reality, these goals are not only unattainable but undesirable. For the existentialist, freedom of choice is the highest good. Other high-ranking values are personal love and commitment, individual dignity, and creative effort.

Existentialists use the fine arts as a major means of communicating their outlook on human life, Themes such as freedom, anguish, terror, dread, abandonment, and death dominate their literature and art. In general, existentialists do not subscribe to the traditional criteria of art. Each artist sets up his own criteria and so long as he expresses his subjective feelings, his free choice, and his own engagement in life's struggle he has achieved the goal of the arts.

The educational implications of existentialism are somewhat limited by the failure of its advocates to wrestle with educational problems. Commentators have made the following suggestions for educational theory and practice:

The primary purpose of the school is neither intellectual nor social; it is to develop free, moral individuals. The subjects contained in the curriculum are not as important as the approach to these subjects. It is the personal involvement of the student in whatever subject he is taking that makes it worthy of his time. Every subject and activity (even vocational training) must be studied in the context of the total human situation. There is no such thing as the detached study of science, or mathematics, or history. In the use of teaching methods and evaluational techniques, the teacher must respect the freedom and individuality of the student. In methodology, the existentialist expresses the greatest preference for the Socratic method. Most traditional and progressive methods need major modification before they can be acceptable to the existentialist. Even though personal freedom is the highest good for the existentialist, he offers little advice on how to maintain order in a classroom; he merely asserts that individual freedom must not be violated. Pupil freedom can be honored by allowing free choice of studies, activities and, especially, freedom of expression in written and oral composition.

BIBLIOGRAPHY

Blackham, H. J.*Six Existentialist Thinkers.* London:Routledge &Kegan Paul, 1952.

Breisach, Ernst*Introduction to Modern Existentialism.* New York: Grove Press, 1962.

Buber, Martin.*I and Thou.* Translated by R. G. Smith. Edinburgh: T. & T. Clark Co., 1937.

Bullough, Max. "On Dewey andLindeman: Some Philosophical Foundations Towards Cultural Liberation from Educational Hegemony."*International Journal of Lifelong Education.* Oct/Dec. 1988. pp. 285-299.

Cochrane, Arthur C. *Existentialists and God.* Philadelphia: Westminster Press, 1956.

Collins, James. *The Existentialists.* Chicago: Henry Regnery Co., 1952.

Denton, David E. "Albert Camus: Philosophy of Moral Concern," *Educational Theory,* XIV, No. 2 (April, 1964), 99-102.

Friedman, Maurice S. "MartinBuber's Philosophy of Education," *Educational Theory*, VI, No. 2 (April 1956), 95-104.

Greene, Norman N*Jean-Paul Sartre - The Existentialist Ethic.* Ann Arbor: Univ. of Michigan Press, 1960.

Grene, Marhjorie.*Dreadful Freedom.* Chicago: Univ. of Chicago Press, 1948.

Harper, Ralph. "Significance of Existence and Recognition forEducation,"*Modern Philosophy and Education.* 54th N.S.S.E. Yearbook. Chicago: Univ. of Chicago Press, 1955.Ch. VII.

Jaspers, Karl.*Existentialism and Humanism.* New York: Russell Moore, 1952.

Kaufman, Walter*Nietzsche.* New York: Meridian Books, 1956.

Kerlinger, Fred N. "The Implications of the Permissiveness Doctrine in American Education," *Educational Theory*, X, No. 2 (April, 1960), 120-27.

Kierkegaard,Soren. *The Journals.* Translated by A.Dru. Oxford: Oxford Univ. Press, 1938.

Kneller, George.*Existentialism and Education.* New York:Philosophical Library, 1958.

Kneller, George. "Education, Knowledge and the Problem of Existence," *Proceedings, Philosophy of Education Society.* Lawrence: Univ. of Kansas of Press, 1961. Pp. 132-51.

Morris, VanCleve. "Existentialism and Education,"*Educational Theory*, IV, No. 4 (October, 1954), 247-58.

Morris, VanCleve. "Existentialism and the Educative Process,"*Educational Theory*, VIII, No. 4 (October, 1958), 231-38.

Morris, VanCleve. "Existentialism and the Education of the Twentieth Century Man,"*Educational Theory*, XI, No. 1 (January, 1961), 52-60.

Morris, VanCleve. *Philosophy and the American School.* Boston: Houghton Mifflin Co., 1961Chs. III-X, XIII.

Ozmon, H. A. andCraver, S. M.*Philosophical Foundations of Education.* Columbus, Ohio: Charles EMerril Co., 1981. Chap. 5.

Patka, Frederick.*Existentialist Thinkers and Thought.* New York: Philosophical Library, 1962.

Reisman, David.*The Lonely Crowd.* New Haven: Yale Univ. Press,1950.

Robinson, E. "Education for the 1980s and Beyond: An Interview with Carl Rogers.'*Humanistic Education.* Mar, 1985. pp. 98-110.

Salvan, Jacques.*To Be and Not To Be*. Detroit: Wayne State Univ. Press, 1962.

Sartre, Jean-Paul*Existentialism*. Translated by B.Frechtman. New York: Philosophical Library, 1947.

Sartre, Jean-Paul*Existentialism and Humanism*. Translated by P. Mairet. London:Metheun & Co., 1948.

Sartre, Jean-Paul.*To Freedom Condemned*. ed. J.Streller. New York: Philosophical Library, 1960.

Vandenberg, Donald*Human Rights in Education*. New York:Philo sophical Library 1983.

Wahl, Jean.*A Short History of Existentialism*. New York: Philosophical Library, 1949.

Winetrout, Kenneth. "Buber: Philosopher of theIhou Dialogue,"*Educational Theory*, XIII, No. 1 (January, 1963), 53 - 57.

Wirth, Arthur G. "On Existentialism, the Emperor's New Clothes and Education,"*Educational Theory*, V, No. 3 (July, 1955), 152 - 57.

Chapter IX

A Proposed Solution

In the preceeding chapter a solution to the conservative-liberal conflict was proposed. By redefining liberalism, the existential thinkers offered a synthesis of the two positions rather than a mere middle-of the-road escape between the opposing camps. The theorists discussed in this chapter advance a different idea, namely, that much of the argument between the opposing factions is about words rather than real problems. To resolve the confused situation, the analysts recommend the use of rigorous linguistic analysis and scientific methods. Just what does the analytic philosopher suggest that is different from the views expressed throughout this text?

Most of the philosophies discussed thus far have been very comprehensive in scope, providing answers to the many questions proposed throughout this text. Such answers were offered because the advocates of the various philosophies consider it their task to synthesize all knowledge which man acquires about himself, about his physical and social environment, and, in some instances, about the world outside of sense experience (supernatural realm). This construction of a world-view or *Weltantchauung*, as it is called, has been considered one of the major occupations of philosophers throughout the ages. Plato, Aristotle, St. Augustine, Thomas Aquinas, Kant, Hegel, Spencer, Dewey, and many others have sought to systematize all human experience and knowledge into a unitary philosophy.

Another important aim of many of the philosophers studied, especially those in the conservative camp, lies in their search for some ultimate principle or cause for all existence and events in the world. This search led them to posit certain ultimate truths, ultimate realities, absolute values, and final principles as the foundation for their philosophical systems. Plato found his ultimate in God; Aristotle, in the First (un-caused) Cause; Thomas Aquinas, in the Christian God; Hegel, in the Absolute; Spencer, in some natural force.

In the first few decades of the twentieth century a group of thinkers felt that these two aims of philosophy were wholly unattainable. In reality the history of Western philosophy shows that philosophical chaos and confusion resulted from trying to achieve the two goals. Dualism, monism, pluralism, mechanism, vitalism, and a list of other "isms," all of which were supposed to synthesize or *unify*, tended to divide the intellectual world. Similarly, the search for an ultimate cause or an *absolute* led to almost as many absolutes as there were searchers. It was felt, therefore, that the philosophers' prime task should be to clear up the confusion rather than to add a new "ism" to the already existing heap. This is to be accomplished by logical *analysis* of the language of everyday usage and of science, by pointing out fundamental assumptions of the contending points of view, and by asking for operational definitions of terms.[1]

Thus the thinkers of the analytic school pose one significant question, "What do you mean?" rather than the many questions philosophers have usually asked. Certainly, this is not a new question for philosophers. From Socrates to Dewey we find philosophers asking this question, especially of their opponents. But after devoting some time to meaning, they set out to tell their hearers or readers exactly what man's nature is, what is true or false, how one arrives at truth, and what is good and beautiful. The analytic philosopher, on the other hand, contends that his primary concern is for the first phase; he does not consider it his function to advise people what to believe or how to achieve certain goals.

The chief difference between the role of the analytic philosopher and others might be made more understandable by citing the experience of an American college graduate who received a Rhodes scholarship. His philosophical training in an American college had led him to accept realism. He had anticipated that he would be expected to defend this position in the British university, where he attended lectures and discussions on

---

[1] The study of language and meaning has become a specialized discipline in recent years. Its scope is too broad to be included in one text. The student can consult many excellent books on the subject: S.Hayakawa, *Language in Action* (New York: Harcourt, Brace & Co., 1941.); C. Morris *Signs, Language and Behavior* (New York; Prentice -Hall, 1946), Max Black *Language and Philosophy* (Ithaca, N.Y.: Cornell Univ. Press, 1949); K. Burke, *A Grammar of Motives* (New York: Prentice-Hall, 1945); Korzybski, *General Semantics* (Lakeville, Conn.: Institute of General Semantics, 1947); N. Brooks *Language and Language Learning* (New York: Harcourt, brace & World, 1964).

philosophy. Much to his surprise neither his teachers nor his fellow students asked him to give his reasons for his views on the philosophical questions which he considered so important. Rather, they asked him what he *meant* when he said man had a mind which was essentially different from his body. They asked him what his assumptions were when he argued that there was some guiding force in the universe. They wanted a clarification of his statement that certain human acts were good and others evil. What did he mean by good? What criteria was he using to evaluate human acts? In fact he was never asked to defend his or anyone else's point of view on the major issues of philosophy. After his teachers and fellow discussants had determined what he meant by the various statements he made, the exercise came to an end. He retained his beliefs, and no one seemed to care what he believed.

Apparently, the analysts do not feel that the philosopher should tell people what is true or false, right or wrong, beautiful or ugly. This does not imply that they believe that people need or want no guides for determining moral standards and truth. But giving such guidance is not the responsibility of the philosopher as a philosopher. His obligation ceases as a philosopher when he has pointed out the logical structure of decisions about truth and morality and stimulated an understanding of the implications of such decisions. However, as a person and a member of society he must share every man's responsibility to be concerned with all problems of living.

If the analytic philosopher views his task as such a limited one, it might appear that he has little to offer the teacher, administrator, or guidance counselor. For this reason, perhaps analytic philosophy had no effect on educational theory until the mid-twentieth century. Then, a few educational philosophers recognized the service that the analytic approach might render to educational theory and practice. The analyst is not expected to provide general doctrines or principles to guide administrative and classroom practice, nor is he expected to state the goals of education and the means of achieving such goals. But he can clarify the terms and concepts used in education and point up the beliefs underlying choices being made and the logical foundation and implications of methods and evaluation. He can detect inconsistencies in the assumptions underlying certain theories and practices. He can analyze the major theoretical and practical differences between the various competing parties regarding major educational issues of the day by indicating the presuppositions of each competitor and the possible consequences of his view.[2] In other words he can be of great help

---

[2]For a more detailed explanation of this view, see C. Hardie, "The Philosophy of Education in a New Key,'*Educational Theory*, X (October, 1960), 255-61.

to educational theorists and practitioners if he does nothing more than clarify a confused situation so that the participants in the educational enterprise know what is at stake.[3]

The selections in Scheffler's book represent philosophical analysis in action in educational contexts. It is worth noting that the majority of the authors devote their efforts to clarifying the situation by removing or pointing to linguistic confusions and underlying assumptions of the conflicting viewpoints. Perhaps the most specific statement of the role of philosophical analysis in education is the following:

1. To discover the neglected meanings which particular terms and expressions are given through the ways they are used in different contexts.

2. To uncover conceptual blunders and to lay bare erroneous lines of reasoning which result from failure to understand how language is being used in a given situation.

3. To clear away pseudo-problems and pseudo-questions that exist only as a result of confused and unclear conceptions and the vague, ambiguous use of language.

4. To explore the dimensions of educational terminology and to gain a clearer understanding of the relationships between thought, language, and reality, and thus to broaden the basis upon which we ground our beliefs about reality and our convictions of value.

5. To lay bare unrecognized logical inconsistencies which result from the uncritical use of language.[4]

The selections which the authors present as examples of analysis applied to education are not designed to defend any ism (even though the authors might be advocates of an "ism") or to solve the many theoretical and practical problems in education. Rather, they are selected as exemplars of clarity in thinking, demonstrating that unless the disputants are using the same meanings for the same words they cannot even determine where the disagreement lies.

It seems evident then that analytic philosophy is not a philosophy in the

---

[3]See *Philosophy and Education*, ed. IsraelScheffler (Boston:Allyn & Bacon, 1958), pp. 1-6.

[4]*Language and Concepts in Education*, ed. B.Othanel Smith and R.HEnnis (Chicago:Rand McNally & Co., 1961), Preface.

same sense that most of the others treated in this text are. It does not set out to build comprehensive theories of knowledge, metaphysics, and values. It is more a way of approaching philosophy rather than a systematic philosophy. However, not all philosophers who use analysis as their method remain aloof from the problems we have been considering throughout this text. Because of the limitations of space only one such group, choosing to call themselves Logical Empiricists (Positivists), can be studied here. This school of thought has been very influential and has its advocates in practically every large university in America and abroad.[5] Since it had its beginnings only three decades ago, there must be something quite appealing about this philosophy. Perhaps its appeal lies in its exclusively scientific orientation, a feature which will be emphasized in succeeding pages. As each question is presented to the logical empiricist, note his concern with meaningfulness and the extent to which he draws his answers from the empirical sciences.[6]

WHAT STATEMENTS ARE MEANINGFUL?

As indicated, the analyst's first concern is with meaning. Thus, before it can be decided what man is or what truth is, one must know what constitutes a meaningful statement. The logical empiricist maintains that a statement is meaningful only when it can be put to a direct or indirect empirical test. For example, the statement "copper conducts electricity" is meaningful since one can test it directly. Simply touch a piece of copper to an electrical current and find out whether it conducts the electrical charge. Similarly, the statement "wood conducts electricity" is meaningful, since it can also be tested directly.

In the examples just used, note that the concern is not with the truth or falsity of the statement but with its testability. In both instances the statements can be tested directly by scientific means and are, therefore, meaningful. The fact that the statement "wood conducts electricity" is false is beside the point. The situation becomes more complex when a statement

---

[5]See *Twentieth Century Philosophy* ed. D. Runes (New York: Philosophical Library, 1943), pp. 371ff

[6]Needless to say, the logical empiricists, like other philosophers of the same "school," are not in agreement on all fundamental issues. this chapter will attempt to describe one view, leaving to the student the opportunity to consult the suggested reading for others.

such as "the temperature of the surface of the sun is 11,000,000 degrees F." is under consideration. At the present time no one can get near enough to the sun to plunge a thermometer into its surface. Even if one could make a direct test, no thermometer now in existence could record such temperatures. However, certain indirect means are available for determining the temperature of the sun. Thus the statement "the temperature of the surface of the sun is 11,000,000 degrees F." is meaningful. A statement is not to be considered meaningless simply because technical or practical difficulties do not permit one to make an empirical test. When the technical difficulties are solved an answer will be possible.

Yet another example should help to clarify the positivistic criterion of meaning. Some of the educational philosophers discussed in this book stated that "Man possesses a spiritual soul." By definition, the existence of a purely spiritual substance cannot be determined by empirical tests. Thus, according to the meaning criterion, the statement "Man possesses a spiritual soul" is meaningless. No question of truth or falsity is involved. In general, a great number of statements made by the educational philosophers mentioned in this text, especially those of the conservatives, are meaningless since they are derived from revelation, faith, or pure reason. In fact, nearly all *speculation* about the nature of man; of the universe, of God, of goodness, and of beauty which occupied the attention of classical philosophers is meaningless. Also, a great number of educational theories and propositions fall into the same category.[7]

This meaning criterion is often referred to as the "verification principle." Admittedly, it is a limiting one and is considered too strong even by some positivists. Therefore, instead of applying the verification criterion of meaning, some have proposed the "falsifiability" criterion. This criterion serves the same purpose as that of verification, i.e., it distinguishes meaningful from meaningless statements. But it does so in a negative rather than a positive way. Thus, if a statement can be shown to be false by experience or science, it is considered meaningful. In other words, the falsifiability criterion simply distinguishes statements which have empirical content from those which have other kinds of content. This criterion seems

---

[7]See A. Ayer, *Language Truth and Logic* (New York: Dover Publications, 1946), pp. 5-25, 36. Ayer's rigorous criterion of meaning has been modified somewhat by recent analysts. That they have not changed the foundation for this criterion, however, is apparent positivistically-oriented works. See K. Nielsen, "Philosophy and the Meaning of Life," *Cross Currents* XIV (Summer, 1964), 313-35.

to admit the possibility that some statements might be meaningful even if no empirical evidence is available for their verification. Of course, such statements could make no claim to scientific truth"-they must be defended on other grounds. Such seems to be the case in some of the views expressed by positivists regarding the question of moral behavior.[8]

As the basic philosophical and educational questions are posed in the following pages, one will note that both the verification and the falsifiability criteria will come into play.

WHAT IS MAN?

The question of what man is, which is of central importance to most philosophers and to which so many different answers have been given, poses no serious problem for the logical empiricist. In effect, he says it is not his business as a philosopher to answer this question. The psychologist, sociologist, and anthropologist are the experts who must answer the question for the educator.

The philosopher can be of some assistance in the sense that he can clarify language and point out assumptions of the statements made by the scientists in each of these fields. He might note that certain statements made by psychologists are not warranted by either the subject matter being studied or the methods used. For example, some behavioristic psychologists made the statement that since all man's actions are determined by hereditary and environmental factors he does not have the power of free choice, A group of philosophers applied logic and linguistic analysis to the problem and showed that the statement was unwarranted.[9]

What can science tell the educator about man? The geneticist, anthropologist, and other scientists will give important information about man's evolutionary origin. The psychologist will provide key concepts and theories about human behavior, especially learning. The sociologist and social psychologist will describe and explain man's social behavior. And, as these various sciences improve their techniques, they will be able to give a more detailed and complete answer to our question "what is man?"

It is not necessary to repeat what the behavioral sciences have to say

---

[8]See K. Popper,*The Logic of Scientific Discovery*(New York: Science Editions, 1961), pp. 40ff.

[9]See Univ. of California Associates, "The Freedom of the Will,"*Readings in Philosophical Analysis,*ed. H.Feigl and W. Sellers (New York: Appleton-Century-Crofts, 1949), pp. 595-615.

about man, The student will find such knowledge in the basic texts required for each of these sciences. The significant point, for the philosophy of education, is that the logical empiricist bids the questioner to seek his answers about man's nature from sources other than philosophy.[10]

HOW DO WE KNOW?

The logical empiricist considers questions concerning the theory of knowledge one of his main concerns. It is in this area, he feels, that the analytic philosopher can make his greatest contribution. Critical analysis of the knowledge acquired by everyday experience and through the exact sciences *is* the philosopher's fare.

It was noted that a statement is meaningful when it can be subjected to a direct or indirect empirical tests. The assumption underlying this meaning criterion is that experience is a valid mode of knowing. Much of man's daily living entails this kind of knowledge, For example, if someone says that there are bears in Yellowstone Park, one can find out for oneself by searching the parks, This type of everyday experience is a perfectly legitimate way of arriving at knowledge.

The other way of acquiring knowledge, and perhaps the most important in our age of science, is through the sciences. But many people, both past and present, have claimed to be employing science in their search for knowledge. The medieval and modern theologians and metaphysicians considered their disciplines sciences. the logical positivist rejects this claim since the methods employed did not meet the standards of the scientific method. Only those activities which have the following characteristics can claim to be truly "scientific."

1. Intersubjective testability or objectivity: This criterion has two features: first it demands that the person be free from any *a priori* or preconceived notions and biases in his search for knowledge; second that the claims which a scientist makes for his findings be capable of test by others who are competent in that particular field. Thus, a physicist who claims he has discovered a very important principle in the behavior of atoms but refuses to disclose the nature of his discovery so that other physicist can check his theory, has no right to claim scientific respectability for his work. Similarly, when Aristotle claimed that "prime matter" existed but that it could never be found in objects, he was not speaking as a scientist

---

[10]See Hardie, *op. cit*, pp. 258ff.

but as a metaphysician. Aristotle's prime matter theory is factually meaningless since, by definition, it cannot be tested.

2. Reliability: This criterion demands that scientific statements be based on repeated testings all of which have approximately the same results. The statement that "copper conducts electricity" is reliable since repeated testings have shown that when an electric charge is put to a piece of copper the current passes through the copper. but when the astrologer claims that a certain day will be the best one to begin a battle or plant a crop there is no opportunity to check the reliability of such a proposition. Even if the battle were won or the crop proves to be a good one there would be no way of demonstrating that it was the position of he stars which had any effect on the outcome.

3. Definiteness and precision: This criterion demands that the terms and concepts used in the science be clearly defined and delimited. If the concept "matter" for example is used in physics it must be clearly distinguished from older meanings such as the "prime matter" of Plato and Aristotle. In education, such concepts as "intelligence,   motivation," "learning," "discipline," "the democratic classroom," call for operational definitions based upon empirical evidence.[11]

4. Coherence or systematic structure: In order to satisfy this criterion, a haphazard collection of facts or information is not adequate. Gathering of data must be done in a systematic manner and accompanied by a statement of certain laws and theoretical assumptions. There must be no contradiction between the various laws, assumptions, and facts of the case. A study of modern explanations of learning will reveal that the psychologist is attempting to construct a coherent or systematic theory. The important auxiliary tools in this endeavor to attain coherence are logic and mathematics (statistics).

5. Comprehensiveness: All truly scientific activity must be characterized by the endeavor to include all possible knowledge related to the problem at hand. The knowledge acquired by the unaided senses is merely the beginning; all of the technical tools of modern science must be employed. The astronomer of today could not claim scientific adequacy for his work if he failed to use the high-powered telescopes available. The biologist without an electron-microscope cannot do a comprehensive study of his subject. This criterion also bids the scientist to stay up-to-date on all new discoveries, techniques and equipment in his own and related fields. The tasks of science are never completed; the scientist should never succumb to the temptation to believe that all the problems of his field have been

---

[11]An operational definition gives the meaning of a concept or term by a set of operations.

solved.[12]

When these criteria are applied rigorously many disciplines which claim to be scientific must be ejected from the family of legitimate science. Mythology, theology, metaphysics, aesthetics, spiritualism, and astrology are, for example, nonscientific.

The relationship of the knowledge acquired in everyday experiences and in the pure sciences is an important one for the logical empiricist. Very often the ordinary person and the scientist are observing the same phenomenon. But the purposes of their observations differ. To illustrate, one might gaze at the stars just to admire their beauty. This constitutes an experience for the observer. But an astronomer has quite different purposes. First, he wishes to give a systematic description of the various heavenly bodies. Second, he presents an explanation of what he has observed by proposing various laws (e.g., gravity) and theories (e.g., relativity). Finally, from his observations, laws, and theories he attempts to predict the behavior of the heavenly bodies, such as eclipses, the appearance of comets, and so forth. The ordinary observer of a phenomenon may stop at simple observation or perhaps attempt some kind of description. Seldom does he offer or is he capable of scientific explanation and prediction.

Clearly, then, the logical empiricist limits knowledge claims to the realms of experience and science. The methods of faith, revelation, mysticism, and pure reason are not regarded as valid means of arriving at knowledge. But what proof does he offer for the validity of scientific (inductive) method, since he uses criteria of scientific method to rule out the validity of other modes of knowing? The empiricist is willing to admit that one cannot demonstrate the validity of the principle of induction by appealing to induction-that would be question begging. Rather, he asserts that "it is a principle of procedure, a regulative maxim, and operational rule." If one proceeds according to this rule, he will be able to "do" science; if he does not choose to do so, he may be indulging in other activities (poetry, art, etc.), but not in scientific activities.[13]

---

[12]For a more comprehensive discussion of these criteria of scientific method, see H. Feigel, "Naturalism and Humanism," *Readings in the Philosophy of Science,* ed. H. Feigel and M.Brodbeck (New York: Appleton-CenturyCrofts, 1953), pp. 10-13.
[13] See H. Feigel "The Logical Character of the Principle of Induction," *Readings in Philosophical Analysis*(New York: Appleton-CenturyCrofts, 1949), pp. 297-304.

WHAT IS TRUTH?

From the foregoing sections, it is evident that the logical empiricist must reject the conservative notion of truth. Since the statements of theology and metaphysics are meaningless, the question of the truth or falsity of such statements need not be considered. Consequently, the empiricist's reservoir of truths will contain only the findings of science and ordinary experiences. But even the latter must be capable of a scientific test before they can be considered true. If one is unwilling to subject an individual or personal experience to public test, he can make no knowledge claims for such experience. Thus a person who claims to have some mystical contact with the spiritual world (which no one can objectively check) can not claim any truth value for his experience.

In reality the empiricist holds that scientific activity produces the major truths which can claim general or public acceptance. It is important then to know which disciplines can lay legitimate claim to the title, science, from which truth is derived.

The sciences can be divided into the formal and the factual. The formal sciences are logic and mathematics (deductive sciences). From these, formal or analytic truth is derived. The factual sciences from which synthetic truths are derived are divided into the pure and applied sciences.

Diagram I

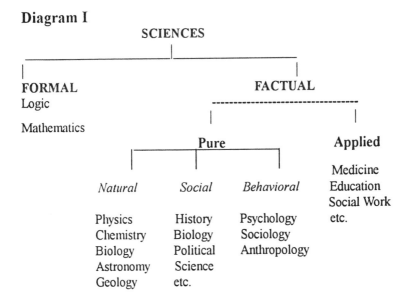

The applied sciences, such as medicine, education, and social work, are based upon knowledge derived from the pure sciences. The pure sciences are divided into the natural, social, and behavioral sciences. The natural sciences include such disciplines as physics, chemistry, biology, and astronomy; the social sciences include economics, history, political science, and the like; the behavioral sciences include psychology, anthropology, and sociology. (There are various combinations of the sciences such as physical chemistry and social psychology and many subdivisions of each major science, e.g., mineralogy is a subdivision of geology.) Diagram 1 shows the relationship among the various sciences. There is a final question which the philosophers must seek to answer: "Are the truths of science immutable (absolute)?" The logical empiricist's answer to this question is that the conclusions of the formal sciences (logic and mathematics) are, in a certain sense, absolute. For example, in the deductive syllogism X is Y and Y is Z, therefore X is Z, the conclusion derived from the two premises follows of *necessity* from them. Mathematical deduction is of the same nature. Perhaps it is more accurate to speak of *necessary* truths in the formal sciences and eliminate the term absolute with all its metaphysical connotation.[14]

In the factual sciences, however, there are no absolute or immutable truths. In other words, the factual sciences yield only *probable truths*. The degree of probability will depend to a great extent upon the degree of refinement and scientific accuracy which the particular science has developed. For example, the findings of the natural sciences boast a higher degree of probability than those of the social or behavioral sciences. Even if the findings of the factual sciences are probable, how does one know when a scientific statement is factually true or false? "When it corresponds or does not correspond to observed fact," answers the empiricist. But when the statement *does* correspond to an observed fact, why can it not be considered an immutable truth? Simply because the correspondence of the statement with the observed fact is only incompletely or indirectly indicated. Therefore the logical empiricist is wont to use the terms confirmed or disconfirmed to describe the conclusions of factual science.[15] To support the wisdom of this position, he will point to the history of science which is as much a record of errors and misconceptions as it is one of confirmed truths. Even the brute facts of history have undergone constant revision because of

---

[14]Some argue that modernmultivalued logical and mathematical systems constitute and exception to this general rule.

[15]See Feigl, "Naturalism andHumanism,"*op. cit*, pp. 9-13;Ayer,*op. cit*, Ch. V.

penetrating historical research.

The logical empiricist readily admits the skeptical nature of his view of knowledge and truth. But, he considers it a healthy skepticism and a sign of intellectual maturity. Only the immature demand certainty.

To summarize the logical empiricist's views on truth, it can be asserted that truth is equated with the findings of the sciences and with experience (when it can be checked empirically). Metaphysical and theological conclusions have no factual validity and therefore cannot be considered true or false.

WHAT IS GOOD?

When the logical empiricist is asked to distinguish good from evil, right from wrong, beautiful from ugly, he is in a difficult position. Certainly, he makes choices in his day-to-day living which involve these questions. And many of these choices have great significance not only for himself but for his fellowmen; he answers ethical questions every day of his life. However, as a philosopher he views this whole matter from the coldly analytic point of view. His first question will be, "Are statements about good, evil, and the like meaningful?" Some are. For example, the following propositions are meaningful. "Some primitive peoples believe that it is wrong to kill a member of one's own tribe but right to kill a foreigner"; or "Polygamy is considered right by certain oriental peoples"; "Most literary critics say Shakespeare's works are more beautiful than those of Milton." These statements are meaningful because anthropology or sociology or a survey of literary critics can prove them right or wrong-they are capable of a scientific test. But closer scrutiny will show that they are not value judgments at all, but statements of fact; they are descriptive.

The crucial question of meaning arises when prescriptive statements are involved, that is, those which advise or command people how to live. The Ten Commandments and the moral codes of different races, countries, or cultures are statements of this type. Applying the meaning criterion, one sees that all such moral prescriptions are factually meaningless simply because no empirical test can be made of them. Even when the "Thou shalt not" is omitted from the statement, it is still meaningless. For example, the statement "It is wrong to steal" must be meaningless since it can never be shown to be true or false empirically. All such statements represent an expression of one's feelings, emotions, or preferences and an explicit or implicit desire that others will accept the same view and live according to it.[16]

According to this view of values, statements about the beauty or ugliness of natural objects or works of art are also devoid of factual meaning. They, too, are simply expressions of one's feelings or preferences. There seems to be nothing for the analytic philosopher or the logical positivist to talk about in connection with values of any kind. He can make no ethical pronouncements; he must "resist the role of expert moral guide" as Scoffer says. As a philosopher he must limit his task to giving an analysis of ethical terms and clarifying the logical structure of moral decisions. But as a human being, he must go on living, making ethical and aesthetic choices. This he does, but he makes no claim for the truth or objectivity of his choices; he admits they are merely expressions of his preferences.

Many logical positivists argue that the emotive theory of ethics is the only legitimate position they can hold. Other members of the same school believe that in the realm of the arts the emotive theory is wholly adequate, but they find it inadequate in the treatment of ethical values. To put matters of good and evil in the same category as matters of taste in food and art is to overlook a significant difference between the two. They note that there is a general tolerance in matters of taste which does not exist in the realm of *fundamental* morals. Modern technologically advanced peoples and primitive tribes condemn robbery, murder, rape, stealing, greed, lying, and the like. Also, most people consider prohibitions against sub behavior binding on all men. Consequently, the radical empiricist commits the reductive fallacy when he reduces all ethical statements to meaningless propositions.[17]

Does the moderate empiricist grant ethical statements the same status as factual ones derived from the sciences? For example, are the statements "Copper conducts electricity" and "Stealing is wrong" of the same kind? It seems not; as Feigl says "ethics is not, and cannot be, an exact science." However, it appears that the sciences of man, especially anthropology and sociology, can be of assistance in determining what the fundamental moral values are. But the various applications of these basic values which result in different ethical systems such as naturalistic, pragmatic, or Thomistic ethics

---

[16]See Ayer, *op. cit.*, pp. 20-22, Ch. VI. This view of value is called the Emotive Theory.

[17]H. Feigl, "Aims of Education for Our Age of Science: Reflections of a Logical Empiricist," *Modern Philosophies and Education*, ed. N.B. Henry (Chicago: Univ. of Chicago Press, 1955), p. 326.

represent legitimate alternatives. All the alternative systems hold certain moral principles in common but also have certain differences. The essentials are "morals," the differences mores or folkways.[18]

Admittedly, however, the position described above as moderate is not generally accepted among analysts and positivists. Yet it is felt that the analyst has something practical to contribute to the whole field of ethics. Thus certain analysts following Wittgenstein's lead argue that ordinary language is a tool for conducting human affairs. Moral discourse, then, is a practical kind of speech designed to guide people's behavior rather than to describe or predict factual situations. Obviously, people's preferences for certain kinds of behavior are contained in ethical statements. But, these statements also reflect what people actually believe to be good and evil. As such these statements do have a real meaning, though not a scientific one. Most people know what you are talking about when you say, "It is wrong to steal." Someone might disagree with you, but he cannot say he does not know what you mean.

Herein lies the task of analytic ethics. By analysis of moral statements the analyst can correct many popular misconceptions. For example, he might show that what is proposed as an absolute in morals may actually be only a relative prescription. Or he might show that what one holds to be a moral truth may be only an expression of a certain personal prejudice. Yet another result of such analysis might demonstrate that no increase in factual information can compel opposing moralists to agree on ethical or ideological principles. Perhaps even more valuable is the assistance the analyst can give in pointing up how a particular way of life will include certain prescriptions, commendations, rewards, and punishments, in other words a whole moral code, whereas a different way of life might have quite another moral code.

A very practical outcome of this analytic endeavor might be a greater tolerance for the moral beliefs of other cultures as well as those of other individuals. Furthermore, such analysis will assist people to clarify their language, removing many of the current moral squabbles. Only after such linguistic confusions have been removed can people actually do an intelligent job of clarifying the fundamental goals of life.

Thus, according to this view, the analytic philosopher and the logical positivist have a role to play in the centuries-old field of moral philosophy. But their role is "not to prescribe but to analyze and clarify." The fulfillment of this role will have practical value for the moral philosopher, the man on

---

[18]For an analysis and description of moderate empiricism, see *ibid.*, pp. 323-30.

the street, the politician, and the teacher.[19]

WHAT IS THE PURPOSE OF THE SCHOOL?

Early in this chapter it was noted that the analytic philosopher contends that it is not his function to tell educators what to do in their schools. The logical empiricist is in general agreement with this view and tends to shy away from answering educational questions unless scientifically derived answers are possible. It does appear, however, that certain answers to basic educational questions would be in harmony with the scientific outlook of the logical empiricist whereas others would be completely foreign to their views. Obviously any answers drawn from theological or metaphysical sources would be wholly unacceptable.

Regarding the first question, "What is the purpose of the school?", one logical empiricist states that the school's primary obligation is to develop "rationality." More specifically this aim includes the fostering of (1) clarity of thought, (2) consistency and conclusiveness of reasoning, (3) objectivity, (4) scientific (factual) accuracy and reliability, (5) the selection of proper means to achieve desired ends, and (6) moral rationality, i.e., adherence to standards of justice, equity, benevolence, impartiality, and abstention from violence.[20]

It is worth noting that the objective of rationality is related closely to the criteria of science listed on p. 251. Evidently, then, the logical empiricist wants the school to develop a "scientific mentality" in pupils. This is its primary obligation. If teachers, administrators, and others concerned with the operation of schools wish to include purposes such as physical fitness, social adjustment and vocational competence they might do so in response to local or national needs. Thus some communities or nations might choose to give the school the job of developing vocational competence. Others may feel that agencies other than the school should be responsible for this task.

---

[19]H.D. Aiken, "Moral Philosophy and Education,"*Harvard Educational Review*, XXV, 1 (winter, 1955), 39-60. See M.Schlick, "What Is the Aim of Ethics?" and C.L. Stevenson, "The Emotive Meaning of Ethical Terms," in*Logical Positivism*,ed. A.Ayer (Glencoe, Ill.: The Free Press, 1959),Chs. XII, XIII.

[20]H. Feigl, "Aims of Education for Our Age of Science,"*op. cit*, pp. 335f.

WHAT SHOULD BE TAUGHT?

To ask the analytic philosopher or the logical empiricist to formulate a very detailed curriculum for the school would be to no avail. As a parent, teacher, or school board member he might participate willingly in curriculum planning. As a philosopher he is more apt to make statements like Feigl's "There is much in progressive education that appears sound and hopeful," or "Too much concern with the past is fruitless." "I am pleading for a golden-mean solution of the issue between progressive and classical education." But he soon betrays his scientific orientation, especially if be refers to himself as an empiricist. Then, he avers that a "large part" of the curriculum should be devoted to the study of the natural, social, and applied sciences throughout elementary, secondary, and higher education.

The actual pattern of courses is not important to the empiricist. He does insist, though, that subject matter has a definite place. By subject matter he does not mean mere facts, formulae, principles, and rules, although these are important. The study of mathematics and the sciences should include an examination of the role these disciplines play in our scientific age, "the methods of discovery and the validation of knowledge." Surely, no twentieth-century empiricist would ever argue that science education should be excluded from the school curriculum.

Even though the sciences will constitute the heart of the empiricist's curriculum, he admits that "man does not live by technologically enhanced creature comforts alone." Therefore, history, literature, and the fine arts should be an integral part of the course of study. These two categories, science and humanities, will make up "general education. Vocational training might be added to this central core at both the elementary and secondary level. Also, the curriculum of higher education should represent a balance between general and specialized education.[21]

One final point should be made about the logical empiricist's view of the curriculum. As an advocate of analytic philosophy he would wish to have all teachers in all subject-matter areas be especially attentive to training students in linguistic analysis. This training will enable them to distinguish the various ways in which language is used. The differences between fact and value, propaganda and truth, poetry and philosophy should be made clear. In other words, students should be trained in philosophical analysis throughout their educational careers.

---

[21] For the recommendation of a logical empiricist and the views just mentioned, see *ibid.*, pp. 336-41.

HOW SHOULD ONE TEACH?

The logical empiricist, unlike many of the educational philosophers discussed in this volume, does not feel that the controversies about how to teach are especially important. His first recommendation for resolving the conflict would be to employ the tools of logic and linguistic analysis to clarify the issues involved. Ludwig Wittgenstein, for example, felt that such analysis would remove the main source of most controversies the misunderstanding of meanings. Remove the source of the problems and the problems will disappear (therapeutic positivism).

The role which linguistic analysis can play in clearing up the confusion about teaching-learning methods is exemplified in certain recent works. Several chapters of *Language and Concepts in Education* are devoted to this topic. Also Scheffler's *Philosophy and Education* has a number of selections on teaching methods.[22] In general, however, the authors are not arguing that one teaching method is better than another. Their chief concern is for the clarification of the language, pointing up logical inconsistencies in arguments and noting the basic assumption of each point of view.

In the last analysis, then, the logical empiricist and his fellow analysts would advise the educator to seek answers for his question "How should one teach?" from those doing research in that field and from everyday experience or common sense. After all, the question of methods and means is a practical one. Thus, the natural method advocated by liberals may not be practicable under all conditions; some of the techniques and methods used by conservatives may get the job done better than modern techniques; one teacher's personality traits might make it inadvisable for him to try progressive methods. Some of this common sense approach to teaching method is noted in Feigl's comment that the dry-as-dust method of teaching science should be "replaced by an exciting intellectual adventure in science." Also, learning by doing and the natural method have their limitations in our modern complex civilization. In many subject-matter areas the teacher can achieve more by using the systematic approach of the traditional school.[23]

It was mentioned that the analytic philosopher and the empiricist would recommend that the educational theorist also look to research for the answer to the question "How to teach?" During the past thirty years much

---

[22]See Smith andEnnis, *op. cit*, Chs. I, III, IV, VI, X;Scheffler,*op. cit*, pp. 32, 92, 146, 205.

[23]Feigl, "Aims of Education for Our Age of Science*op. cit*, p. 337.

research has been done in the field of educational methodology which the empiricist would regard with skepticism. Many of the studies lack adequate control of the numerous variables involved in the teaching-learning process. Terms and concepts are inadequately defined; assumptions are not clearly stated; the broad conclusions drawn are not warranted by the data or findings. Recently, however, the canons of scientific method have been applied to research in teaching. In one study, which fulfills the rules and requirements of analysis and empiricism, the procedure is as follows: (1) The term teaching is clearly defined and delimited, (2) teaching and learning are adequately distinguished, (3) the system of actions involved in teaching is stated Specifically, (4) a pedagogical model is constructed pointing up the independent, intervening, and dependent variables in relation to linguistic, performative, and expressive behavior (for both teacher and pupils), and, finally, (5) the limitations of the research design and the conclusions are noted.[24]

It seems, then, that both the analytic philosopher and the logical empiricist have the same answer to the educator's questions regarding how one should teach: use your own experience, common sense, and the findings of research studies.

HOW SHOULD PUPILS BE EVALUATED?

The empiricist would agree with philosophers of other persuasions that evaluation should be in terms of the stated purpose of the school. Do the objective or essay examinations which are in use adequately measure clarity of thought, consistency, objectivity, and the like? Do current examinations or other means of evaluation determine the students' knowledge of and attitudes toward justice, equity, impartiality, and benevolence? Obviously, the answers to these questions must be based upon valid research. Again, this is not the task of the philosopher, but of the experts in the field of measurement and evaluation. The philosopher might lend his assistance by acting as a critic of the language and concepts used and by pointing up underlying assumptions, logical inconsistencies, and the like, but he will not tell the educator *how* to evaluate pupils.

---

[24]Smith and Ennis, *op. cit*, pp. 86-101.

HOW ARE DISCIPLINE AND FREEDOM TO BE HARMONIZED?

The answer to the question of how discipline and freedom are to be harmonized, which is of great concern to those who run schools and teach in classrooms, is not to be found in the works of the analytic philosophers or the logical empiricists. And this is as it should be since they do not believe that the philosopher should concern himself with such questions. Of course, the tools of linguistic analysis will aid in the clarification of the problem for the educator but will not give him the solution. The problem must be solved by teachers and administrators in terms of the objectives of the school, the type of society in which the school operates, the personality traits of teachers, and other practical concerns.

Even though most of the analytic philosophers and empiricists mentioned thus far express a preference for democracy as a form of government, they make no explicit or implicit inference that democracy should be practiced in the classroom. Thus, unlike either the conservatives who are opposed to the idea of the democratic classroom or the liberals who favor it, the empiricist does not commit himself. He tells teachers, "This is your problem; solve it to the best of your ability."

CHAPTER SUMMARY

The analytic movement in philosophy differs radically from the other philosophical points of view mentioned in this text. The analysts do not believe in the construction of world views or the search for absolutes or ultimate principles. Rather, they look upon the function of philosophy as one of service to common sense and the sciences. The analysis of language, pointing up assumptions and logical inconsistencies, and clearing away pseudo-problems are important functions of the analytic philosopher.

One group of philosophers within the analytic movement, the logical empiricists, do offer specific answers to some questions posed in our text. Their analytic orientation, however, is evident in their answers. In general, they hold the following views on philosophical or educational questions: Man is what the behavioral sciences say he is-an evolving organism with certain needs, drives, and desires and living in a society having norms for behavior, customs, and so forth. Experience and science constitute the valid ways by which man acquires knowledge about himself and the world around him. Truth is contained in experience and the findings of the sciences. Aesthetic values are merely expressions of individual or group preferences. For some empiricists ethical values, too, are expressions of preferences. For others, certain fundamental moral values are rooted in man's nature and can be empirically determined; the different applications and implementations of these fundamental values to daily living result in alternative ethical systems.

The application of empiricist philosophy to educational questions provides the following answers: The school's primary goal is to develop rationality. The curriculum should contain a good balance of scientific studies and the humanities. The methods of teaching and evaluation should he determined by common sense and educational research. Harmonizing freedom and discipline is a practical problem, the solution of which will vary among different social groups and teachers.

BIBLIOGRAPHY

Ayer, Alfred. *Language, Truth and. Logic*. New York: Dover Publications,1946.

Beck, Robert N. *Perspectives in Philosophy*. New York: Holt, Rinehart and Winston, 1961. Parts IV, V.

Broudy, H. S. "The Role of Analysis in Educational Philosophy," *Educational Theory*, XIV, No. 4 (October, 1964), 261-70.

Burns, Hobert W. "The Logic of Educational Implication," *Educational Theory*, XII (January, 1962), 53433.

Feigl, Herbert. "Aims of Education for Our Age of Science: Reflections of a Logical Empiricist," *Modern Philosophies and Education*. 54th N.S.S.E. Yearbook. Chicago: Univ. of Chicago Press, 1955.

Feigl, Herbert, and Sellars, Wilfrid (eds.). *Readings in Philosophical Analysis*. New York: Appleton-Century Crofts, 1949.

Hospers, John. *An Introduction to Philosophical Analysis*. New York: Prentice-Hall, 1953.

Lauglo, J. "Concepts of General Education and the Norweigian Basic School." *Scandinavian Journal of Educational Research*, 1985.

Lightfoot, S. "On Goodness in Schools: Themes of Empowerment" Presentation at Vanderbilt Univ. Nashville, Tenn. Oct. 3, 1985.

Mehta, Ved, "The Battle Against the Bewitchment of Our Intelligence," *New Yorker*, XXXVII, No. 43 (December 9, 1961), 59-159.

Nielsen K. and Sleeper, R. W. "Linguistic Philosophy and the Meaning of

Life" "Linguistic Philosophy and Religious Belief." *Cross Currents*, XIV (Summer, 1964), 313-59.

Proceedings of the Philosophy of Education Society. Lawrence: Univ. of Kansas Press, 1959. Pp. 15-23, 59-64, 41-48. Also 1960 Proceedings. Pp. 19-23, 42-56.

Reichenbach, Hans. *The Rise of Scientific Philosophy*. Berkeley: Univ. of California Press, 1951.

Runes, D. (ed.). *Twentieth Century Philosophy*. New York: Philosophical Library, 1943. Pp. 371-417.

Scoffer, Israel. *Philosophy and Education*. Boston: Allyn & Bacon, 1958.

Smith, B. Othanel, and Ennis, Robert H. (eds). *Language and Concepts in Education*. Chicago: Rand McNally & Co., 1961.

White, Morton (ed.). *The Age of Analysis*. Boston: Houghton Miflilin. Co., 1955.

Chapter X

Educational Psychologies

Many readers might consider educational psychology a discipline with its beginnings in the twentieth century. To some extent, this notion is understandable since psychology as a "behavioral science" is relatively new. But it must be noted that practically all of the theorists mentioned in Chapters 1-VIII espoused views which legitimately might be labeled their "psychology." Their views of human nature treat such questions as how the mind and body are related, how individuals come to know themselves and the world around them, how the individual learns, how teachers should teach and the like. This aspect of their theory has been variously referred to as philosophical or rational psychology. In fact, the English word is taken from the Greek, meaning the study or science of the mind (soul). Johann F. Herbart (1776-1841) might be considered the first theorist to blend philosophical psychology with educational practice. His efforts to "make education a science" and to test his theories in a "laboratory school" might justify naming him the first educational psychologist.

Chapters IX and X, however, treat the philosophical views mainly of early and mid-twentieth century thinkers. One might expect a commitment to a specific psychology of education. But, as mentioned, these theorists generally are not concerned with the application of their theories to educational practice. In reality, many of them deliberately shy away from giving specific recommendations for curricula, teaching methods, evaluation and discipline. It seems, then, that their influence has been felt through the psychological theories which are at least partially rooted in these philosophical beliefs.

The two dominant psychologies in education of the past decades have been the behavioristic and humanistic approaches. Of these two "camps" the behaviorists have had the greatest influence on education especially because of the work of B.F. Skinner in the field of learning theory.

BEHAVIORISM

Of the philosophies discussed in this text, Skinner's theoretical position is most closely related to that of the positivists (or Logical Empiricists). His psychological antecedents can be traced to the work of Ivan Sechenov and Ivan Pavlov, the eminent Russian psychologist. The latter devised the well-known experiments with dogs in which the animals responded to certain stimuli other than the original (natural) stimulus, food. After continued pairings of food and the sound of a bell the dogs salivated at the sound of the bell alone. Perhaps the experiments themselves are not as important as the theory (later developed by other behaviorists) that learning is a matter of "conditioning" rather than a conscious choice of the individual to learn.

J.B. Watson, the American psychologist, contributed to the early development of behaviorism by rejecting any psychology of human beings other than that derived from objectively observable and measurable behavior. Further, Watson rejected the notion that instincts are causes of behavior.[1] Edward L. Thorndike echoed these same sentiments when he stated anything which truly exists can be measured or it simply does not exist. This dictum became the watchword of the objective testing movement in the United States. Thorndike, too, was the first to propose that rewards were better reinforcers than punishment because they strengthened the connections between the stimulus and the desired response.

It was Skinner who seized upon this notion of positive reinforcement and made it the cornerstone of his theory of operant conditioning. Teachers, therapists, and parents have all used this technique in some form or other. (The old adage, one can catch more flies with a spoon of honey than a gallon of vinegar, reflects this same notion). Since teachers, counselors, and the like are concerned mainly with those behaviors that can be strengthened by reinforcing consequences, Skinner's learning theory has played a major role in the process of education. In fact, he believes that all "good" and lasting education is that based on positive reinforcement.[2] Since Skinner is the best known of the behavioral theorists, it might be well to derive his answers to the main questions asked in the preceding chapters. "Derive" is a proper term since Skinner himself may not always address these questions

[1]J.B. Watson, "Psychology as the Behaviorist Views It," *Psychological review* 20, (1913), 158-177.
[2]B.F. Skinner, "The Shame of American Education," *American Psychologist* September 1984, Vol. 39, No. 9, 947-954.

directly. In fact, he seems to imply that he has no philosophical presuppositions.[3]

WHAT IS MAN?

It is helpful that Skinner's title for Chapter 9 of *Beyond Freedom and Dignity* is: "What Is Man?" For the behaviorist, human nature is what the behavioral sciences say it is. Thus, human beings are biological organisms existing in a sociocultural environment which determines their "nature or essence." A combination of their genetic history and environmental influences make the individual, the race, and the culture what they are. One cannot, therefore, speak of a given "essence" such as rationality as many traditional thinkers did. (Therefore, Skinner rejects any mind-body, spirit-matter dualism.) Even certain traits or characteristics, formerly attributed to human nature such as the "will to succeed," and the "hunter or warrior instinct" are due to external conditioning. Both of these behaviors persist because of past positive reinforcement.[4] Also, because of evolution the human species has under-gone changes and will continue to change.

If all behaviors are due to conditioning, obviously, human beings are not free agents, i.e., they do not possess "free will" in the traditional sense of the term. Freedom, then for Skinner is an illusion. We have been conditioned to believe we are free.[5]

What does the behaviorist say about the individual differences in human beings about which traditional thinkers made so much? It follows from their notion of the conditioning influence of environmental factors that individuals differ mainly because of the effects of their different environments. Genetic differences do exist, e.g., eye color, but even these differences can be changed by "genetic engineering."

Finally, behaviorists would, of course, reject the notion that humans are "innately" inclined to evil or good. Again, these so-called human tendencies are due to environmental forces which determine the individual's behavior.

---

[3]B.F. Skinner and Carl Rogers, *Dialogue on Education and the Control of Human Behavior.* N.Y. Psychology Today (Audio Cassettes).
[4]B.F. Skinner, *Beyond Freedom and Dignity* Chaps 1 and 5.
[5]Ibid. Chapter 2.

HOW DO WE KNOW?

The answer to this all-important question is quite simple for the behaviorist. Science! Of course, the sciences include the behavioral sciences and thus our knowledge of human beings is derived from these sciences, not philosophy or theology.[6] Skinner clearly states that empirical psychology provides the only reliable knowledge of human behavior just as physics, chemistry, biology, etc., provide the only reliable knowledge of the universe.[7]

WHAT IS TRUTH?

Theorists of the behaviorist persuasion adhere to the criterion of meaning and truth discussed in Chapter X. They would agree that for a statement about human behavior to be meaningful it must be testable. For example, if one were to assert that the spiritual soul moves human beings to behave in a certain way, it would be a meaningless statement simply because the existence of the soul is (by definition) empirically untestable. This and similar statements are devoid of any factual content and therefore cannot be labeled as either true or false. But if a statement about human behavior is verifiable by experimental means, are such statements immutably true? The answer is that the "truths" garnered from empirical psychology are probable, not absolute or changeless. Most behaviorists will admit that the behavioral sciences have not yet achieved the high degree of probability found in the physical sciences, but that will come with the improvement of their theoretical structure and the new techniques being devised by behavioral scientists.

WHAT IS GOOD?

The behaviorist does not deny that people hold "values" such as honesty, sympathy, brotherly love, and a host of other "goods" which are found in our culture. The important point Skinner makes is that these values are not innate, not due to the inner voice of conscience, not "written into the heart of man." Nor are they derived from some source external to human experience

---

[6]See Chapter X sections on "How Do We Know What is Truth?"
[7]Skinner and Rogers *Dialogue on Human Behaviors* tape 1.

such as God's commandments to the human race. Since humans are not free to decide what is good and act upon that knowledge, they act in certain ways that are considered good or bad because of their "genetic endowment traceable to the evolutionary history of the species and the environmental circumstances to which an individual has been exposed."[8] Values, then, simply are expressions of (or preferences for) those forms of behavior which have been reinforced, the most basic of which is survival. Others such as honesty is the best policy" are acceptable values because they provide positive reinforcement to both the individual and society. But, what about values such as those involving civil disobedience which do not result in pleasant consequences (imprisonment) either for the individual or society? The answer lies in the fact that not all reinforcement must be immediate. For example, students may subject themselves to many unpleasant courses, examinations, and sleepless nights to get a degree which makes them eligible for admission to medical school. Acts of civil disobedience, then, may not provide immediate reinforcement. Further, it is not necessary to be able to demonstrate that this "decision" is based on any particular experience(s) since so many uncontrolled variables in the individual's past experiences may have entered into the "decision."

Even those values expressed in a nation's preference for democracy can be traced to the greater positive reinforcement individuals and groups receive from a democratic rather than from an autocratic structure. This "higher level" value, then, may be considered a cultural value as distinguished from an individual or personal value.[9] Somewhere between the individual and cultural values Skinner posits social values such as justice and honesty. Thus, dishonesty among people in any society proves not to be positively reinforced in the long run even though it might "pay off" for an individual. The "white collar" criminal might gain by his embezzlement, but his behavior does not bring satisfaction to the rest of society.

If moral values are derived from experience and are retained because the greatest positive reinforcement has been realized, then, too, aesthetic values are acquired by the same process. No piece of art, be it in music, painting, sculpture, or literature is *inherently* better than some other piece. One might assert that certain types or genres of art are preferred (or survive longer) because they provide the greatest positive reinforcement to the readers, listeners, or viewers. So, too, an individual might prefer one art piece or art form over the other for the same reason.

---

[8]Skinner,*Beyond Freedom and Dignity*, Chap. 6, p. 96.
[9]Ibid. Chap. 8.

Aesthetic values, then, just as moral values, may be held individually, socially, or culturally. An individual might prefer "rock to Bach"; a social class might prefer symphony and opera to "Country Western" and a culture (Oriental) might develop a quite different kind of music from that preferred by another culture (Occidental).

It seems clear that the behaviorists derive their theories from a set of philosophical beliefs radically different from those mentioned in earlier chapters. (Even Dewey, the eminent twentieth century thinker, wished to distinguish his psychology, functionalism, from theirs.)

WHAT IS THE PURPOSE OF THE SCHOOL?

The fundamental behavioristic beliefs about human nature and values suggest that the school's goals or objectives encompass the entire range of human activity. Thus, the purposes of schooling should be satisfying individual, social, and cultural needs. Just what these needs are will change from generation to generation, and their identification will come from the behavioral sciences. In this respect behaviorists reflect the earlier thinking of Herbert Spencer who proposed a hierarchy composed of survival, vocational, familial, social, and leisure time needs.

One point the behaviorists will make about all educational objectives is that they be stated in "behavioral terms" so that the results can be measured objectively. Skinner is especially critical of "useless goals of education such as excellence or creativity." Unless these goals of education can be translated into behavioral objectives, they are absolutely meaningless. He chides the authors of many reports of the 1980s on "excellence" in education and "creativity" in the sciences for their failure to specify what they mean by these terms. He faults the politicians that mouth the same clichés and the legislative bodies that pass laws to improve education" for their complete lack of understanding of the educational process and the means to achieve certain goals.[10]

WHAT SHOULD BE TAUGHT?

The sections above on How Do We Know? and What Is Truth? suggest the content of the curriculum. Again, one is reminded of Spencer's answer

---

[10]Skinner, "The Shame of American Education," p. 951.

to the question, "What knowledge is of most worth?" Who shall decide what knowledge is of the most worth? It is clear that such decisions will be based on the findings of the various sciences. Skinner maintains that the sciences can provide the answer to "what ought to be taught?" Such decisions, Skinner says, need not be left to philosophers and theologians because these decisions are presumed to be beyond or above the realm of science.[11]

With the sciences providing a clear framework of the content of the curriculum, the specific subject matters should be put into "programs" covering the essentials of each area. Every program will contain behavioral objectives and means for the objective evaluation of the students' success in achieving the stated objectives.[12] In response to critics who claim a curriculum providing for "discovery" is the best means of learning, Skinner responds that "working through a program is really a process of discovery" and "trying to teach mathematics or science as if students themselves were discovering things for the first time is not an efficient way of teaching." After students have finished the programs, they will have acquired the skills and knowledge which might assist them to "actually make a genuine discovery." Also, Skinner points out that the time saved by using programmed materials will give the teachers time to listen and talk to students, read what students write, counsel them on careers, and the like.

The general content of the curriculum will have been determined beforehand by the experts in curriculum design and the subject matter fields. The choice of subjects and the material to be covered in each area will be determined by the individual, social, and cultural needs of the learners.[13] The following example might illustrate this approach to curriculum construction. It can be demonstrated (by the sciences) that children need reading, writing, and computing skills to meet their individual needs. Also, these same skills are needed for the survival of modern society. In a similar manner, mastery of a foreign language may be needed by some students to achieve a personal or individual objective such as work in the foreign service. Also, it might meet a cultural need such as understanding people of another nation or culture.

A final note on the curriculum design of the behaviorist pertains to its permanence or tentativeness. Because of biological and social evolution, any curriculum must be tentative. What serves the needs of the individual, society, or the culture in the last decades of the twentieth century may be

---

[11]Skinner,*Beyond Freedom and Dignity*, p. 97.
[12]Skinner, "The Shame of American Education," p. 951.
[13]For and example of this approach, see*Individually Guided Education* Eighth Annual Report 1971-72. R & D Center for Cognitive Learning, Madison WI.

completely different for people in the 23rd century. Therefore, behavioral scientists must provide continuous guidance for curriculum designers to update the "programs" to meet changing needs.

HOW SHOULD ONE TEACH?

Skinner and many advocating his position are opposed to teaching large groups of students the same content at the same time. Because of individual differences it is impossible to expect students to advance at the same rate. Also, he says, tracking is a "feeble remedy." The solution, then, is *Individually Guided Education* using programmed learning and teaching machines. (Computers are merely more complex teaching machines.) Students know what the objectives of each are and are immediately reinforced when they achieve those objectives. Thus, the problem of motivation is solved. Skinner reports on a visitation he made to a classroom where students were learning by this method. When he entered, they paid no attention to him. The teacher tried to get their attention, but to no avail - the students were so absorbed in their individual programs.[14]

What does a teaching machine do? It succeeds in modifying the behavior of the learner. The term "behavior modification" is now widely used to cover the act of teaching. But behavior modification can be used in many settings other than with teaching machines. Communicative disorders can be corrected with specific behavior modification techniques. Therapy provided in mental health and penal centers frequently apply such techniques. In all of these situations, however, the application of positive reinforcement for reproducing the desired behavior is essential. Thus, even if one does not agree with Skinner that the teaching machine or computer is the "best teacher," there are other techniques which are based on the same behavioral principles.

How does the behaviorist respond to the critics (chiefly the humanists) of this approach to teaching who maintain that behavior modification is "training," not education? The answer is quite simple: Education is training of the highly evolved species called humans. It has been going on for thousands of years in the educational process, but only with the advent of the behavioral sciences have the principles and techniques for effective training been devised.

---

[14]Skinner, "The Shame of American Education," p. 952.

HOW SHOULD PUPILS BE EVALUATED?

As mentioned above in the section on What Is The Purpose of The School?, the stated behavioral objectives must be coupled with the means of objectively determining whether the learners have achieved these objectives. Obviously, objective examinations constructed by experts in the behavioral sciences and the subject areas fit well into this scheme. Since most students in U.S. schools have been "tested" for "just about everything" from kindergarten through graduate school, they know what objective tests are and need no explanation of their function. But, one might ask the behaviorist if all human behavior can be measured by objective tests. The answer lies in what one means by objective tests. For example, if one wishes to measure achievement in a speech class it is possible to list certain behavioral components in a good speech such as diction, eye contact, organization of material, and the like. The trained observer then can determine to what extent the speaker has displayed these behaviors. Thus "competency-based" tests can be constructed which measure the speaker's mastery of the skills involved. Such competency-based tests are now available in many fields and, strictly speaking, are not the "paper and pencil" tests to which most students are accustomed. They are, nevertheless, "objective," since they assess observable behavior.

HOW ARE FREEDOM AND DISCIPLINE TO BE HARMONIZED?

As noted above, the behaviorist wishes to dissociate himself/herself from the traditional notion of freedom, Freedom is an illusion - human beings behave in certain ways because they have been conditioned to do so. Also, they do not believe that discipline - law and order - can be achieved only by punitive measures even though they recognize that punishment may eradicate certain undesirable behavior under certain circumstances. Rather, behaviorists contend that positive reinforcement is the best means of promoting "good discipline" in schools. If desirable behavior is rewarded, it will be sustained. If undesirable behavior is not rewarded, generally it will be extinguished. One need not resort to punishment to eradicate undesirable behaviors, especially in the young.

Finally, "discipline problems" should not even arise if students are actively engaged in completing their "programs." Most discipline problems arise when the learners are not absorbed in the task at hand. If some students have serious behavioral problems, they can be directed to specialists in behavior therapy who will attempt to eradicate the undesirable behavior by behavior modification techniques. To summarize, discipline problems are not caused by "bad students" or "poor teachers" but by the environment which creates these problems. Unless the culture is willing to accept the scientific findings of the behavioral sciences (behaviorism) and the technology which they advocate (behavior modification), discipline problems will remain an educational dilemma.[15]

HUMANISM

A simplistic description of the humanistic approach might be phrased as follows: If behaviorists say that a statement is true, humanists will say its contradictory is true. Behaviorists: Human beings are determined (not free). Humanist: Human beings are not determined (free). This use of formal logic would save many pages, for all the reader would have to do is put a T or F after each statement attributed to the behaviorist and posit its contradictory for the humanist. But, all is not that simple. First, one does not find the general agreement on theoretical principles among the humanists which one finds in the behaviorist camp. Thus, one may speak of a "behavioristic model." Second, the term humanist covers a wide range of thinkers embodying a variety of philosophical persuasions. Third, individual humanists are apt to insist that they do not wish to be restricted by any "system." In other words, there is no one "humanistic model."

However, having stated these limitations, it appears that some common elements emerge in the humanistic theories. Also, since not all the humanists suggest answers to all the questions raised in this text, when a certain author addresses the specific questions, his/her answer is noted. For example, Carl Rogers' work, *Freedom To Learn*, presents answers to many of the questions posed whereas A. Maslow, Rollo May, or Perls may not do so.

WHAT IS MAN?

Few humanists will deny that one's genetic history and environmental circumstances influence the individual's behavior. Likewise, few will deny

---

[15]Ibid. p. 953.

that the behavioral sciences can tell us something about human beings. But the point humanists emphasize is that the behavioral sciences only describe one small (and the least important) aspect of human behavior. (The same is done for rats, pigeons and pigs in much of the behavioral research.) The behavioral approach deals only with "objective" man or rat, not "subjective man." And it is this subjective aspect, the human situation, which is the real subject matter of psychology.

This subjective element in human beings gives them the capability of acting upon or interacting with the objective world. Unlike animals, human beings can "choose" to behave in a certain way rather than simply acting because of external stimuli. In reality, humans can choose to act in a manner contrary to the forces of external stimuli. In other words, human beings are not determined by environmental circumstances but are free to choose their own course of action.[16]

HOW DO WE KNOW?

Humanistic psychologists do not deny that the behavioral sciences supply much information about human behavior. But the major concerns of human existence cannot be examined by the empirical methods of the sciences. A different method of arriving at knowledge is needed to enlighten the individual on so many matters which are unique to each person. "My experiences are not the same as yours." Therefore, human experience cannot be "systematized" - no generalizations can be drawn from the elements of personal experience since they are unique to each individual.

This notion of subjective experience is especially crucial in education and therapy. If each individual comes to know himself and the world around him in his own subjective way, it is futile to attempt to educate people or treat clients as though all will respond to the same stimuli in the same way. Michael Polanyi, in his book *Personal Knowledge*, goes one step further and says that even scientific knowledge is "personal" and not purely objective. Each committed person responds in his/her own way to what he/she is perceiving.[17]

What, then, are these important matters about which individuals seek knowledge? One's relationship with others, death, alienation, anxiety, fear, value choices, and the like are essentials of the human situation about which the individual seeks to know something. The behavioral sciences are of little

---

[16]Skinner and Rogers *op. cit.*, Tape 1: Carl Rogers *Freedom to Learn*, p. 259.
[17]Ibid. p. 272.

help in providing knowledge of such subjective matters. The individual must look into the "inner-self" for answers to the questions which make a difference in one's life. For this reason, Rogers states that diagnostic testing is a contradiction since the individual must "look into himself" to find out what is causing the anxiety or fear- such knowledge cannot be acquired from objective tests!

In some respects, this mode of knowing is similar to the introspective method of the early psychologists which the behavioral scientists reject. Perhaps a better designation of this mode is "phenomenological method" since it is broader than introspection. Also, psychologists such as Jung argue that the phenomenological method provides evidence of cultural realities (collective unconscious) as well as of individual experience.[18]

WHAT IS TRUTH?

The humanistic notion of the subjectivity of knowing implies the subjectivity of truth. Since individuals perceive themselves and the world differently from other individuals, it is not necessary that all hold the same "truths." For example, scientists who make "original discoveries" do so because they see the object of their study in a way quite different from those who merely master the observed facts of past scientists. Likewise, the poet who writes about a sunset perceives that phenomenon in a very unique way, and the poet's description is just as "true" as that of a physicist.

Another characteristic of truth for the humanist is its relevance to the knower's purposes. For example, it is useless to speak of "truths" or facts to be mastered by students if they have no meaning to the students. Whitehead stated that knowledge or truth which is no relevant (inert ideas) is like dead fish - it soon spoils.[19] For the humanist, then, the most important kind of truth is personal experience. It is the most important because it is relevant to the person's life and activities. It comprises all those truths upon which the individual makes the significant choices for life and death.

WHAT IS GOOD?

Perhaps, a belief about values which humanists hold in common is that

---

[18]See A. La Fond, *Jung's Psychology of Religion*, Doctoral Dissertation, Marquette University, 1984.
[19]A.N. Whitehead, *Aims of Education*, Chap. 1.

values (both moral and aesthetic) are much more than behaviors which have been positively reinforced. Also, many humanists would not deny that conditioning does play a role in the determination of values and that some members of the human species do not rise above "being conditioned." Thus one implicit value seems to emerge - freedom. If one does not value freedom, one cannot be truly human.

But how do humans arrive at moral and aesthetic values if not through conditioning? Rogers suggests that conditioning plays the major role in determining value preferences among infants and usually involves immediate reward in the form of food, warmth, and the like for the infant. Later, the child moves beyond this stage of self-satisfaction and tries to please others. In this later process, conditioning again plays a role insofar as the child receives approval for pleasing parents, relatives, teachers, and others in authority. As youngsters move into adolescence, they begin to question the notion of social approval as the criterion for value and may decide to behave in ways that do not conform to social norms. Finally, mature persons develop values based on life-experiences, feelings, and thoughts and arrive at a synthesis of all these experiences. But the key element in this mature valuing process is personal choice. Thus, certain behaviors may be valued even if they do not conform to social norms or even do not provide personal satisfaction.[20]

Just what these values are will depend much on each individual, and they will not always be constant. However, certain values in addition to freedom seem to find favor among humanists. Authenticity might rank near the top in a hierarchy of values (Unto thine own self be true). Openness, empathy, concern for "the other," acceptance of oneself and "the other" as "I am" or "they are" rather than in any preconceived notion of what I or they should be. Maslow's peak experiences might be classified as value experiences. Individuality, as opposed to conformity, should rank well up in the hierarchy.

Finally, one is not likely to find values such as wealth, power, influence, dominance, force, ease, and comfort among the lists of goods to be esteemed.

WHAT IS THE PURPOSE OF SCHOOL?

Carl Rogers clearly states that the broadest aim of education is the

---

[20]Rogers, *Freedom to Learn*. pp. 239-256.

"facilitation of learning" in an ever changing world.[21] Of course, for Rogers, too, the school is only one phase of education. But, schools, teachers, and therapists have the special mission of helping individuals and groups achieve this goal (just what the facilitation of learning means for Rogers is explained below in the next two sections). Paul Goodman, too, in *Community of Scholars* seems to suggest a similar purpose for the school.[22]

The salient feature of this goal which radically differentiates it from the behaviorist purpose is its flexibility relative to each individual engaged in the educational process. Whereas the behaviorist could specify what the school should "do to" each student, the humanist will encourage learners to devise their own personal goals. The school's purpose, then, is defined by the learner's purpose. Ivan Illich made the point very powerfully when he argued that society must be "deschooled" simply because the school's stated purposes were not those of the clientele they were supposed to serve.[23]

The school's purpose, then, is not to make carbon copies of the adults who control schools, be they parents, teachers, or administrators. Nor should the school be devoted to making everyone read, write, spell, compute, or "master" science, history, literature, or foreign language. Even more abhorrent to the humanist would be setting the goal of surpassing Japanese, European, or Soviet students in achievement. These may be "national goals" devised by politicians and experts in the various fields, but they are not the goals of the individual learners.

WHAT SHOULD ONE TEACH?

In general, humanists do not propose a fixed curriculum designed for all students. If human learners are truly free, then why must they be subjected to a predetermined curriculum? A devoted humanist must be quite irked with all the "reform movements" of the 1980s in which presidential commissions, state governors, and legislators demand that every student have four years of English, science, mathematics, history and the like. If one believes that human beings are free, such action constitutes a contradiction since no time remains for students to learn what they want to learn or what they consider important and relevant.

Carl Rogers asserts that the curriculum should be largely self-chosen by

---

[21]Ibid. pp. 107 and 305.
[22]Paul Goodman, *Community of Scholars*, Chap III.
[23]Ivan Illich,*Deschooling Society* New York:Harper and Row, 1972.

the learner; each student should set his/her own assignments rather than have to complete assignments set for all.[24] Goodman, too, castigates those who insist on pre-programming the curriculum for all the years of compulsory education. This approach, he says, robs the learners of the best years of life when their personal interests and needs might lead them to exciting learning. Instead, they have to complete assigned lessons and pass useless tests which simply show that they have responded acceptably to certain stimuli.[25]

In addition to the theoretical reasons for opposing predetermined curricula, standards, and the like, humanists cite some very practical reasons for their opposition. First, students learn rapidly what they themselves choose and are apt to retain what they have learned. On the other hand, they soon forget what they were forced to memorize or master because it had no meaning for them. Second, the high drop-out rate in many schools might be attributed to an irrelevant curriculum and even students who remain in school may become "discipline problems" for the same reason.

HOW SHOULD ONE TEACH?

The humanist is more concerned with learning than with "instructing." Instructing implies imparting knowledge or skill. It also implies that the instructor knows what the students should know whether they want to know it or not. Paul Goodman, John Holt, and Carl Rogers reject the assumptions underlying these beliefs. Goodman calls it *Compulsory Miseducation*. Obviously, then, the lecture would be the most infrequent mode of instruction because there is no assurance that student learning is taking place.

But if one rejects both the traditional modes of teaching and behavior modification as humanists do, "How Should One Teach?" There is no one answer to this question. Since each teacher and each learner is a unique individual, no two will fulfill the teaching-learning function in the same fashion. Perhaps it would suffice then to point out some guidelines suggested by Rogers to "facilitate learning."

1) True learning takes place only when the learner perceives what is to be learned as being relevant to his or her interests or needs.

2) Learning is facilitated when external threats are at a minimum.

---

[24]Rogers, Ibid., p. 9.
[25]Paul Goodman, *Compulsory Miseducation*, Chap. 6.

3) Learners should participate in the teaching-learning process and not be passive observers or listeners. This includes much of what the early liberals and Dewey advocated under "learning by doing."

4) Significant learning involves the whole person - emotions, cognitive processes, choices, and the like.

5) Independent learning in all matters is the ultimate goal of teaching; that is, learning how to learn is perhaps more important than what is learned.[26]

But, one might ask Rogers or Goodman, "Do you need teachers at all?" The response is that the teacher still has a significant role to play in the facilitation of learning, namely, providing a suitable environment. Providing this suitable environment might involve some of the following:

1) Openness to and trust of learners.

2) Assistance in clarifying individual and group purposes.

3) Reliance on individual choice of learners in providing assistance.

4) Provision for a wide range of resources.

5) Availability of teacher as a resource person.

6) Recognition of differences in students' emotional and intellectual responses to different content and situations.

7) Sharing with students as a co-learner and recognizing the teacher's own limitations.

8) Alertness to students' expressions of such feelings as fear, anxiety, lack of self-esteem, pain, conflict, and tension accompanied by a willingness to assist students in their own therapy.[27]

In summary, humanists affirm the independence of the learners and that they can learn without teachers. But teachers with humanistic attitudes can be of assistance in facilitating learning.

HOW SHOULD PUPILS BE EVALUATED?

Rogers states that the first principle of evaluation is "self criticism and self evaluation. Evaluation by others is of secondary importance."[28] Only by these means will the learner achieve independence, creativity, and self-reliance. From this perspective, standardized tests lose their meaning, and grades based upon objective tests lose the importance given them. If grades

---

[26]Ibid. pp. 157-164.
[27]Ibid. pp. 164ff.
[28]Ibid. p. 163.

are to be given, they should be largely self-determined.[29] Goodman, too, criticizes the emphasis on testing since conformity to predetermined responses is all that is really tested.[30.] Even diagnostic tests used clinically are of little value in most cases since they too are based on predetermined responses and standard norms.

In general, then, humanists suggest few specific means of evaluation. Rather, they contend that, because self-evaluation is the only meaningful form of evaluation, the behaviorist insistence on objective forms of evaluation is not only meaningless but might be downright detrimental to the learner's achievement and personality. For this reason Rogers and others recommend the elimination of the "horrible machinery of tests, examinations and evaluation" in American education.[31] Illich and Goodman are perhaps more sweeping in their condemnation of the test mentality of American education and go so far as to recommend the "de-credentialing" of society. The current practice of requiring credential for almost all activities from that of the mechanic to the M.D. should be replaced by "performance" of the tasks. They recognize the difficulties involved in eliminating the billion-dollar testing programs but see it as necessary in order to free the individual from dehumanizing effects of the testing movement.

HOW ARE FREEDOM AND DISCIPLINE TO BE HARMONIZED?

The answer to this question appears to be the same for both the behaviorists and the humanists: namely, if students are actively engaged in learning, discipline problems will not arise. But the rationale for what appears to be the same answer is different for each. Whereas the behaviorist contends that external stimuli bring out proper behavior in students, the humanist argues that it is brought about by internal motivation. Both parties admit that in spite of the ideal situation they would like (no discipline problems) there may be an occasional student who becomes a severe discipline problem. Again, the solution is different for each. In such instances, the behaviorist recommends therapy by behavior modification; the humanist suggest ways of helping the problem students see their own problems and devise their own ways of solving them. In the former, the

---

[29]Ibid. p. 9.
[30]Goodman, *op. cit*, p. 87.
[31]Rogers p. 201.

external therapy resolves the problematic situation; in the latter, the problem student "decides" to change his or her behavior. This latter approach, Rogerian psychotherapy or client centered therapy, stresses the therapists' attitudes that would lead to changes in the client. The success of Rogers' approach to changing behavior by means other than behavior modification (external stimuli) is claimed as evidence that clients can and do change their behavior by their own volition.

CHAPTER SUMMARY

The two psychologies which have influenced education and therapy significantly in recent years are behaviorism and humanism. The philosophical roots of the former seem to be in positivism; the latter draws more from existential thought. Behaviorists view human beings as evolving organisms determined or conditioned by their genetic history and environmental circumstances; humanists view human beings as undetermined (free) individuals or persons who have some control over their own destiny. For the behaviorist, knowledge and truth are derived only from the empirical sciences; for the humanist the most important knowledge and truth (i.e., about the human situation) is personal and subjective. Values for the behaviorist represent behaviors which have been positively reinforced; for the humanist values are freely chosen and based on life experiences.

The application of these two psychologies leads to quite different answers to the educational questions. For the behaviorist, the school is the agent for conditioning learners for individual, social, and cultural survival; for the humanist, the school should provide an atmosphere where learners can freely achieve selfhood (self-realization) and ultimately become what they want to be (create their own being). The behaviorist sees the curriculum as a scientifically predetermined program designed to meet individual, social, and cultural needs; the humanist sees the curriculum as a series of "activities" freely chosen by the learner. The behaviorist defines "teaching" as conditioning and learning as modification of behavior; the humanist prefers to view teaching as the facilitation of learning. Evaluation for the behaviorist consists of the objective measurement of behavioral changes; evaluation for the humanist is the subjective estimate of the learners of their own achievement. The behaviorist believes in external conditioning as the means of achieving discipline; the humanist believes that the only true discipline is self-discipline.

In conclusion, one might ask if behaviorism and humanism are the only psychologies influencing education and therapy. Obviously not! Freud's psychoanalytic theory has especially influenced therapy even to this day. But it is difficult to find much direct or even indirect influence on educational theory and practice. One might cite the "Summerhill" schools of A. S. Neill as examples of Freudian philosophy applied to child rearing or schooling. Neill mentions Freud in the introduction to *Summerhill* but a closer examination of the Summerhill program reveals great similarity to what has been classified as humanistic practice in this chapter.

BIBLIOGRAPHY

Allport, Gordon. *Pattern and Growth in Personality*. N.Y.: Holt, Rinehart & Winston, 1961.

Bellack, A. S. and Hersen, M. *Introduction to Clinical Psychology*. N.Y. Oxford University Press, 1980.

Fromm, E. *Man For Himself* N.Y.: Holt, Rinehart & Winston, 1947.

Goodman, Paul. *Compulsory Miseducation and The Community of Scholars*. N.Y.: Vantage Books, 1964.

Holt, John. *How Children Fail and How Children Learn*. N.Y.: Dell Books, 1970.

Illich, Ivan. *De-Schooling Society*. N.Y. Harper-Row Co., 1972.

Kneller, George F. *Movements of Thought in Modern Education*. N.Y.: John Wiley & Sons, 1984. Chaps. 2 and 5.

Neill, A.S. *Summerhill*. N.Y.: Hart Pub. Co., 1960.

Maslow, A. H. *Toward a Psychology of Being*. 2nd Ed. Princeton, N.J.: Van Nostrand, 1968.

Matson, Floyd W. *Without/Within: Behaviorism and Humanism*. Monterey CA: Brooks/Cole Pub. Co. 1973.

Rogers, Carl R. *A Way of Being*. Boston: Houghton-Mifflin Co., 1980.

Rogers, Carl R. *Freedom To Learn*. Columbus Ohio: Charles E. Merrill Co., 1969, 1983.

Rogers, Carl R. and Stevens, Barry. *Person to Person*. N.Y.: Pocket Books, 1971.

Skinner, B. F. *Beyond Freedom and Dignity*. N.Y.: Bantam books, 1972.

Skinner, B. F. *Science and Human Behavior*, New York: Macmillan Co.,1956.

Skinner, B. F. *Walden Two*. N.Y.: Macmillan Co., 1962.

Watson, J. B. *Behaviorism*. Chicago: Univ. of Chicago Press, 1924.
Watson, Robert I. *The Great Psychologists*. N.Y.: J. B. Lippincott Co., 1971.

Chapter XI

Postmodernism

Postmodernism has evolved in the latter part of the twentieth century. It informs us of another paradigm shift in the way educators look at schooling. As society has placed less emphasis on materialism, reductionism, and a reliance on competition, it has begun to place greater significance on holism and integration.[1] The premodern era can be demarcated between the years 1000 B.C.E. - 1450 C.E.(Common Era). The modern era spanned 1450 C.E. - 1960 C.E.; the postmodern era encompasses 1960 C.E. onward, heading toward the third millennium.[2] It has been linked clearly to changes in social structure and belief systems about what it means to exist. It does not fall clearly under either a conservative or liberal model of education. Postmodernism includes elements from both although it has more in common with a liberal framework.

The 20th century has been witness to social, political, and technological upheaval. An educational response has accompanied each. For example, Eisner notes that radio, TV, and computers have come on the scene only in the last 50 years.[3] Concomitantly, the modern classroom seems incomplete without multiple personal computers with CD ROM capability, laser disc technology, and access to world wide computer networks. This has in turn affected educational expectations for all pupils from preschoolers through graduate students.

Historical underpinnings of the postmodern era that support this paradigm shift include the threat of nuclear annihilation and its resultant peace education, the end of the cold war between the United States and the former Soviet Union, environmental concerns, a movement toward global thinking rather than being limited to nationalism, changes in patterns of family and social structures, and civil rights movements. Postmodernists wish to fuse ideals consistent with an agrarian society while maintaining the

---

[1] F. Capra. The Turning Point (Toronto: Bantam, 1982).

[2] P. Slattery. *Curriculum development in the Postmodern Era* (New York: Garland, 1995).

[3] E. Eisner. *The Educational Imagination (3rd Ed.)*. New York: Macmillan, 1994).

advantages of a highly technological world. Descriptive terms such as "harmony with nature," "post-matriarchal vision," "post-scientistic," "post-Eurocentric view," and seeing the world as an "organism, not a machine" are associated closely with postmodernistic thinking.[4] Theological discussion as it pertains to academic content is also included.

Postmodernism, sometimes referred to in discussions on reconceptualization, constructivist learning theory, multicultural education, and/or feminist pedagogy, focuses on the significance of the person in the learning process and the way in which meaning is constructed in the educational experience. This is different from a purely liberal, student centered education as illustrated in the following diagram.

	Conservative Model	Liberal Model	Postmodern Model
Content chosen by:	Teacher Chooses Content for Learner	Teacher Supplies Content Chosen by Learner with Some Constraints	Learner Chooses Personally Relevant Content with Teacher - Also Evolves During Learning Process
Instruction:	Teacher Directs	Teacher Guides	Teacher Supports Process
Learner interacts with the content:	No	No	Yes

The teacher controls the content and the manner in which it is delivered in the conservative model. The learner is a receptacle for the content. In our previous discussions of liberal models, they were found to be learner centered; however, the teacher still plays a significant role in content

---

[4] Slattery, p. 17

decisions. The teacher may begin with student interests and learning styles but teacher opinion plays a significant role in instruction. Both the liberal and conservative views of education still focus on information coming into the student be it teacher directed or student choice. Postmodernism is characterized by the student interacting with the content. It is student-centered in that the student seeks learning experiences that are personally relevant. They may be accomplished within a state curriculum framework; yet, the learning begins with a liberal focus on where the student is at educationally. The meanings students construct regarding the content are central to the learning process in postmodernism, a significant difference between it and liberalism. The teacher undergirds the process of learning, acting as a facilitator for exploration rather than a dispenser of knowledge. The teacher is more concerned with the way the student uses the material rather than the quantity of facts that can be regurgitated in written or oral exams.

There appears to exist some overlap between the liberal model and postmodernism; however, the latter focuses on celebrating the individual. Dewey referred to the learner as a biological entity and studied education scientifically in order to find better ways to foster development. The postmodern educator wants human development to occur because the learner is inherently special. These concepts will be developed further as we examine postmodernism within the framework of the nine philosophical and educational queries.

WHAT DOES IT MEAN TO BE HUMAN?

The postmodernistic movement embraces constructivist learning theory in which people are the sum of their experiences and more. They construct their world reality according to how the data is organized via perceptual filters.[5] Even siblings may have similar growing up experiences while perceiving them or constructing different meanings about them according to their own perceptual filters. Thus, children enter classrooms with individual notions of their world. An example can be illustrated by asking children to describe what it feels like to be cold. Children who have lived in snowy climates will bring a different experience of cold to the discussion when compared to those who have lived their lives in moderate climates. Innacurate measurement occurs when educators attempt to use standardized

---

[5] J.V. Wertsch. *Vygotsky and the Social Formation of Mind*. (Cambridge: Harvard University Press, 1985).

assessment tools to compare disparate experiences.

Contrary to conservative philosophy, postmodernists would never characterize children as being born evil. Children are simply brought into the world with certain biological tendencies and a spiritual nature that will be developed. To exist encompasses interacting with the environment, making sense of it all. Tendencies toward wrongdoing are seen as either defined within a specific culture or a response to some stimulus be it benign or as traumatic as child abuse. The mind-body dualism espoused by early conservatives has been replaced by holism. Mind and body exist as an integrated unit. The spiritual world is as important as the physical.

Tsunesaburo Makaguchi wrote eloquently about what it means to be human. He was a Japanese educator some have compared to John Dewey. Due to his beliefs as a Buddhist pacifist during World War II, he was imprisoned and consequently died of malnutrition. His philosophy which is characteristic of postmodernism, became the foundation of the Soka schools which were established to create peace through culture and education. Makaguchi described the human spirit as "something innate that guides the life of each individual."[6] Echoing Maslow, he also discussed the necessity of providing for material needs in order to allow the individual to explore spirituality. Quoting the Chinese philosopher, Kuan-tsu, Makaguchi wrote, " 'When the granaries are full then you can attend to matters of etiquette and integrity; when you have sufficient clothing and food then you can worry about honor and disgrace '". [7]

Paulo Freire, a theorist cited by many postmodernists, discusses humanity in the context of forming relationships.[8] The individual is worthy of respect and is valued despite gender, culture of origin, ethnicity, physical ability, and/or sexual preference. The masculine and feminine natures of humans must be valued equally and brought into harmony. It should be reflected in all facets of education including language. Thus, one task assumed by humanity is to rectify past social inequalities. The American civil rights movement and the feminist movement are historical examples of turning points when people demanded their equal place in society.

The modern definition of family is another meaningful example of the postmodern definition of humanness and changing social mores. In the late 1990s the traditional mother-father parent structure has metamorphosed to reflect modern family units that have been amplified by alternative models.

---

[6]D.M. Bethel (Ed.). *Education for Creative Living:Ideals and Proposals of Tsunesaburo Makaguchi* (Ames: Iowa State University Press, 1989), p.18.

[7]*Ibid.*, p.41

[8]P. Freire.*Education for Critical Consciousness*(New York:Seabury, 1973).

Children may derive from families headed by grandparents, aunts and uncles, foster parents, single parents of either gender or two parents of the same gender. Each model is considered a family by postmodernists for whom the term human is all encompassing. This line of thinking has not been embraced by all.

As the current American curriculum has been altered to reflect postmodern ideas of humanity, a strong reaction by Christian Fundamentalists has emerged. They question the notion that it is appropriate to perceive being human in a way that conflicts with their beliefs. They have organized politically and been rather effective in removing objectionable ideas regarding social structure and human sexuality from the school curriculum. Their attempt to present Creationism as an equally valid theory to evolution has been less successful.

HOW DO WE KNOW?

Plato's world consisted of immutable truths; an objective reality existed which theoretically could be experienced and perceived by the individual. The postmodern thinker sees reality as a construction by the perceiver. Each person knows the world within her/his personal context that may be subject to revision as new knowledge is encountered. We know by interacting with the environment or "The knower cannot be separated from the known."[9] Postmodernists draw from the quantum physics research acknowledging that purely objective observation is not possible. The observer affects that which is observed. Thus, knowing is interactive rather than passive. Humans manipulate the environment to learn. The very act of observation is an effect resulting in learning. [10] Plato's absolute knowledge cannot exist in this reality.

Knowing is not limited to cognitive learning activities. The learner is a fusion of mind and body. Thus, information about the world is gathered via cognition, the senses, and intuition. [11] For example, the student may be able to learn chemical formulas and interactions. That is considered a purely cognitive and limited way to learn. When she performs experiments, observes the results, and applies the learning to novel situations, learning takes place at additional levels of thinking which access sensory and

---

[9] Slattery,*op.cit.*, pp.20.

[10] Capra,*op.cit.*, 1982.

[11] B. Clark.*Growing Up Gifted*(2nd Ed.). (Columbus: Charles E. Merrill, 1983).

intuitive domains of the brain.

This integrated way of knowing can be noted historically in the work of psychologists such as Jean Piaget and Jerome Bruner. Before becoming involved in educational research, Bruner wished to ascertain the methods in which individuals learn. He identified three levels of "knowing". [12] He labeled the first level enactive representation. It is experienced by infants and is characterized by the perception of a connection between children and the world they encounter. The manipulation of an object and the object itself, are inseparable to very young children. Iconic representation, the second level, was noted to occur in early childhood. Objects have a separate identity and can be imaged when absent from view. Symbolic representation, the third level, would take the form of language or other complex activities such as sign language.

Bruner illustrated this framework by discussing the way in which a child would perceive the emptiness or fullness of a cup. A child using enactive representation would note that the cup could either be turned over (empty) or was about to overflow (full). In either case, action was the medium for obtaining information. Children who perceived the cup as being empty or full due to the amount of water or empty space in the cup were using iconic representaion. A child who used symbolic representation was able to integrate numerous observations and previous knowledge such as the ratio of water to empty space and the capacity of the cup. Bruner then concluded that "the heart of the educational process consists of providing aids and dialogues for translating experience into more powerful systems of notation and ordering ... a theory of development must be linked to a theory of instruction, or be doomed to triviality." [13]

More recently, Howard Gardner's work on multiple intelligences has gained support among educators. His research focuses on identifying the multiple ways in which people know their world. Gardner identified first seven and not long ago, eight intelligences which include: 1)Verbal/Linguistic, 2)Logical/Mathematical, 3)Visual/Spatial, 4)Body/Kinesthetic, 5)Musical/Rhythmic, 6) Interpersonal, 7) Intrapersonal, and 8) Naturalist. He believes that people possess all the intelligences but develop them in differing degrees. The least used intelligences can be activated and developed further. The challenge for the

---

[12] J.S. Bruner. *Toward a Theory of Instruction*(Cambridge:Belknap, 1966), p. 23; J. Bruner. *In Search of Mind* (New York:Harper & Row, 1983); B.Inhelder. "New Currents in Genetic Developmental Psychology." InS. Bruner & A.Garton (Eds.).*Human Growth and Development*(Oxford:Clarendon, 1978).
[13] *Ibid*, p. 21.

educator is to activate the various intelligences throughout the curriculum.[14]

WHAT IS TRUTH?

Humans interact with each other and with the environment; thus, they learn and construct a truth around the experience. Each person's individual truth is real. Since reality is constructed by the individual, each reality is equally valued and justified. The intersection of different people's realities implies agreement.

Postmodern truth reflects a society that is continuously in flux. The perception of the world is altered as new technological advances are made or social structures undergo transformation. Thus, we see again that Plato's immutable truths do not conform to a postmodern view.

Truth in transformation can be illustrated by the example of the way people perceive their places in society. Postmodernists describe social engineering put into place by the dominant culture. It implies a reality in which different groups of people are placed in hierarchal levels of social strata with all the inherent advantages and disadvantages. It may appear to be in the best interest of the dominant group to maintain a degree of political and economic power to the detriment of the non-dominant group. Experience shows us that this social structure leads to conflict. However, a social construct that is perpetuated as truth and justifiable, i.e., "we are superior; they are inferior," is thus engineered and established.

Webster discusses the social engineering accomplished using racial categories.[15] He argues that race is an obvious example of a categorization system that has been perpetuated in order to maintain one group's economic and political dominance. Examining racial categories within the context of the argument that they are artificially constructed by anthropologists, causes the entire social-racial hierarchy to disintegrate. It is certainly to the advantage of the dominant group to perpetuate the system as truth.

Truth that is static is easily transmitted from one generation to the next. That which was true for the parent generation is still true for the children. There is no need to question interpretation or analysis of past events. Postmodern truths are continuously questioned. Current generations dispute their parents' interpretations of events and the manner in which policy was dictated. Truth in flux does not make for a placid dialogue between generations.

---

[14] H. Gardner. *The Unschooled Mind* (New York: Basic Books, 1991).
[15] Y. Webster. *The Racialization of America* (New York: St, Martin's Press, 1992).

WHAT IS GOOD?

Good is not a moral issue for postmodernist thinkers. It is an answer to questions surrounding the human condition. That which is good can be decided according to what is best for the community. Thus, an importance is placed on living together peacefully, a viewpoint reminiscent of rational humanistic philosophy.

For example, peace education represents a postmodern response to the great political turmoil of the current century. World peace is the only means for humankind to not only survive but thrive. The United States alone has participated in numerous armed conflicts. Probably the most significant political realignment has come as a result of the reconciliation of the U.S. and the former Soviet Union or the end of the Cold War. When President Dwight D. Eisenhower delivered a speech on November 13, 1957 in Oklahoma City, he raised the alarm over the Soviet threat stating, "'Young people now in college must be equipped to live in the age of intercontinental ballistic missiles'". [16] Thus, began federal involvement to direct the best and the brightest students into math and scientific endeavors. A generation of children was perceived as "human resources for the benefit of industrial and corporate leaders"[17] with the goal being to surpass all other countries, especially the Soviet Union, militarily and industrially. With the end of the Cold War the threat of global annihilation lessened; however, with the rise in terrorism and continued human rights abuses, the educational response in the social studies curriculum continued to be active. Peace education continues, most noticeably under the aegis of curriculum that focuses on the celebration of cultural diversity and globalism. Each person has a vested interest in the human community that is good. Consequently, while the postmodern individual is valued, the good of the community must take precedence.

---

[16] Spring, J. *The American School 1642-1993, 3rd. Ed.* (New York: McGraw-Hill, 1994), p.392.

[17] *Ibid.,*. p. 371

WHAT IS THE PURPOSE OF THE SCHOOL?

The development of critical thinking skills is central to the educational process. In order to cultivate a thriving population, it is believed that people must be able to think logically and to make clear decisions. School must be a place where children are challenged intellectually and encouraged to reason adeptly. Problem solving is an important part of the curriculum and accomplished in light of the total community be it local or global.

The postmodern school emphasizes democracy and community over competition. Makaguchi argued for a cooperative system of living when he wrote, "The purpose of education is to enable children to become responsible, healthy cells in the social organism, to contribute to the happiness of the society, and, by so doing, to find meaning, purpose, and happiness in their own individual lives."[18] Accordingly, the Soka schools were founded in Japan on the philosophy that people should strive to evolve personally and live for the good of the community.

The following table illustrates how the accumulation of material goods is emphasized in the competitive model; individuals take from the community. A cooperative living model is one that emphasizes mutual giving and spirituality. However, the individual is not lost within the community; school provides an opportunity to discover and develop interests and abilities.

Competitive Living	Cooperative Living
⇨ Individual ⇦ Individuals	Individuals ⇦⇨
•Emphasis on Material Goods Gathered by the Individual	•Emphasis on Spirituality and Giving Back to Community

The postmodernist rejects the application of Ralph Tyler's mechanistic model for the purpose and organization of school. That model is perceived

---

[18]Bethel, *op.cit.*, 1989.

to be far too limited and lacking in flexibility. Postmodernists also veer from liberal philosophers such as Rousseau. They believe that children should develop while remaining in the larger community. School is a place for the child to grow and to be nurtured. Simultaneously, school is a place to learn to participate in a democracy and to learn to live peacefully within the community. The value of life is fundamental and thus the development of respect for all people and the resolution of conflict in a nonviolent manner must be part of the educational experience. In some ways, the school takes on the role of what was formerly the sole province of home and church. The difference between right and wrong or good and evil are addressed under the aegis of values awareness. Thus, the formation of values shifts from a moral framework to one that stresses the good of all people.

The postmodern school also acts as a social entity, righting past injustices such as gender inequality, racial and ethnic discrimination, and the rampant depletion of world resources. This is accomplished by instituting a curriculum that addresses these issues explicitly as well as implicitly. For example, the school is considered an ideal place to role model recycling programs and cleanup the environment days. The school will also implement behavioral policies such as anti-sexual harassment edicts, gang prevention programs, substance abuse groups, youth interest clubs, and conflict resolution strategies.

WHAT SHOULD BE TAUGHT?

Postmodernist curriculum is student centered, experiential, and interactive. It is an "encounter between the word and reader." [19] Curriculum that requires students to analyze and think creatively is emphasized. Ecology, our interdependence with the environment, and globalism are the foci of the social and biological sciences. The fine arts are necessary to provide the student with a balanced course of study and expanded world view. Postmodernist curriculum is somewhat remindful of conservatism in its inclusion of theology and spirituality. World religions are studied in a historical context. The student's choice concerning practicing a particular faith is left to the province of the family. "This epochal transition . . . is a movement toward a new global understanding of various denominations where religion and education, along with art and

---

[19]Slattery,*op.cit.*, p.77.

politics, will be central to understanding the intellectual character of our time."[20]   Subject matter that is seen as denominational or proselytizing is not appropriate; however, as argued by   feminist theologian Rosemary Radford Ruether, nurturing wisdom is a worthy pursuit.

Postmodernist educators continue to debate with conservative educators the need for studies of ethnicity, gender, and the self. They argue that in order to nurture personal evolution, one of their visions of education, the curriculum must facilitate growth of positive self-concept.   This is accomplished by ensuring curriculum is relevant to students' lives and represents the target population. Thus, one of the results of the American Civil Rights and women's movements was a commitment to rectify the lack of mention of the contributions of those groups in the school curriculum. It was pointed out that studies in history and literature concentrated primarily on a Euro-centric focus. Multicultural curriculum, one focus of postmodernism, embraces an inclusive perspective in the study of history, literature, fine arts, math, and science. For example, textbooks in the United States have been revised to provide the learner with a more thorough understanding of historical events. The perspectives of all the participants are examined rather than limiting study to that of the dominant group or victor.   Curriculum also has been revised to include the contributions of women and ethnic groups who have been considered minorities.   High school literature classes read authors such as Alice Walker, Rudolpho Anaya, Langston Hughes, Maya Angelou, Sandra Cisneros, and Amy Tan. as well as the traditional writers.   A multicultural curriculum is believed to have greater relevancy to students who derive from a variety of backgrounds.

Multicultural writers have been accused by some theorists of rewriting history by omitting important events and putting greater emphasis on unsavory parts of our past. Postmodernists counter that the revised history is more truthful and provides the learner with a more effective tool for understanding ourselves as a nation.   James Banks defines multiple acculturation as a mechanism by   which minority cultures influence dominant cultures. Consequently, their history is intertwined or shared. Banks argues, "the emphasis, rather, should be on how the common U.S. culture and society emerged from a complex synthesis and interaction of the diverse cultural elements that originated within the various cultural, racial,

---

[20]*Ibid.*, p, 69.

ethnic, and religious groups that make up American society."[21]
Consequently, the legacy of slavery in the United States is considered a
critical piece of African-American history.   The postmodernist would
contend that slavery is part of shared history. They do not mean to infer that
all Americans were equally discriminated against.   Rather, all Americans
are affected in some way by the decisions and actions of their ancestors.

Social evolution is another aspect of the changing curriculum.
Postmodernism   requires students to make a thorough exploration of
advances in science and technology as well dramatic changes that have
taken place in the last 50 years. For example, an elementary math
curriculum can no longer be an end to itself.   Concepts mastered as
adequate end-products at the beginning of the century are now perceived by
postmodernists as essential preparation for algebra, geometry, and calculus.
In turn,   the higher level math is a prerequisite for completing modern
physics, biology, chemistry, or engineering courses in secondary school.

Finally, the postmodern curriculum must balance the positive results of
advancing technology within an environmentally sensitive framework.
Besides studying environmental sciences, potentially damaging practices
are examined and debated. The depletion of the Amazon Rain Forest serves
as an illustration. The needs of urban society are no longer taught as taking
precedence over long-term global effects.   A Brazilian farmer's individual
needs must be weighed but in light of the ramifications of the global
community. The issues are debated and acceptable solutions are supported
with evidence.

HOW SHOULD ONE TEACH?

The postmodernist teacher is described as a "fellow traveller."[22] The
student's perspective is at the center of the learning experience. Teachers
support their student's quest for knowledge. They may guide or point to
possible directions but the student is in charge of following the instructional
path and making sense of it all. This does not imply that teachers do
nothing. They begin with the student's individual needs and strengths. The
content can then be adapted affording the student the opportunity to find
meaning. The teacher does not have to state the meaning; the student's

---

[21] J.A. Banks. "Integrating the Curriculum with Ethnic Content: Approaches and
Guidelines." J.A. Banks and C.A.McGee Banks (Eds.)*Multicultural Education:
Issues and Perspectives*(Boston: Allyn & Bacon, 1993), pp. 189-207.
[22]Slattery,*op.cit.*, p. 97

answer is derived critically and is considered valid.   Collaborative learning strategies are encouraged as a method of de-emphasizing competition. The liberal Progressive model for providing students with field experiences or lab activities is believed to make the learning more relevant and accessible. Seminars are encouraged as they place more responsibility on the learner.

The ideal of learning a set of immutable truths is rejected as impossible to achieve when one considers that each person brings her/his own perceptual filter to the classroom.   Thus, students will encounter the curriculum and interact with it in a variety of undetermined ways.   That process must be supported by the educator as opposed to a conservative model of emphasizing conformity in thinking.   Teachers facilitate learning interactions by employing methods that fit the situation and content. The student's individual relationship to the content is foremost.   One must listen to students' life stories and integrate them into the learning experience. Greater importance is placed on personal analysis.   Since each student brings different experiences to the learning, it follows that a variety of interpretations of the curricula (such as of historical events or poetry) will surface.

James Banks discusses four approaches to changing current curriculum.[23] The first two levels describe the Contributions and Additive approaches which are superficial addenda to the existing curriculum. They consist of celebrating different cultural holidays, learning about historical figures, and/or historical events deemed important by the author.   The Level 3 or Transformation approach to curriculum is one in which "the structure of the curriculum is changed to enable students to view concepts, issues, events, and themes from the perspectives of diverse ethnic and cultural groups."[24] Metanarratives, written by outside observers who cannot keep their own perceptual filters from contaminating the work are not to be emphasized.   Primary documents provide the learner with a more personal glimpse into the participant's thinking or descriptions of an event.   The Second Treatise of Civil Government by John Locke, The Declaration of Independence, The Articles of Confederation, The Constitution of 1787, and The Bill of Rights are examples of primary documents that can be analyzed by the students rather than by relying on that of the textbook author's.

Incorporating the use of primary documents in one's teaching opens the door to what the participant was thinking and feeling rather than the way a

---

[23] J.A. Banks & C..A.McGee Banks (Eds.)*op.cit.*, 1993.
[24]*Ibid.*, p.192.

third party reports those feelings or actions. The student hears the history told from a person who experienced it directly. Voices From America is an example of a collection of personal accounts of people involved in the Civil Rights movement.[25] One example of an oral history is that told by Melba Pattilllo Beals. She related her thoughts about being one of the Little Rock Nine students who entered Central High School in Little Rock, Arkansas in 1957. Her account illustrates one way to present a richer and deeper appreciation of American history. Reading personal histories also represents diverse opinions which are analyzed by students who are encouraged to begin to form their own opinions.

I went in not through the side doors, but up the front stairs, and there was a feeling of pride and hope that yes, this is the United States; yes, there is a reason I salute the flag; and it's going to be okay. The troops were wonderful. There was some fear that they were dating the girls in high school, but I don't care what they were doing: they were wonderful, they were disciplined, they were attentive, they were caring. They didn't baby us, but they were there. So for the first time I began to feel like there is this slight buffer zone between me and this hell on the other side of this wall. They couldn't be with us everywhere. They couldn't be with us, for example, in the ladies' bathroom. They couldn't be with us in gym. We'd be showering in gym and someone would turn your shower into scalding. You'd be walking out to the volleyball court and someone would break a bottle and trip you on the bottle. I have scars on my right knee from that. After a while, I started saying to myself, am I less than human? Why did they do this to me? What's wrong with me? And so you go through stages even as a child. First you're in pain, then you're angry, then you try to fight back, and then you just don't care. You just, you can't care; you hope you do die. You hope that there's an end. And then you just mellow out and you just realize that survival is day to day and you start to grasp your own spirit, you start to grasp the depth of the human spirit and you start to understand your own ability to cope no matter what. That is the greatest lesson I learned.[26]

---

[25]H. Hampton & S. Fayer with S. Flynn. *Voices From America* (New York: Bantam, 1990).
[26]*Ibid.*,pp. 48-49.

Slattery suggests that student apathy may be more a symptom that teaching strategies must change to meet the needs of postmodern students. Teaching subjects in an interdisciplinary model was espoused by the Progressives and has gained popularity recently.   Courses that team literature and history instructors are reminiscent earlier thinking and are found with greater frequency in high schools. Teachers combine the two classes into a two-hour block interweaving literature and history. Students can see how literature and history are fused; they can see how neither takes place in a vacuum.

Finally, for effective learning to take place, there must be time for introspection and reflection on the content. It is a necessary component of the school day, not a luxury. Thus, the teacher's day looks quite different from that of the conservative instructor's.   Teaching that is accomplished through facilitation of learning removes the instructor from a lecture model. An observer of a postmodern classroom may have difficulty locating the teacher upon entering. She may notice a noisy group of students over in a far corner, discussing the best way to complete a project.   They shift positions and there is the teacher, sitting amid the group, observing the process and only intervening when it seems necessary.   The next hour begins with the teacher giving a short introduction about the task followed by instructions for students to analyze their favorite character, in the novel, illustrate a symbolic representation of the character's traits, and write a narrative explaining their work. The teacher will analyze the products, reflecting on whether they are demonstrative of critical thinking and individual creativity. She makes notes for the next time she assigns this task to maintain it as is or to revise if needed. She even notices how different students react to the task. She observes that some students find the drawing enjoyable while others struggle with that medium. Therefore, the teacher can ensure that all   students have the opportunity to experience their favorite learning style.

HOW SHOULD PUPILS BE EVALUATED?

The ideal postmodern evaluation reflects the shift in thinking about the learning experience from an emphasis on product to one on process. Conservative evaluation focused on mastery of subject matter. Liberal and postmodern evaluation is more concerned with noting growth of the whole student.   Authentic assessment is considered to be more thorough as it includes samples of student work, learner self-evaluation, and the instructor's evaluation of student progress. The emphasis on developing critical thinking skills requires a different type of assessment. Evaluation by examination is considered to be limited and incomplete. Rote memorization of facts takes second place to the student's interpretation of events. Exam questions should elicit responses that demonstrate the student's grasp of the ramifications of the content under study.

The analysis of the American Revolution serves as one example of assessment that requires students to demonstrate a deeper understanding of a historical event rather than simply listing various battles, naming the participants, and identifying the victor. Students might be asked to defend British policy in the North American colonies between 1763-1774. These dates are critical to student's understanding of British policy. The year 1763 marks the end of the French/Indian War and the escalation of the colonist's perception of British oppression. This type of exam requires inclusive thinking about events that led up to the Revolutionary War, a traditional practice. Rather than confining the discussion to the colonist's points of view, students must demonstrate understanding of the positions of the various participants. They must also show evidence that they understand the ramifications of everything that took place at that time and its effect on future events, even into the present time. Students are not told what to think. They take a point of view and write a defense whether or not they agree with it, propelling them into critical thinking levels essential to the postmodern curriculum.

The teacher evaluates the quality of the thinking. Is the argument logical? Does it fit the historical events? Does it include all points of view? Do students consistently support their ideas with evidence? Do they make justifiable assumptions? Are their conclusions reasonable?[27]

HOW ARE FREEDOM AND DISCIPLINE TO BE HARMONIZED?

The postmodern teacher struggles with maintaining a delicate balance between the student's rights and anarchy. The child's freedom must not be stifled. The child must be allowed to develop a sense of democracy; yet, there is a recognition that learning will not be very effective amidst chaos. While, the child's self-esteem must not be compromised by undue criticism

---

[27]R. Paul and Y. Webster. *The Infusion of Critical Thinking* (Los Angeles: California State University at Los Angeles, 1994.

and personal attacks. Respect is valued, two-way, and should be modeled by the teacher.

Discipline is for the good of the community and enables individual growth. Individual freedom is valued but not at the expense of the group. However, by shifting discipline away from a moral issue the postmodern teacher must look to alternative motivation for requiring cooperation. The emphasis is shifted from "being good" to encouraging students to be helpful.

The conservative model of a quiet classroom with students reading silently at their desks is considered far too rigid and even a hindrance to learning. The postmodern educator accepts some degree of classroom interaction and values an energetic group of students. The class will be one in which students learn to value learning and care for each other as well as the world.

CHAPTER SUMMARY

In summary, postmodernism is the most recent educational philosophy to emerge in our discussion. It encompasses numerous sub-movements such as multiculturalism, feminist pedagogy, human rights, environmentalism, and theological studies.   Postmodernism displays some elements of conservatism and many of liberalism. It will likely be considered separately by educational philosophers due to a shift first from the conservative, teacher-centered classroom: second, to the liberal, student-centered model: finally to the teacher/facilitator-learner process orientation.

Postmodernism embraces the idea that humans are born good and equal with no justification for a caste system. We know by interacting with the environment and constructing meaning around our observations. Sensory, cognitive, and intuitive input are equally valued ways to know. Thus, the school becomes a place to facilitate growth of the whole child. The curriculum encompasses content that raises consciousness about basic human rights. The teacher facilitates student development of critical thinking skills. Freedom is deemed paramount but not at the expense of the greater good of the community.

Examining postmodernism in a historical perspective presents some difficulty due to the ongoing nature of its development. In other words, it is difficult to look back on something until it is complete. One thing we know, each educational action precipitates a public reaction. Protest against some postmodernism curriculum changes have been noted in this chapter. Whether or not another equally strong but opposing educational philosophy surfaces in the third millennium remains to be seen.

BIBLIOGRAPHY

Banks, J.A.. "Integrating the Curriculum with Ethnic Content: Approaches and Guidelines." J.A. Banks and C.A. McGee Banks (Eds.) *Multicultural Education: Issues and Perspectives*(Boston: Allyn & Bacon, 1993).

Bethel, D.M. (Ed.).*Education for Creative Living: Ideals and Proposals of Tsunesaburo Makaguchi* (Ames: Iowa State University Press, 1989).

Bruner, J.S. *Toward a Theory of Instruction*(Cambridge: Belknap, 1966).

Bruner, J.S. *In Search of Mind* (New York: Harper & Row, 1983).

Capra, F.*The Turning Point*(Toronto: Bantam, 1982).

Clark, B.*Growing Up Gifted*(2nd Ed.). (Columbus: Charles E. Merrill, 1983).

Eisner, E. .*The Educational Imagination (3rd Ed.)*(New York: Macmillan, 1994).

Freire, P. *Education for Critical Consciousness*(New York: Seabury, 1973).

Gardner, H. *The Unschooled Mind*(New York: Basic Books, 1991).

Hampton, H. & Fayer, S. with Flynn, S. *Voices From America* (New York: Bantam, 1990).

Inhelder, B. "New Currents in Genetic Developmental Psychology." InS. Bruner & A. Garton (Eds.).*Human Growth and Development*(Oxford: Clarendon: 1978).

Paul, P. and Webster, Y. *The Infusion of Critical Thinking* (Los Angeles: California State University at Los Angeles, 1994).

Slattery, P. *Curriculum development in the Postmodern Era* (New York: Garland, 1995).

Spring, J. *The American School 1642-1993, 3rd. Ed.* (New York: McGraw-Hill, 1994).

Webster, Y. *The Racialization of America*(New York: St, Martin's Press, 1992).

Wertsch, J.V. *Vygotsky and the Social Formation of Mind.* (Cambridge: Harvard University Press, 1985).

Chapter XII

Unity Within Diversity

The preceding chapters have sketched the broad outlines of the development of educational thought from the first systematic theory proposed by Plato to the modern varieties of educational philosophies. Educational thinkers. and systems have been classified as either conservative or liberal depending upon their answers to the four basic philosophical questions and the five educational questions posed throughout the text. We have noted that the Platonic beliefs about man, knowledge, truth, and value (with adaptations to fit the Christian view of life) were not seriously challenged until the seventeenth century. It is true that there were numerous liberal ideas suggested and even tried by educational theorists. But these new ideas did not result in radical and far-reaching changes in the educational scheme of the times. The revolt of Rousseau might be considered the first instance of a *complete* rejection of the old way.

The seventeenth and eighteenth centuries witnessed the rise of many, often disconnected attacks on conservatism and the proposal of many new philosophical beliefs and educational practices. The influence of these radical departures from centuries-old theories was not greatly felt in Europe where the theories originated but rather in the rapidly growing United States. Here, great dissatisfaction with the classical education which our ancestors brought to this country encouraged experimentation with many of the new educational ideas, especially those which promised an educational program close to life. But even these early liberalizing innovations were without any unifying set of philosophical beliefs and educational principles.

This feat was accomplished by the liberal philosophy of John Dewey. Just as Plato had done twenty-two centuries before, Dewey succeeded in constructing an educational theory which was in accord with his political and social philosophy, his theory of knowledge and truth, and his ethical doctrines. For Dewey, philosophy was viewed as a theory of education. This integral unity of education and philosophy is perhaps one of the main reasons for the phenomenal influence which Dewey's liberalism exerted on American education. Its rapid spread throughout the teacher education institutions might be compared to the rapid spread of the ideas of the Protestant Reformation.

But just as the Reformation had its Counter-Reformation so, too, the conservatives began a counter reformation against Dewey's liberal philosophy. Many of the advocates of older philosophical systems which had done little for educational theory began in earnest to construct educational theories which would be consistent with their philosophical views and at the same time stand as refutations of Dewey's system. Thus in the first half of the twentieth century a fierce verbal battle ensued between conservatives and liberals in education. The resolution of the conflict is far from complete.

In the preceding chapters we have examined possible escapes from the either-or dilemma of the conservative-liberal conflict. But at this writing, it seems correct to assert that even these attempts to resolve the difficulty have not received much attention from educators. This rather unsettled situation will certainly bewilder the layman, the student, or the beginning teacher. One can rightfully ask, "If the experts can't decide which philosophy is best suited for American education, how can you expect me, a novice, to do so?" Actually, this question can be divided into two separate, though related, parts. The first involves the individual student's choice. The second involves the selection of a philosophy of education for the American public schools.

Obviously, these are not easy questions to answer or there would be nothing to fight about. Individuals can resolve the difficulties for themselves by siding with the conservatives or the liberals or by espousing one of the solutions suggested in the last few chapters. Regardless of which position is taken, they will be able to give many good reasons for their choices. If such were not the case there would not be so many varied points of view on the issues discussed in this volume. Also, one must acknowledge that the advocates of the various positions are sincere in their efforts to seek and propound the truth as it applies to educational theory and practice.

Since it is not the purpose of this book to convert the readers to any point of view, no evaluation of the various positions is offered. But, if the readers reflect seriously on these problems of educational philosophy, they will undoubtedly feel drawn to one of the schools of thought, or even to several of them. The only word of warning your authors have for the neophyte is to beware of unsystematic eclecticism. This intellectual disease often found among teacher education students (and even experienced teachers) consists in picking and choosing from several or all of the philosophies those items which one likes. Of course, the major pitfall in this approach lies in espousing contradictory views.

When the individuals make a choice and advocate one philosophy their problem is only half solved. As soon as they join a teaching staff they encounter other points of view.

The next important question, then, is, "Which educational philosophy is best for America?" That other countries have an official or quasi-official philosophy has often been cited by critics of American education as the main reason for their superiority to American education. France, Italy, Germany, Switzerland, the British Isles, and other European nations also appear to be less divided on the issues of educational philosophy or even on educational practices. (A few exceptions to this general rule are noted at the end of Chapter VI.) The students in teacher education institutions are generally schooled in what we have called the conservative view. When they serve on elementary or secondary school faculties they are in general agreement with their fellow teachers on the primary purposes of the school, they use much the same teaching and evaluation methods, and they follow a national syllabus. Even those foreign visitors, including Americans who do not agree with the educational philosophy of these countries, will generally admit that national systems are quite successful in achieving their purposes.

That the schools of America do not have a unifying philosophy is recognized by most Americans and foreigners. Some say that this is to be expected in a young nation where each group of early settlers brought theological and educational beliefs to their own isolated colonies. Each had a somewhat different outlook on life. For example, the Puritans were aggressive, energetic, and efficient in realizing the goal of material success in this world. Thus Puritanism emphasized the value of education and the necessity of its availability to all to achieve this end. On the other hand, the non-Puritan colonies, such as Maryland, reflected the religious and cultural values of their European tradition. Because of the isolation of the colonies, each one fostered its own pattern of education without interference from its neighbors. Under such circumstances, local autonomy both in administration and philosophical outlook was the most natural pattern of educational development. No attempt was made to propagate an educational philosophy acceptable to all the colonies, and the great influx of European immigrants during the nineteenth and early twentieth centuries did nothing to direct the young nation toward a central educational purpose. Some educators feel that this great divergence of views about education should be retained. Others argue that America needs unity of educational purpose.

Let us look at some of the responses to the question "What philosophy is best for American public education?" The liberals, of course, will say that the greatest democratic nation and recognized leader of the free world should adopt a liberal philosophy of education. The conservatives, believing that their philosophy should prevail, will maintain democratic government is not an outgrowth of liberal educational theories. Democracy has flourished, they will say, in the British Isles, France, and many other nations which espouse educational conservatism. Furthermore, they maintain, the purpose of education is not to make little democrats or any other political species out of children but rather to give them knowledge and develop their intellectual powers so they can make wise political choices when they become voters and rulers in adult life. At any rate, there seems little likelihood that either of these two camps will allow the other to dominate.

As we have seen in Chapter X analytic philosophers or logical positivists do not conceive of their role as one of telling educators what to do. Similarly, they would hesitate to tell those engaged in the huge task of American education what set of philosophical and educational principles should guide the schools of the nation. Undoubtedly they would be willing to assist educators in the important job of clarifying the language and the fundamental assumptions underlying the issues of the discussion. With their analytic tools they might even convince educators that many of their problems are pseudo-problems. Certainly, this would do much to diminish the conflict between the liberals and conservatives. But by their own admission the analytic schools do not provide the philosophical and educational principles needed to guide the American school system.

It might appear that all the alternatives have been exhausted. However others are proposed. The first to come to mind is that there is no need to have one philosophy of education for American public education. Heeding the postmodern argument, an educational philosophy must be flexible. If other countries wish to institute national educational philosophies that is their business. Perhaps certain advantages accrue from such uniformity. On the other hand, one can point to certain disadvantages. The rigid lockstep pattern of European schools, for example, stifles creativity and initiative. Educators from the former Soviet Union have admitted that their completely undiversified program of general education did not always bring out leadership qualities and creativity in youth.

Since the application of one philosophy of education at all educational levels limits freedom one might argue for the application of different philosophies at the various levels. In reality, such seems to be the case at the present time. Most public elementary schools adhere to the liberal philosophy, whereas most senior high schools reflect conservative educational thinking. Generally it is believed that the junior high schools are supposed to bridge the gap between the two levels and the two philosophies. Colleges and universities, especially academic departments, tend to favor a modernized version of conservatism. Dewey's educational philosophy finds its greatest critics in academic departments. However, academe at all levels has not been immune to the momentum of the postmodernist movement. Professors in all disciplines are being asked to examine their courses to assess whether or not they are sensitive to cultural diversity, gender issues, and changing technology.

This educational pluralism, based on the different educational levels, is not the only alternative to a national philosophy of education. Some educators have contended that each community should make the decision for itself.

Your authors have worked with large school systems which apply both liberal and conservative philosophies within the same system. For example, one school system has three or four secondary schools possessing all the characteristics recommended by modern conservatives. The principal, other administrators, and practically all the teaching staff agree that the school is designed to develop intellectual power and transmit knowledge. Great emphasis is placed on the disciplinary value of certain subjects like foreign languages, both classical and modern, and mathematics. The curriculum consists of separate subjects - there are no integrated areas such as social studies or general science. All nonacademic activities are strictly extracurricular and take place after school. Teaching methods are teacher-centered with lectures taking much of class time. Evaluation of pupil progress is exclusively in terms of academic achievement. Those students who do not receive a numerical grade of 70 or above fail and must retake the entire course. No student graduates or receives a diploma unless he has passed all of the courses. Discipline is very strict, and students are suspended from school after several infractions of the rules of conduct.

There are several other schools in the same system which exemplify in most respects the liberal philosophy. Administrators and staff do not view development of intellectual power and mastery of subject matter as the most important goal of their school. They are much more concerned with the practical needs, interests, and desires of their students. With the exception of English there are few strictly academic courses and these are electives. Even the English classes are concerned with practical problems such as letter writing and reading popular periodicals rather than with rhetoric, composition, or literature. Great emphasis is placed on students becoming productive and well-adjusted members of their community. Current events, contemporary issues, and practical projects occupy most of the class time. Club, athletic, and social activities are recognized as essential parts of the curriculum. The lecture method and other teacher-centered methods are seldom used. Grading and promotion practices are very liberal and pupils are seldom failed. Only pupils with extreme discipline problems are suspended, and teachers allow considerable freedom of choice and action in their classes.

Finally, a few other schools are experimenting with both conservative and liberal ideals within the framework of postmodernism. Students read original historical documents. Their reading list in literature classes covers a diverse collections of writers from all over the world. Male and female poets are represented equally. Science classes study the effects of pollution and ponder global warming. Students tackle analysis of local issues and global events.

SYNTHESIZING POSSIBLE SOLUTIONS

No doubt this type of pluralism exists in many cities throughout the nation. Indeed there is much to be said in its favor. It permits a great amount of flexibility and experimentation. Parents and children can select schools which fit their philosophical preferences. Teachers can request placement in a school suited to their own philosophical bent. Top level administrators need not officially espouse any one of the opposing philosophies. Thus great diversity is found even within one school system. Perhaps this same diversity might be recognized as the only acceptable approach to education in a pluralistic society.

Thus far several answers have been suggested for the question "Which philosophy is best for American education?" Americans could demand that conservatism, liberalism, or one of the proposed philosophical solutions become the official philosophy for this country. Or they might wish to retain one of the pluralistic arrangements just mentioned.

Professor George Barton, past president of the Philosophy of Education Society, believes that some form of ordered pluralism might be better than the rather haphazard types now found operating in American school systems. He argues that the espousal of any one philosophy for American education would result in an intolerably dreary uniformity. Further, he contends that pluralism is not only desirable but inevitable in this country simply because there are multiple ways of being right (just as there are multiple ways of being wrong) on the many issues dividing educators. Even the absolutist has a legitimate place in this scheme.

The following statements contain the broad outlines of Barton's ordered pluralism. (His use of the term "man" rather than the more inclusive "human" has been retained). He contends that there are different ways of looking at life. The first, the purposive vision, seeks to determine the purpose of all things (including the school) and how these purposes are achieved. Thus one might ask, "What is the purpose of science or religion and what means are used to achieve these purposes?" Some thinkers (e.g., Plato, Aristotle) will be much more engrossed in searching for purposes than others, but at least all will give the problem some consideration if for no other reason that to find reasons for rejecting purposiveness.

The second way to look at life involves the search for organic relations. This approach presses one to look for the interrelatedness of the parts which form one unit. How does a man who is composed of so many parts, act as a unit, a person? How does an institution, such as the school, function as a unit? How do the various parts of a symphony form one composition?

The third way to view life considers the mechanical relations in persons or things. Which of man's actions are purely mechanical? In what sense is man or animal similar to a machine? Which school activities are related only in an automatic or mechanistic way? What types of learning are purely mechanistic, purely stimulus-response?

The fourth vision of life deals with classification of things, activities, and the like. Is history to be classified as a social science or a science of a quite different kind? Is teaching to be classified as an art or a science? Is the pupil a highly evolved animal or should he be classified as a rational animal?

The next facet of ordered pluralism is one in which Barton considers the different educational ages of man. The first, the age of exploration, is at the root of all learning. This has been variously described by philosophers of different persuasions as the innate desire to know, as a systematic doubt, or as a felt difficulty. Whatever it is called, this age provides the motivation for learning from which the teacher can prod, urge, and assist the learner to further awareness, understanding, appreciation, or contemplation. Children display this quality in a most evident manner; they are always probing into everything to find out "what makes it tick." However, the urge to explore never ceases to be operative even at the advanced stages of achievement and learning.

Man's second educational age, the age of conversation, involves discussion of the problems, questions, or subject matter with others. In an educational setting, the conversation would normally be between student and teacher and other learners, However, the conversation can be broadened beyond the classroom and its personalities by consulting the recorded thoughts of the ancients, medieval man, or more recent thinkers. At this stage, however, the learner will not settle upon final answers or solutions; he is trying to learn more about the questions and problems that bothered him in the age of exploration.

The age of resolution is the time for settling upon answers and solutions. Such answers and solutions should, at first, be only tentative. But the learner must at some time reach some firm if not immutable conclusions; he cannot go on forever exploring and discussing without making some decisions. Different kinds of resolutions will be achieved: The test of experience will solve one kind of problem; intellectual insight will give some answers; aesthetic perception will result in ordering of the parts or elements into a unified whole; moral judgement will make the distinction between good and evil; and religious faith will lead to commitment to a god. It is during this educational period that the learner begins to specialize in some field of knowledge or technical skill. The vastness of the world around him and the variety of persons he comes in contact with convince him that he cannot learn everything about all things.

The fourth and final educational age is that of consummation. In this phase the learner decides on a way of life and actually commits himself to it. Any new learning is built into his accepted pattern of thinking and acting. He relates general knowledge to his field of specialization. All of these new acquisitions may be motivated by exploration and discussion with others and a solution may be reached, but they will be integrated into the learner's accepted pattern of beliefs and ways of doing things.

The next question Barton raises in his ordered pluralism is how the different ways of looking at life and the four educational levels can be applied to teaching-learning situations within the classroom. Much like Whitehead, he argues that the age of exploration calls for student-centered teaching. By this he means that the needs and interests of the students should be the central focus during this period. Subject matter is not to be disregarded, but rather it should be subsidiary to student needs and interests. Also all of the ways of looking at life will be considered but the purposive will be dominant.

In the age of conversation, teaching is concerned with arranging for the student to meet the world around him so that he can converse with it. This calls for an examination of all sides of questions and issues in the natural and social sciences and the humanities. These studies will take the student well beyond his own needs and interests and bring him in contact with the world. During the age of conversation the teaching process seeks primarily to establish the organic relationships, though the purposive, mechanistic, and classificatory are not neglected. The occasion might arise in the student's study of the world when the latter ways of looking at life are needed to illuminate the organic relationships.

The age of resolution lends itself best to that type of teaching which focuses on the acquisition of definite knowledge and specialization. This calls for rather systematic work in the arts, sciences, technologies, professions, and crafts. At this stage the learner is ready for the self-discipline demanded by rigorous acquisition of knowledge and the mastery of the life's vocation. The mechanistic view of life, that concerned with external relations, will dominate this phase of the teaching-learning process. Again, the other views might come into play, but they will be secondary.

The age of consummation is the period of self-education. At the stage the student should be competent enough to be his own teacher. He has decided on his way of life, his patterns of belief and action. He might still seek the assistance of other sources, teachers, experts, books, and the like. But in the main, the learner at this stage must be self-taught, for he must continue to learn after the days of formal schooling are over. In this final stage the classificatory view of life dominates. The learner has made the others (purposive, organic, and mechanistic) so much a part of him that conscious attention must be paid to them only occasionally. When a new question or problem arises or when new knowledge is acquired the learner classifies it according to its essential ingredients -he places it in its proper category and in the right perspective.

Professor Barton's ordered pluralism is designed to give a place in the educational scheme for what we have called conservatism and liberalism. The purpose of the school is given in very broad terms which advise that one purpose be emphasized at a certain time in the teaching-learning process and another at a different time. It allows and encourages educators to use various methods of teaching, both teacher- and student-centered. Problem and subject-matter centered curricula seem to find their niche. Evaluation is in terms of both growth and mastery of knowledge. General education and specialization (vocational education) are put on an equal footing; both are viewed as good and necessary. Both external and internal control are emphasized in the management of behavior and action. The solutions of Whitehead, the work of the analysts, positivists, and postmodernists also can be accommodated in ordered pluralism.

In the philosophical realm, ordered pluralism purports to encompass all the views of humanity, the various modes of knowing, the different kinds of truth, and the great variety of ethical codes and aesthetic theories. The only requirement seems to be that all these be ordered according to some logical pattern.

Just how much acceptance ordered pluralism will find among educators is unpredictable at this time. The proposal is of such recent origin that it will be some time before it can be put into practice in the schools. It has certain advantages over what we have called the haphazard forms of pluralism which now exist in American schools, the chief of which is the conscious ordering of the various approaches to educational problems according to certain educational ages and certain views of the world. Also, it gives educators a certain freedom to emphasize those educational principles which appeal most to them. Thus in the age of exploration, for example, the Postmodernist would be more apt to emphasize the recognition of difficulties and problems as the starting point for learning. On the other hand, the Aristotelian realist might emphasize the innate drive to know as the starting point for learning. In the age of resolution, the Deweyan liberal would be apt to concentrate on the testing of proposed hypotheses whereas the realist would more than likely see to it that the learner be given or lead to the right answers. Each of the other educational ages might receive different emphases from teachers holding different philosophical viewpoints. In a similar manner, each of the different views of life will be emphasized by teachers according to their philosophical preferences. However, ordered pluralism seems to imply that although educators might emphasize one approach the other possibilities should not be completely ignored. In this manner the learner will have some experience with the great variety of approaches that exist within the broad framework of human activity. Thus the learner will also be familiar with ordered pluralism.

In summary, it seems that students have two questions which they must answer. The first is, "Which of the many points of view presented in this text shall I choose as the guide to my professional work as a teacher?" The students' home backgrounds, personality traits, and educational experiences will influence their choices. The views of their high school teachers and especially of their college professors will undoubtedly have some effect on their choices. These many influences might entice students to go in several different directions at the same time leading them into eclecticism. Perhaps this is good, especially for neophytes since it takes many years of study and experience to comprehend all the intricacies of the competing philosophies. But, as students mature, study more about educational history and philosophy at the graduate level, and acquire added teaching experience, they will more likely than not cast their lot with one of the schools of thought.

The second question, and by far the more difficult one to answer is, "Should there be a philosophy of American education?" Other countries have achieved great educational unity by espousing a single philosophy for their schools and some influential American educators, politicians, scientists, and business leaders are demanding this kind of unity for American education.

Furthermore, as the federal government plays a greater role in education through aid programs and the like the reality of a national system is not as remote as some might believe.

The alternative to having a national philosophy to guide educational practice is educational pluralism. If the American public (and their educators) agree that no official philosophy is needed or desirable this agreement in itself constitutes a certain type of unity.

BIBLIOGRAPHY

Brameld, T. *Education For the Emerging Age*. New York: Harper & Row, 1965. Ch. XXIII.

Brauner, C. J. *American Educational Theory*. Englewood Cliffs, N.J.: Prentice-Hall, 1964. Ch. XVII.

Brubacher, J. S. *Modern Philosophies of Education*. New York: McGraw-Hill Book Co., 1962. Ch. XV.

Grambs, J. D., & McClure, L. M. *Foundations of Teaching*. New York: Holt, Rinehart and Winston, 1964. Ch. XIV.

Gunnison, H. "The Uniqueness of Similarities: Parallels of Milton, H. Erikson and Carl Rogers." *Journal of Counseling and Development*. 1985, (63).

Ozmon, H. A. & Craver, S. M. *Philosophical Foundations of Education*. Columbus, Ohio: Charles Merrill Co., 1981. Pp. 271-280.

Rogers, C. *Journal of Counseling and Development*, 1985. (63)

Rugg, H. *Foundations of American Education*. New York: World Book Co., 1947. Ch. I.

Smith, H. *Condemned to Meaning*. New York: Harper & Row, 1965. Ch. III, IV.

Ulich, R. *Philosophy of Education*. New York: American Book Co., 1961. Ch. XVIII.

Walker, W. *Philosophy of Education*. New York: Philosophical Library, 1963. Pp. 28-38, 106-19.

Woodring P. and Scanlon, J. *American Education Today*. New York: McGraw-Hill Book Co., 1963. Pp. 188-97.

Appendix

It is no surprise that professors teach according to their philosophies of education. However, it can be useful to examine the manner in which others have used a certain text or designed a particular course. In the search for interesting and thought-provoking activities, teachers have found that they can adapt activities from many disciplines. Even the most gifted teachers admit that they are effective scavengers. When I began teaching Educational Philosophy at Loyola Marymount University, I sought out syllabi and advice from colleagues both in and out of my own university. With the encouragement and feedback from Dr. Alfred Lightfoot, I found the following strategies to be successful for teaching this course in a way that supports the students' reflection on, and construction of, a succinct personal philosophy of education. Their articulation is not intended to be conclusive. It is the beginning of the life-long discussion mentioned in chapter 12.

Exploring the Chapters

A. Model of Instruction

My philosophy of education course is conducted as a seminar which requires each class member to bear significant responsibility for course content. Historical trends, specific philosophy models, and the writings of leading educational philosophers (past and present) from all over the world are read and discussed.

The majority of students are at a place in their education where they are fully competent to present the manner in which they made sense of the philosophy being discussed. In order to discourage students giving a type of book report presentation, they are required to merge the chapter they present with current thinking they uncover in the literature. Additionally, the literature they examine should be culturally diverse in nature. Although western education systems have been influenced greatly by early Greek and Roman models, noting similarities, difference, influences, and thinking of diverse educators is informative and effective in the current global, social/political climate. Writing their reaction to the philosophy they present is a critical step in the construction of their own philosophy of education.

Student Instructions for Chapter Presentation

I. Summarize the reading according to the nine focusing questions used in the chapters.

II. Include 2-3 articles or readings that relate to your topic and use them as examples that either support or negate the philosophy your are discussing. The use of examples is extremely important in the illustration of your reading. The presentation should not consist of reading an outline that is culled from the author, without any of your personal input. The inclusion of personal illustrations may help explain the orientation of the philosophy you are outlining. It also gives you the opportunity to use your creativity and personal interests to clarify the information. Examples of personal illustrations might include anecdotal evidence or readings from other disciplines.

III. Each class member will be responsible for reading the chapter being outlined and discussed.

IV. Each student will present her/his own session making the outline available for all class members.

V. Structure for the outline
   Introduction : summarize the philosophy in a paragraph or two.
   Answer Dupuis' nine questions.
   Summarize: What is your opinion of this philosophy? Why?
             What leads you to say what you do?

B. In-class Writing
   Writing on related topics is used to facilitate students' reflection on issues raised in the course of discussion. Generation of topics during the class is also recommended. It is interesting to be part of a learning process in which it is not possible to plan every outcome.

C. Personal Philosophy of Education

Examining one's personal philosophy of education is a task we undertake at numerous stages in our students' education at Loyola Marymount University. The nine focusing questions used to structure the chapters have provided a very useful model to help students focus their provided a very useful model to help students focus their thinking. Students are required to cite the current literature which again represents diverse views. The goal is to finish the semester with a coherent picture of their philosophy of education. It may change with time, appropriately so, but in the context of a strong and well thought out foundation asking; "why do I now believe this way?" "Why have I altered direction?"

D. Portfolio Assessment

This type of assessment documents both the assignments completed for the class, and the students' growth within the context of this class. The portfolio includes:

A. Reader response journal writings. These are completed and discussed in class, each session.

B. Written outline of each of the class presentations. Copies of the outlines are made available by the presenter for all class members.

C. Final paper on one's personal philosophy of education.

literature which again represents diverse views. The goal is to finish the semester with a coherent picture of their philosophy of education. It may change with time, appropriately so, but in the context of a strong and well thought out foundation asking; "why do I now believe this way?" "Why have I altered direction?"

Index